Never Ask Permission

Never Ask Permission

Elisabeth Scott Bocock of Richmond

A Memoir by Mary Buford Hitz

University Press of Virginia • *Charlottesville and London*

The University Press of Virginia

© 2000 by the Rector and Visitors of the University of Virginia

All rights reserved

Printed in the United States of America

First published in 2000

⊛ The paper used in this publication meets the minimum requirements of
the American National Standard for Information Sciences—Permanence of Paper
for Printed Library Materials, ANSI Z39.48-1984.

Never Ask Permission was designed and typeset in Centaur by Kachergis Book Design,
Pittsboro, North Carolina; and printed on 60-pound Glatfelter and bound by
Thomson-Shore of Dexter, Michigan.

Library of Congress Cataloging-in-Publication Data

Hitz, Mary Buford, 1941–

   Never ask permission : Elisabeth Scott Bocock of Richmond: a memoir / by Mary
Buford Hitz.

     p. cm.

   Includes index.

   ISBN 0-8139-1993-2 (cloth : alk. paper)

    1. Bocock, Elisabeth Scott, 1901–1985.   2. Richmond (Va.)—Biography.

3. Richmond (Va.)—Social life and customs—20th century.   4. Historic preservation—Virginia—Richmond.   5. Women—Virginia—Richmond—Biography.

6. Elite (Social sciences)—Viriginia—Richmond—Biography.   I. Title.

F234.R553 B634 2000

975.5'451043'092—DC21

[B]

00-025951

This book is dedicated to my family, both immediate
and extended, and to the memory of Mother and Father,
who transmitted to their children the importance of
the tribal ties that bind.

Contents

Illustrations

Preface

Some towns, for reasons that it is doubtful anyone understands, produce extraordinary women. New Orleans is such a place and Boston is another. Richmond in the early twentieth century produced a galaxy of such extraordinary and diverse characters as Ellen Glasgow, Mary Cooke Branch Munford, and Lila Meade Valentine. Elisabeth Scott Bocock, though of a slightly later generation, carried on the tradition and established a high standard of achievement in an aura of personal eccentricity. Her contributions to the well-being of her city were numerous and important, and her personality, which is the focus of her daughter's memoir, is fascinating.

This is no standard biography. In addition to being a very good read, this book reveals a great deal about the elite families who are dignified by sociologists as "the power structure," as well as about their relationships with all sorts of other people. The reader will gain many insights into the now lost world of the early twentieth century.

But to begin one should get into the spirit of this child's retrospective view of a most interesting parent. Not since Clarence Day has an author writing about a real-life parent done so with such verve. We see before our eyes a traditional southern lady who is also a far-sighted visionary moving into areas few "ladies" would have ventured to enter. In giving us her perception of her mother, Mary Buford Hitz also offers a fascinating discourse on the life cycle, moving through her mother's childhood, young adulthood, and old age and through her own early years.

Elisabeth Scott Bocock's approach to parenting may not have been unique but it was unusual. Lively details about manners, domesticity, cooking, dress, and elite-servant relationships, as well as the nature of an extended family, all tell us about the inwardness of family life. There are very few such honest memoirs of life among the well-to-do. Thanks to the interest social workers and reformers have in them, poor people have perhaps been overdocumented, but the rich, the movers and shakers, have been able to protect their privacy. It is only when a perceptive child comes along to write about (in this case) life with Mother that we can begin to pierce that veil and understand that the well-to-do are as complex and contradictory as their working-class contemporaries.

While part of a tradition, Elisabeth Bocock was far from a conventional club woman. The appearance, even the shape, of Richmond owes a great deal to her skill as a lobbyist, and her determination to save the historical "built environment." She was a talented, opinionated, one-woman dynamo whose methods were highly personal, even when she was seeking cooperation. Historians of women need to understand that not all women of achievement are cut from the same cloth, and this book will be instructive to them.

Although she would probably never have used the label, Bocock was certainly a feminist—one who could persuade powerful men to do her bidding. In this way she resembled, but vastly outdistanced, many southern women reformers of her day.

Anne Firor Scott

Acknowledgments

Foremost thanks go to Anne Freeman, teacher of writing, who pushed this parachutist out of the plane, jumped behind her, and kept the gentle criticism and encouragement coming right down through the soft landing of the first version of the memoir. I am equally indebted to Patricia Cecil Hass, fellow Richmonder, friend of Anne Freeman and an editor at Knopf, who became the bulldozer for the project, giving me the crucial editorial support I needed to turn the memoir I had written into the more substantive book that the University Press of Virginia was after.

Nancy Essig, director of the University Press of Virginia, took a chance on a middle-aged freelance writing her first book, and through the ups and downs of various outside readers stayed behind the project. I am honored that Anne Firor Scott, preeminent in the field of women's history, was willing to write the preface for the book.

When Mother died, we gave her papers to the Special Collections Department of the James Branch Cabell Library of Virginia Commonwealth University. When I needed to do extensive research, their willingness to let me take this material back to Alexandria, Virginia, made my job infinitely easier. My thanks to Betsy Pittman and Ray Bonis for their help guiding me through the collection.

The collections of the Richmond Public Library, the Library of Virginia, the William Byrd Branch of the Association for the Preservation of Virginia Antiquities, and the Valentine Museum all yielded useful information. I thank, also, all the individuals who gave of their time to be interviewed.

Encouragement came from many sources, but I am deeply grateful to the persistent votes of confidence I got from my husband, Fred; daughter, Eliza; sister, Bessie Carter; sister-in-law and brother, Berta and Freddie Bocock; niece Natalie Turnage, and friends Alice Digilio and Rosalie Kerr. Rosalie came to my rescue each time that my computer ignorance threatened to overwhelm me. Zofia Smardz also helped me over technological problems.

They, in addition to Anne Freeman and Pat Hass, read and reread the manuscript in the eight years that it took to get from the beginning of this project to the end. The rewriting, which went on for three years, was by far the most tedious and discouraging part, and it was in this period that their support made the difference. Sadly for all of us, my brother-in-law, Bobbie Carter, died during the writing of the book, as did both Fred Reed and Bill Reed.

Never Ask Permission

Elisabeth Scott Bocock, a radiant Salvation Army Christmas Mother for Richmond, with me beside her, 1107 Grove Avenue, 1942 (Copyright Richmond Times-Dispatch; *used with permission)*

Prologue

I AM SEVEN YEARS LATE starting to write about my mother, and here I
am, a half sentence into the project, already having violated one of her
chief commandments—never begin a letter, a sermon, or any other piece
of writing with the pronoun *I*. Mother's Victorian upbringing, combined
with a well-born southerner's passion for privacy, made talking about oneself
a sin second only to the sin of talking about money. She was born in 1901, the
year that Queen Victoria died, and we often teased her by pointing out that
she had been born to carry on the tradition. As unconventional as she was by
nature, her manners and mores remained Victorian.

Tied to the sin of talking about oneself was the taboo against washing
one's linen, dirty or otherwise, in public. As a family, we hadn't much dirty
linen. We ran more to exquisitely soft, threadbare but expertly mended, hand-
washed and ironed clean linen. It was neatly stacked on the shelves of the
walk-in closet on the second floor of 909 West Franklin Street, Richmond,
Virginia, the house that Mother had grown up in. No unspeakable skeletons
shared the closet with the linen, because conflict wasn't allowed in our house,
at least not the kind that is openly expressed.

Conflict in our family was reduced to a subterranean battle of wills, and
the outcome was always preordained for a very simple reason—Mother had
the strongest will. Decorum reigned and battles never broke out above ground
because, if you did things her way, life was as interesting, as unpredictable and
unconventional, as lively as it ever gets. All four of us, Father, Bessie, Freddie,
and I, made our separate peace with her, each of us starting from very different vantage points but all of us, without ever talking about it, agreeing on tactics in Life with Mother.

Her ability to scramble, and in scrambling to reenergize a day's plans, her
impatience, her refusal to be hemmed in by the conventional expectations of
Richmond society, her originality—of expression, of opinion, of dress, of
operation—her delightful eccentricities and her not-so-delightful inconsis-
tencies, her temper, her deep interest in people and the energy and generosity
she expended in trying to connect each person she met with everyone else she
knew, powered our family, the community she lived in, and ultimately a whole
city.

To be in her family was not so much to ride in her wake—for she was a strong promoter of her husband and her children—as to be propelled ahead of her, like a small plane trying to outfly a thunderstorm, into all kinds of experiences, all kinds of work, all kinds of excitement one hadn't bargained for. To be her child was to not even begin to figure out, until she died in 1985 when we were in our forties and fifties, where she left off and we began. I can't imagine having a parent that exerted a stronger influence over her children than Mother, yet paradoxically few parents could have worked harder to encourage their children to develop their own talents.

The trouble was that, in her boundless optimism, she often saw talent where precious little existed, as when she decided that my clear singing voice meant that I was destined to be an opera star. No matter that my natural self-consciousness indicated that stage performances might not be suitable for me—this could all be overcome with training. So I took the bus out Grove Avenue to have voice lessons week after week until, mercifully, I went off to boarding school. The irony of it is that it was she who had the personal attributes of a great opera singer. Her sense of presence, her total lack of self-consciousness, her physical grace and beauty would have made her a natural. She adored opera, and was not to be disturbed in the course of the Saturday afternoon broadcasts of the Metropolitan. She would put her fingers to her lips to shush me as I tiptoed into her dark room, curtains still drawn from her nap, as I brought her requested wake-up tea tray, and tried, by means of a scribbled note on a pad, to get permission to go spend the night with a friend.

She was a tireless public-relations agent for her children, even when we were begging her to stay out of processes like getting into college. Cleaning out her files after her death, I came across a copy of a letter she had written to the dean of students at Smith College, when I was on the waiting list. The letter was a politely expressed reprimand for leaving me hanging for so long (it had been only a month), and suggesting that it was high time that I got in (the opposite decision does not seem to have occurred to her). Stapled to this letter was the telegram that arrived a few days later, informing me that I had been admitted to Smith.

Her enthusiasms were a matter of spontaneous eruption, and the timing of the eruptions often played havoc with school schedules, train timetables, and previously made plans. Boredom and routine were the Enemy, and how to avoid them was a daily challenge. I was born when she was forty, and by that time she had two passionate interests in her life (besides her family, which was her constant passion): horticulture and historic preservation. She was a founder of the Historic Richmond Foundation, and before that a mov-

ing force in the Association for the Preservation of Virginia Antiquities. Her
interest in horticulture expanded, in the 1940s and 1950s, into broader environmental interests, and for her there were both practical and aesthetic links
between environmental and preservation issues.

Richmond in the fifties was doing its blindfolded best to destroy its historic architectural heritage without even considering (as Savannah and
Charleston had already begun to do) that it was also destroying the foundation for one of the fastest-growing future industries in the South—tourism.
At the same time that historic buildings downtown were being torn down to
make way for parking lots so that businesses wouldn't flee to the suburbs (a
battle that was ultimately lost, anyway) trees, parks, and landscaping were being sacrificed. For Mother it was all intimately related. The more cars you
brought downtown, the more you needed the trees you were digging up, in order to counteract the carbon-monoxide poisoning you were adding to the air.
The more you destroyed the features that made downtown interesting, the less
people would want to go there. Why are trolley tracks in the first city to have
trolleys being torn up when other cities are busy installing them for tourists?
Why shoot ourselves in the foot while all around us in the South people are
showing the way? Forget the aesthetic reasons and the historic reasons if you
want, but look at where the future is taking us—there's money in it!

The common sense of it all seemed so self-evident to her that she would
be driven into a frenzy over the obstinacy of city agencies responsible for urban policy. Codes were lax in those days, and little notice or justification had
to be given before razing an old building. Sometimes Father and Mother and I
would walk to church on Sunday, down Franklin Street and over to Grace and
down to Capitol Square to Saint Paul's Episcopal Church. Saint Paul's had
been the spiritual home of General Lee and Jefferson Davis and most of the
other Confederate ghosts who peopled our lives so vividly that they seemed to
have imprisoned Richmond's soul in the events of the Confederacy.

This walk was seldom the serene outing it should have been. For starters,
Mother would be late. The same optimism that sent her fearlessly into battle
with city bureaucrats told her that at a quarter past ten there was still time to
plant thirty tulips before changing into church clothes and starting off for
Saint Paul's. Father, who would be ready to start on the leisurely mile-and-a-
quarter walk at 10:20, would stand at the side door, hands jammed in the
pockets of his three-piece suit, hat square on his head, the only sign of his
impatience the jangling of his loose change as the telltale red splotches of
high blood pressure rose above his starched collar line. Because I was small
and the walk was long, we would set out with me in the middle, my arms

stretched above my head as they hurried me over the rough brick sidewalks toward church. Not far past the comfortingly ugly red facade of the Commonwealth Club, as we started uphill, I would be stricken with such a bad split in my side that I'd be allowed to sit on whatever front steps were handy to get my breath.

Franklin Street was *the* premiere residential street in the late nineteenth and early twentieth century. After the fires that devastated Richmond when it was captured in April 1865, the city spread west, and its wealthier citizens built sturdy, spacious Victorian mansions along the streets radiating out from Capitol Square. My interruption of our walk down Franklin would give Mother a minute in which to look around and find that yet another of these houses had a bulldozer parked, ready to attack on Monday. At this, the split in my side would be forgotten; in fact, *I'd* be forgotten, and would be allowed to run parallel to them through front yards and over garden walls, dirtying my church clothes and thoroughly enjoying myself. Furious at one more sneak attack on Richmond's past, Mother would note the address in her little red book, pick up our pace, and send Father and me into church to hold pew 66 while she found a phone in the church office and at least identified the culprit.

We did not often make it in time to find pew 66 empty. Mother was the middle of five children of Frederic and Elisabeth Scott, who had occupied that pew in the first four decades of the twentieth century. Their five children had nineteen grandchildren, providing me with the instant security blanket of first cousins my age who were exceptionally close, even by the standards of southern clans. As a small child I could sense that we were greater than the sum of our parts; our number was partially responsible for this, but so was an almost atavistic need to do things together. The "five little Scotts," as they were called, often moved together in both conscious and unconscious ways, standing en masse at a funeral, combining their gifts to a building fund or a capital campaign, vacationing together and gathering for Christmas dinners that were the highlight of the year.

As we milled around on the steps of Saint Paul's after the service, while the adults talked interminably, my cousins and I would dart around playing tag amid the fur coats and velvet-collared Chesterfields, being reprimanded for knocking pocketbooks askew, and interrupting conversations as we tugged on their coat sleeves, trying to move them down the steps and toward the street. Richmond in general, and the congregation of Saint Paul's in particular, had a large number of genteel old ladies who could be found during the week roving the aisles of Thalhimer's and Miller and Rhoads, the two big, downtown department stores, in a hat and gloves, looking for bargains. Like me, they were bus riders, and I would shrink from their scrutiny as I boarded the Grove Avenue Express and slumped down, out of their line of vision. But I couldn't avoid them on the steps of Saint Paul's on Sunday.

We moved under the rubric of "the Scotts," but we included one family each of Andersons, Bococks, and Reeds, and two of Scotts—the Buford Scotts, who lived in Richmond, and the Fred Scotts, who lived outside of Charlottesville, Virginia. By the time I was born, in 1941, Grandmother and Grandfather Scott were both dead; but our family still followed patterns they had set both in Richmond and at Royal Orchard, an apple orchard straddling Afton Mountain in the Blue Ridge, which they had turned into a family summer paradise. Royal Orchard was, and still is, part of the myth, as its beauty is legendary and its hold reaches down now into the fifth generation.

The Sunday competition for pew 66 was usually won by the Buford Scotts, as Aunt Isabel Anderson was as incorrigibly late as her sister Elisabeth, despite prodding from Uncle Edward, and Aunt Rossie and Uncle Billy Reed had to drive twenty miles into town from Sabot Hill, their farm in Goochland County overlooking the James River. The late arrivals grouped themselves in a phalanx around the home base of pew 66, greeting with elaborate politeness those too new to the congregation to realize that they had invaded sacred territory.

On December 9, 1985, as we passed pew 66 and squeezed into the front pews on the right, specially reserved that day for us for Mother's funeral, a backward look revealed the same family phalanx, literally wrapping us in a mantle of comfort. I had been afraid I would cry uncontrollably, as I had at seventeen at Father's funeral, sitting in the same spot, leaning into the red brocade of those relentlessly upright pews to try to stem the flow: control of the emotions in public was a family expectation, but one I was powerless to live up to as the piercing sadness of the hymn "The Strife is O'er, the Battle Done" fused in my mind the Easter agony with Father's slow death from what had been referred to only as a "circulatory disturbance."

Father had died too soon, leaving a widow still in the prime of life and a daughter still in school, and his funeral reflected that. On the other hand, Mother, who would have hated the indignities of old age, left life just as she had lived it—in a terrible hurry—dropping dead at eighty-four in her own home. Incredibly, Father's spinster-sister, Natalie (nicknamed Bo) Bocock, died later the same day. She had been senile and under nursing care at Westminster Canterbury Retirement Home for years, and everyone who knew them both felt that ESB—as Mother was often known—whose unorthodox ways often riled her placid, sedate sister-in-law, had stopped by on her way out of town, gathered up Bo, and taken her along, probably having a ladylike argument en route about whether or not it was indeed time to go.

We buried Mother in the morning and Bo in the afternoon of a warm, sunny, December day. A Richmonder once said that, given a choice between a Yankee wedding and a southern funeral, they would take a southern funeral anytime, and Mother's lived up to that choice. It was a real celebration of her life. Saint Paul's is a cavernous church, and it was filled with those whose lives she had touched, many of whom—probably *most* of whom—knew her only slightly. It was her genius that whoever she met in the course of a day's work was of genuine interest to her, and her interest was not snobbish, nor was it of the gossipy kind. She was forever connecting herself to others, not just out of curiosity but out of a deep belief that she and they were part of a community of interest. Richmond was her bailiwick, her field of battle, and the recipient, sometimes reluctantly, of her relentless enthusiasms. Every mall, every parking lot, every four-lane highway that divided and disfigured her city, she was against, and any chance she got to knit in the fabric of neighborliness she took.

She knew the waitresses at the Commonwealth Club—knew which one had a sick grandmother or a college loan to pay off. She knew the man with bursitis who dug the graves in Hollywood Cemetery, and the lady who sold her stockings at the Miller and Rhoads department store and saved eggshells for her so that she could put them on her azaleas. Not to mention Mr. Spence in Mr. Caravati's junk yard who would manage to save the good heart pine flooring for Mrs. B., and those who had fought with her in a myriad of civic battles to save Church Hill, fight the expressway, bring back the trolleys, start the Handwork Shop, plant the trees on I-95, or found the Virginia Vehicular Museum.

They were there that day because they had a visceral sense of that connection, and many of them had stories to tell—of how she had double-parked her antique Mercedes in front of Miller and Rhoads on Good Friday to run in to deliver a potted azalea to the stocking lady, triumphant over their successful joint venture with the eggshells, raced back out to find a policeman in the process of writing her a ticket, and then not only talked him out of the ticket but left him standing guard over the car while she ran into Ratcliffe Florist for some Easter lilies to put on family graves in Hollywood. By the time she returned, he had made the further discovery that her car's inspection sticker was weeks overdue, but this, too, would be overcome by a recitation of more important things than car stickers that had to be taken care of before she got to the inspection station.

Oh, the stories! Everyone there that day had at least one, and family and close friends had dozens. They smiled as her grandchildren read the lessons, prayers, and "The Road Less Travelled" by Robert Frost, knowing how much that would have pleased her. They were able to sing "Once in Royal David's City," as we celebrated the miracle of birth in that Christmas season, and they felt the hairs rise on the backs of their necks when they heard the trumpeter in the balcony soar over the voices singing the closing hymn, "Onward Christian Soldiers." The service was as distinctive as the individual it honored, and it was fitting that it should end with a martial hymn, for there was in Mother's character, not just strength, but something that was fierce and uncompromising. Whether we were a charmed policeman, a frustrated opponent, a co-opted fellow board member, or a child held hostage to her latest passion, we could sense the underlying steel. We had all marched to her orders.

I didn't cry at her funeral, for which I was grateful, and was able to comfort my daughter and my niece as Mother had comforted me at Father's funeral. I had the sense that I had witnessed an extraordinary outpouring, and that, in some mystical way, the strength of feeling present in that church had laid its stamp on me—had held me up and stiffened my spine when I needed it most.

That was seven years ago—that's how long it has taken me to work up the courage to write about ESB. It was not only the hesitation of not feeling up to the task, or the realization of the enormity of the project. Nor was it just the fear of trying and failing. It has been more the terror of being simply a teller of stories, of not being able to flesh her out so that the reader would know in what a unique fashion she gave of herself to her city. I want to be able to convey the electricity of her person—so that the reader can sense the stubbornness, the willfulness, the playful winsomeness of her character. All my excuses for not trying to flesh out this infinitely interesting character have run out. Her life deserves to be chronicled, and Mother would forgive me for trying and not succeeding, but she would scorn my never having tried.

Several months after her death (she liked the finality of that word as much as she hated the word *passing*) we were cleaning out the closets in the lovely apartment she made for herself out of the old servants' wing at 909 West Franklin Street. In an overhead closet in her room, stuffed in with the suitcases and hatboxes, was a long gray-and-white Montaldo's dress box. In it was a washed and ironed, blue-and-white checkered cotton dress. Pinned to the outside of the box was a note in her clear, fluid, bold handwriting, in her signature green ink. It read, "Save for ESB to be buried in. This is the coolest dress I own, and I know it's hot where I'm going."

Bessie, age 17, Freddie, age 15, and me, age 5, taken in 1946

1. 909: *Ground Zero*

I T DID NOT take me very long, growing up, to realize that other people didn't live the way we lived. It wasn't so much that no expense was spared, because Richmond had its share of moderate fortunes founded on the economic boom at the turn of the century; it was more a matter of the formality of our life, which resembled the 1920s more than the 1940s.

During World War II we had moved to Lexington, Virginia, where Father was second in command of the Officer Training School attached to Washington and Lee University. Not long after we returned to Richmond, we moved into 909 West Franklin Street, the house that Mother had grown up in, reluctantly leaving a much cozier house around the corner at 1107 Grove Avenue.

Not much later, Freddie and Bessie, who are ten and twelve years older than I am, went away to boarding school, which left Mother, Father and me rattling around in the vast spaces of a stone mansion whose facade of Corinthian columns made it look more like a public library than a home.

The massive presence of 909 and the yard that surrounds it on three sides dominate the block, and when it was built at the turn of the century it provided all that was necessary for living in high style: a carriage house that bordered the alley, porticos on the east side for entertaining, a porte cochere on the west for loading, first carriages and then cars, out of the rain, a silver safe built into the pantry wall, servants' quarters in the back that were themselves the size of a normal house, and huge, high-ceilinged rooms surrounding, on the first two floors, a massive square entrance hall that rose up the wide main staircase to a third-floor, stained-glass, dome skylight.

The third floor, reached either by a second stairwell in the side hallway at the door to the porte cochere or by an ancient Otis elevator, had more bedrooms, baths, and a formal ballroom. The basement had more servants' rooms and baths, a cavernous furnace room with a coal chute direct from the driveway, a wine cellar with a heavy oak door that it took two keys to open, and a laundry room lined with deep porcelain sinks, ironing boards, and iron drying racks for the proper air-drying of linens. The laundry occupied half of the back of the basement; the other half had built-in glass-fronted cabinets stocked with the extra sets of china, glassware, and linens that came out only for parties.

When it was built, 909 was at the heart of fashionable Richmond, but

An early postcard of 909 West Franklin Street

during the course of the century fashion had moved west, to newer residential suburbs. The house is in the heart of the Fan District, so called because the streets radiating from Monroe Park in the center of Richmond go off from it in the shape of a fan. Since I grew up, the Fan, as it is called, has become a popular residential area, full of young couples restoring interesting Victorian and turn-of-the-century houses. But when I was growing up, the area around 909 was a backwash of seedy boarding houses, decaying commercial strips like West Grace Street around the corner from us, and residential streets that housed people who either liked in-town living or were stuck there. In the middle of all this, like a dinosaur that had outlived the climate that sustained its species, sat 909.

Mother ran the house much as her mother had. In the beginning, the ratio of servants to family was about equal, but when Bessie and Freddie left for boarding school, servants outnumbered family. The heart of the operation was the kitchen, and in my earliest memory it was ruled over by Lucy James, a tiny, wizened figure who had no patience with childish requests or ringing telephones. She had a job to do, and hell could freeze over before she stirred from in front of the commercial-sized gas stove that was her laboratory. When I happened by, she would raise her eyebrows and look at me with disapproval over the tops of her spectacles.

Cora Gardner Jones, who became cook when Lucy retired, began work at 909 as a maid when Grandfather lived there, and remembered using a toothbrush to clean, to his exact specifications, the indentations in the heads of the marble griffins that held up the front-hall table. Unlike Lucy, Cora did not mind doing several things at once, one of which became keeping track of me as Mother got more and more involved in civic affairs. Cora, who had strong maternal instincts, had no children of her own, and so the inevitable happened. Her love and common sense overflowed into my life, and we filled each other's needs—hers for a child to love and mine for normalcy. Gregarious, bright, and endlessly curious about people, Cora might well have been a first-rate detective or psychologist had she not grown up poor and black in the South. The worlds of blacks and whites were completely separate in the Richmond of those days, and Cora stayed abreast of both of them, one actually and the other vicariously. No divorce or scandal in the white world ever surprised her, and whether greeting guests or listening to conversations at a dinner party, Cora stored away the little clues that when added up made for a startlingly accurate portrait of that society. Neither the grocery delivery man nor my aunts and uncles came to 909 without seeking out Cora to bring them up to date.

Cora and Mother had a complex relationship. Cora was Mother's alter ego, her field commander at 909, the one that kept the household to the ordered and measured pace that meant so much to Father. Mother thrived on activity and Father thrived on peace and quiet. It was often left to Cora to keep the center holding. In her I found an ally in my battle against Mother's attempts to civilize me. Cora and I were in cahoots in my campaign to get rid of the French governesses Mother kept hiring to teach me good manners and French, in that order. A succession of governesses found me impervious to instruction and slithery in my escape techniques. I was sure to escape if I smelled Cora's oatmeal cookies baking. These were lacy, see-through things made mostly of butter, brown sugar, molasses, and oatmeal, with just enough flour thrown in to make the main ingredients adhere to each other. Holes formed in them while they were baking, and getting them off the baking sheet was a matter of perfect timing: a second too early, and the buttery mixture regressed into ooze and stuck to the spatula; a second too late, and the rounds were hard and brittle, and broke into pieces when lifted. It took seven or eight of them, hot to the tongue, to go with a glass of milk. Probably thanks to Cora's pleading my cause, Mother finally gave up on governesses. Ten years earlier, Mother had had the opposite problem with Freddie, who loved his French governess, Mlle Gautier, so much that Mother was afraid she would be supplanted, and so let Mlle Gautier go.

The main duty of the governesses was to get me dressed and walk me to school. Getting dressed was never simple because I hated my hand-me-down clothes. I was toward the young end of a line of female first cousins who each spent two years or so in the smocked dresses, dirndls, corduroy overalls, and wool coats with velvet collars, matching hats, and zippered leggings that had begun life either with Bessie or our cousin Leasie Anderson. Good care had been kept of them, but they were dreadfully old-fashioned. My friends at school never had to wear leggings, even in the coldest weather. They dressed in matching skirts and blouses and "store bought" dresses. My dresses tended to puffed sleeves and sashes that tied in a bow at the back, which I learned to undo at school, bringing the ends around and tying them in a knot in front. They were usually a dreary length, with huge hems that showed several different hem lines that refused to be ironed out. There were always several over-sized kilts to choose from, paired with Austrian sweaters that had been darned where moths had eaten them, and whose silver buttons never matched. These were made of scratchy wool and were usually dark green, gray, or navy blue. I was envious of my friends' pink, acrylic sweaters with the heart-shaped, fake mother-of-pearl buttons.

The one item of clothing that Mother approved of buying was shoes, and this was a big event since even my cotton undershirts and lace-trimmed underpants were hand-me-downs. Ask any eight-year-old how important shoes are, and they will tell you that a glance downward gives them an instant clue as to who fits in and who doesn't. The 1950s equivalent of Reeboks were "penny loafers," and although I knew Mother disapproved of these laceless, arch-ruining shoes, I thought if I could stage a tearful last stand at the shoe store I might avoid the brown-and-white saddle shoes that made my long, narrow feet look comical. Part of our problem at the shoe store was in our different views of the outing. It might have been the highlight of the winter for me, but for Mother it was a non-event, sandwiched between, say, a funeral and a dentist appointment. I wanted her to come in and act like a mother, and for us to be indistinguishable from all the other mothers and children in

Hofheimer's shoe store on a schoolday afternoon. But Mother could neither look nor act the part. Dressed for the funeral in the eclectic high fashion that was her style, she would turn every head as soon as she walked through the door. It has always seemed to me unfair that handsome men get more distinguished looking as they get older, whereas the bell curve of most women's beauty peaks in their thirties. Mother was the exception that proves the rule. When I was eight, she was forty-eight, and still at the apex of her beauty.

At five feet nine inches, augmented often by stubby-heeled, lace-up, open-toed French shoes, she held herself regally and did not know how to make an inconspicuous entrance, even into a shoe store. The first thing one noticed about her were her expressive brown eyes, set deep and wide into the bone structure of her face. It was this bone structure that defined her beauty, for as she aged it became more chiseled, and the essential elements of her character became readable in her face. There is a photograph of Mother and Aunt Isabel christening a ship, probably shortly after World War I. They are dressed in the long-waisted style of the flapper era and wearing wide-brimmed hats. What is interesting is that Mother, while handsome in a trendy, rather bored fashion, shows little of the patrician beauty that emerged in her bone structure twenty years later. The vapid expression by then had given way to one of straightforward vigor, amusement, and interest. Her passions registered more in her eyes and in the movement of her eyebrows, but she was always ready to smile, and it took little in the way of a response to evoke one. She disliked frowning, and the admonition "Smile and the world smiles with you, weep and you weep alone" became something of a family motto.

On her prematurely gray head there was usually a hat—not one of the little veil jobs favored by women in those days but more likely a broad-brimmed velvet hat that framed and somehow magnified the sunken beauty of her eyes. Her nose was high and noble, its straight ridge a symbol of her uncompromising nature. She had high cheekbones, and the porcelain-clear complexion and high color of her Scots-Irish ancestors. When she was excited or angry, which was not infrequently, or when she was hot or in a hurry, which was nearly all the time, her cheeks would flame with color. Highlighting this flame were the ruby earrings, pendant, clips, and pin that Father had given her over the years to match the large, deep-red, Indian ruby of her engagement ring. Mother started the day with jewelry, often storing it in her pocket when she was late for a meeting, and then absentmindedly putting it on, one piece at a time, in the middle of a meal, a conversation, or a meeting. Her friends were all used to this and would help with reminders such as, "Elisabeth, you've only

Aunt Isabel and Mother christening a ship, probably at Newport News Shipyard, ca. 1919

got on one earring." Cora, who was forever being asked to find lost jewelry, would check ashtrays if a pocket search did not turn up anything, because frequently Mother would come downstairs with jewelry in her hand, be derailed by the telephone, and leave in her wake a pile of gold and rubies. Her jewelry could also turn up in envelopes, on mantles, in her change purse, which was rarely without an earring or two, and even on the dashboard of her car.

If Cora had failed to find lost jewelry at 909 she could usually track it down by verbally playing Mother's day back to herself, and then following out her hunches on the telephone, finding that "yes, indeed, Mrs. B.'s ring was in Mrs. McElroy's soap dish," or "her bracelets were by the bed where she took a nap at Sabot Hill." At any given point in her adult life, probably a third of ESB's jewelry would be "lost."

Mother carried jewelry around the way most of us carry pencils, her cavalier attitude a result of the fact that her parents had used diamonds and opals to persuade her not to marry a long list of suitors whose worst sin was that they were not Virginians. She had also inherited beautiful jewelry from her mother, since Grandfather Scott, from whom Mother got her quick temper, had called up Raymond C. Yard, Jewelers, in New York City, whenever his temper had sent his long-suffering wife to her bedroom with a migraine headache—which, judging by the stomachers, diamond drop earrings, opal pendants, strings of pearl, and star sapphire rings, must have been fairly frequently. Father often gave Mother jewelry at Chistmastime. Whimsy determined where the jewelry went—often pins went on hats or stomachers dangled from necklaces—but once it was on it stayed on, no matter what changes of clothing the day required. There were not many days when Mother didn't do at least a little gardening, using the last rays of daylight to make her rounds with a trowel in one hand and bonemeal in the other, both wrists dripping with bracelets whose safety catches she had never slowed down long enough to buckle.

If the hat and the jewelry hadn't arrested the attention of the shoe salesman, the rest of her clothing would have. She knew the value of black, and had had several dresses made by couturiers in the 1920s and 1930s that were still serving admirably in the 1950s and 1960s. If the skirt was too confining for her long stride, or if it had been worn so much the material had rotted some place, Mother would have Steve Kulina, the tailor, sew in an enormous kick pleat made of a contrasting color or pattern. If she got tired of short sleeves, she would have Steve sew on long sleeves; if hems changed, he would be asked to circle the bottom of the dress with a contrasting velvet trim—alterations that were so outrageous that they appeared to be the work of a designer who was either a terrible tease or crazy.

Steve operated his alterations business out of rooms on Second Street. He called Mother "the Lady Bocock," and would frown as soon as he saw her get out of the car. His English was halting, but he was downright belligerent when she would bring more clothes to be "carved up" and "ruined." His voice rising and sweat pouring down his agitated face, he would throw the clothes in a pile, dramatically waving his arms and shouting that he shouldn't be asked to commit such barbarities. Some he would work on, others he would just leave in their pile, and Mother would eventually forget they were there. I think Mother measured the success of these ventures by how upset Steve got: if he didn't get riled up, the idea was probably not worth carrying out.

Scarves were the essence of Mother's wardrobe. They could be found stuck up the sleeves of her coat, pinned to her dress and flying out behind her like sails, or wrapped tightly around her throat, for although she was seldom sick, she was prone to laryngitis. In winter, an emerald-green wool scarf would jut out around the Russian fur tippet that she loved. As a child I was scared of it because the fox's head reached around and attached to its feet at the other end, which I thought was disgusting. Plus, I could swear the thing moved.

As with any shopping trip with Mother, I had been dropped off in advance to get the shoes fitted while "I run around the corner and make a quick check on Miss Alice and Miss Marion." The Meredith sisters were spinsters with whom Mother had grown up. They lived like hermits and Mother worried that they were not eating properly or getting out enough. The idea of doing one thing and one thing alone was foreign to Mother. Doing two things at once was a tolerable minimum, but three or more things accomplished in any one outing was really satisfying. Counting on this, I took advantage of my time alone in the shoe store to ask for, and have on my feet when she came in, a brand new pair of penny loafers.

When she did, finally, come in, greeting the salesman in her lilting voice and lighting gracefully, back straight and head held high, on the stool next to us, it was not my feet that drew her attention but the backlit X-ray machine that had just been used to measure my feet for shoes. Horrified by the commercial use of a medical technology that she felt was overused even for strictly medical purposes, within seconds she had turned the shoe store into a lecture hall on the dangers of overexposure to X rays. Did they realize, she asked, that X rays actually killed cells, the good as well as the bad—that it was not a benign technology? Deeply affected by early environmentalists like Rachel Carson and her book *Silent Spring,* and by the work of experimental farmers like Louis Bromfield, Mother was way ahead of her time in her awareness of health and environmental issues and how intertwined they are in modern life. The summer before, coming home by train from a trip out West, Mother got off at Chicago and left Father and me to finish the trip home to Richmond while she paid a visit to Louis Bromfield on his farm in Ohio.

Before she had finished her lecture, the mothers had gathered around, the children were looking at their feet as if they were about to fall off, and the store manager was envisioning lawsuits. Seeing that she had made her point, Mother rose to go, sweeping out without even noticing what was on my feet. I stayed in saddle shoes, and the next day the store manager was sent reams of material on the dangers of overexposure to X rays.

* * *

Soon I was allowed to walk the half mile up Franklin Street to Collegiate School by myself. About this time, Wortham Tinsley came to work as butler at 909. Tinsley was a courtly, white-haired black man who was well intentioned but as slow mentally and physically as Cora was quick. He was ordered around unmercifully by both Cora and Mother, and had the habit of saying "Yes, ma'am" to any request they made, whether or not he had understood it or had any intention of carrying it out. He was famous for lighting fires without checking to see that the flue was open, and eventually "to pull a Tinsley" became a household synonym for not following instructions.

Tinsley had a weakness for alcohol, which had to be kept under lock and key. It was easy to tell if Tinsley had been drinking. If, as he waited on the dining table, summoned after each course from the pantry by the buzzer near Mother's chair, his pace had gone from slow to funereal, that was the tip-off. When the pain of living vicariously became too much for her, Cora, too, would have bouts with alcoholism, but they were mostly on her own time in her other life at home.

Garrett Hardy, who started with the smallest job at 909 and ended up carrying the largest burden for the longest time, came to work part-time for Mother and Father long before I was born, when the family still lived at 1107 Grove Avenue. In the 1930s, his full-time job was with the Railroad Express in the afternoon and evening, which left him time to moonlight for several Richmond families stoking coal-fired furnaces. By the time we moved to 909, he was in charge of much more than just the furnace. He kept the cars serviced and polished, and when Mother needed day laborers to do yard work or move furniture, Garrett would go hire them from the spot at Harrison and Broad where they gathered in the early morning, and supervise them while they worked.

A tireless worker, he was openly contemptuous of slackers and drove anyone who worked with him as hard as he drove himself. A light-skinned black man who was fastidious in his dress and manner, he enforced Mother's prohibition against smoking on the job and looked down on what he considered Tinsley's lax behavior. Mother and Father kept Garrett on in the Great Depression when other families let him go, and by the 1940s recognized his importance in our household by giving him stock at Christmas; over time the stock appreciated, making it possible for him to buy property on a river not far from Richmond where he loved to go to fish and relax. As a result, he took a proprietary interest in 909 and in Mother's and Father's affairs, considering himself their representative. As the years went by, he took on more and more responsibility, retiring from the Railroad Express Company when he was eligible for his pension.

* * *

Mother's and Father's bedroom was a big, high-ceilinged corner room with windows facing, to the front, directly onto Franklin Street, and, to the side, the yard. Both the fireplace and ceiling had decorative friezes; a chintz-covered chaise longue sat invitingly by the fireplace piled with throws and lace pillows; and the wide Victorian windows were hung with heavy curtains. A Persian rug covered the floor, and dominating the room was an enormous four-poster, canopied bed.

Mother's closet and bath opened off of one side of the room and Father's off of the other. A short corridor between Father's closet and bath connected their bedroom with an upstairs sitting room that was home to comfortable reading chairs, a sofa, and Mother's desk. This room opened onto my bedroom, overlooking the back garden; it had been the old nursery when Mother was a child. When I was small, they would move upstairs to this sitting room when it was time for me to go to bed, and I would drift off to the sounds of Father's out-loud reading, reassured by his voice and the soft light that fell over my threshold from his reading lamp. But if I woke in the middle of the night, the light in the sitting room would be off, and I would be gripped by the certainty that now that my parents had gone to bed they had been replaced by the unnamed evil that I was sure lived behind the sofa in the sitting room. I would lie there imagining what was between me and them until terror took hold, and I'd throw off the covers and make a dash for their bed.

I could tell what part of the perilous passage I was in by the feel of what was under my bare feet. There were only about two steps across the carpet under my bed, then the hard floor that came before the five or six steps along the sitting room rug, followed by the hard wood of the little corridor, and finally, when my heart was about to pop out of my chest, the thick Persian rug in their bedroom. After two or three steps on this I would be airborne, landing in the center of their fortress of a bed. They were always good-humored about the arrival of this human projectile, which must have been unsettling even if it didn't happen often. They never made me go back to bed, and I would spend the rest of the night safely wedged between them.

The door between the sitting room and the corridor had a full-length mirror on it, and once I found it closed. I was a nervous, skinny, hyperactive child, prone to moving first and thinking later, and running was my natural pace. I always picked up speed on the dash past the sofa, and so was in overdrive, one night, when I slammed headfirst into the mirror. I was too slight to break it, but that accident caused the kind of pain that is tripled by terror. Crumpled on the floor, I was incredulous that it was my parents, not the unnamed evil, who had done me in. They were horrified, even though they were relieved that I hadn't cut myself. Their explanations as to why the door was shut seemed confused and unsatisfactory. With Bessie and Freddie away, Mother and Father had gone to great lengths to include me in their lives, and it left them little privacy. It wasn't until I was older that it occurred to me that what might have caused them to shut the door—what they would have called "engaging their affections"—could be the only plausible explanation. What my friends and I referred to as "doing it," and spent endless whispered conversations trying to figure out, was not something I could conceivably imagine my parents doing, even when I tried hard to think about it.

It wasn't just that they were older than most of my friends' parents, but that they were both so thoroughly Victorian in their upbringing. They were extremely loving between themselves and with their children, but its expression was chaste. In typical southern fashion, hugs and kisses were exchanged at least every morning and evening. If I came into the breakfast room and everyone else was already seated and eating, I made the rounds, planting kisses on cheeks, not lips, before sitting down. If there were guests, I shook hands, the point being that I made physical contact.

My parents' chief expression of love was respect, and this came through in formal manners that governed discourse and daily life. Men and children were expected to stand when a lady came into the room. An exception was made to this when I was older and allowed to study in the downstairs sitting room with Mother and Father after dinner. If Mother left the room briefly on some quick mission, I was allowed to show my respect when she came back in the room by raising my hand, instead of picking up the books on my lap and rising from the comfortable armchair that I studied in. "Yes, sir" and "no, ma'am" were automatic, not just for parents but for teachers and any adults who addressed us. This habit was hard for me to break at Smith College, where professors considered the habit quaint and comical.

To interrupt a person who was speaking was the ultimate rudeness, as was contradicting a speaker, and disagreement was always prefaced by expressions such as "to the best of my knowledge," or "I beg to differ." Raw, didactic statements of opinion were frowned upon; in fact, disagreement in general was frowned upon, and the dissenter was usually reminded of the famous statement of a great-aunt who, when her story was challenged, responded dismissively, "Hush, Elisabeth! I'm not particular about the facts."

Father called Mother Mama or Elisabeth, and she called him Jack. We called him Pop or Father, but never referred to Mother as anything but Mother. She was definitely not a Mom. I could no more imagine Mother talking to me about the facts of life than I could imagine my parents as sexual partners. What I learned I got from watching cattle at Sabot Hill, browsing bookstores, and pooling my information with friends and cousins. Because we were told so little, we spent endless hours trying to piece together what we knew, trying to translate how humans would perform the bizarre things we saw bulls doing to cows.

The rhythm of daily life at 909 was determined by who was home. Father was there at the beginning and end of the day, and then we all—even Mother—followed regular patterns. In between 8 A.M. and 6 P.M. the pattern zigzagged around ESB's engagements, and how many hoops we jumped through depended on whether or not these events took place at 909.

Breakfast was served in a small, glass-enclosed breakfast room off the main dining room. It had French doors that opened onto the east porch in good weather, and its leaded, small-paned Tudor windows overlooked the garden, the dog yard, and the carriage house to the south. A swinging door connected it to the pantry, and through it Tinsley would come with breakfasts that were very Virginian and very good. Breakfast was as big a meal as dinner, and getting one's vitamin C and fiber was not the point of it. Cora's buckwheat pancakes had been mixed and set overnight, and when she got there in the morning she would add the molasses, warm water, and coffee that reactivated the yeast, and cook them on a cast-iron griddle that rested over two gas burners on her stove. The pancakes were thin and pungent, and as dark as grained mahogany. Before breakfast, Tinsley would roll butter balls between two scored wooden paddles and make a small pyramid of them on the butter dish. The butter balls disappeared fast, melting in yellow rivulets down the sides of the pancakes, mixing with the lava flow of blackstrap molasses and fresh sausage, both made at Sabot Hill.

Sometimes doves that Father or Freddie had shot at Church Point were served for breakfast. Church Point is a farm an hour southeast of Richmond, on the Chickahominy River, which Mother and Father had bought during World War II because it was within gas-rationing distance. The doves were seared fast in a skillet to keep their juices in and then steamed with a little liquid and a top on the pan, until barely cooked through. Fried Albemarle Pippin apples from Royal Orchard, served with sausage, made another wonderful breakfast, but everyone's favorite was roe herring and batter bread.

The roe herring were packed in salt in a wooden barrel that was kept in the basement. A day before they were to be eaten, Cora would soak them in water to lessen the salty taste, changing the water every few hours. The next morning they were patted dry and browned in bacon fat on both sides long enough to make the skin pockmarked and crisp. Opening your herring, you prayed you would find a full, fat roe sack. If it was tiny or nonexistent, everyone at the table would commiserate, and it was family policy that each person would force themselves to cut off a teeny bit of their roe to make you a portion. Sometimes Cora would cook an extra one just in case a herring turned up empty. The roe sack was removed intact, blended with quantities of butter and then—the best moment of all—mixed into a steaming-hot mound of batter bread. Batter bread is a much looser, thinner cousin of spoon bread, and is made with white corn meal. Once the salty roe permeated the bland batter bread, something approaching a perfect taste and consistency resulted—an almost religious experience for a tidewater palate. Purists ate only the roe, but we ate the salty meat of the fish as well, which meant that we all spent a good part of the morning looking for water. Father's tendency to high blood pressure should have put him on a salt-free diet, but he loved roe herring so much that he ate every bit of the fish—roe, meat, and skin.

Such was the sanctity of this early morning ritual that almost nothing was allowed to interrupt it. The "almost" was Cousin Mary Wingfield Scott, whose invasions of 909 at this hour were forgiven by Mother, if not by Father, because she was an early-warning system in the field of historic preservation; and it was she who, long before I was born, had nurtured Mother's interest into passion. The first clue to the invasion would be the sound of the swinging door from the back hall to the pantry, as she shouldered through it with such force that it banged on the wall. Greeting Cora in her deep, masculine voice, Cousin Mary Wing would take several purposeful strides that brought her to the swinging door on the opposite side of the pantry, which in turn banged into the wall in the breakfast room she was entering. Tinsley, intent on serving one of us, would stagger backwards to make way for the whirlwind that had just entered the room. "Elisabeth!" she would shout as she waved the morning's newspaper over her head, "Look at this!!"

Within minutes, Father would have bolted his food and left to wait on the front steps for his friend we nicknamed Mr. Fresh Air Frazier, because he and Father walked downtown together in the mornings. Mr. Frazier's house on Monument Avenue was five blocks west of 909, facing the statue of General Lee seated on Traveller, and he always appeared on the dot of 8:15 A.M. Once Cousin Mary Wing had riled Father's digestion, he preferred to wait for his friend outside. Meanwhile, Cousin Mary Wing had taken his seat at the table and was sounding the alarm about the latest threat to an interesting piece of old architecture. Breakfast-table strategy always involved how to get the house off the market, pronto.

Brilliant, acerbic, and funny, Cousin Mary Wing was the kind of woman the South has never known what to do with. Big and raw-boned, she never fitted the mold of the blushing debutante who could dance as gracefully as she could recite Shakespeare and pen thank-you notes, but who knew better than to voice an independent opinion. Like a smattering of other tough-minded women scattered throughout the life and literature of the old South, she sought on her own the personal and intellectual stimulation that she craved. She raised two adopted boys, although she never married. She devoted her life to researching, cataloging, and writing about the architecture of old Richmond; and she brought to the fight for its preservation a doctorate, a considerable inheritance, and an Irish willingness to do battle. Her book *Old Richmond Neighborhoods* is based on her painstaking examination of old deeds, defining the city as it was in the nineteenth century.

Cousin Mary Wing spent her Sundays exploring old neighborhoods and was often seen climbing into trees, or onto the radiator of her car, to get a better picture of a house that would later appear in her book. Her passion for the houses that early Richmonders had lived and worked in was countered by a complete disregard for Richmond society's passion for genealogy. An article in the *Richmond Times-Dispatch* that appeared in 1957 describes her as saying about herself: "'I should have been a foundling, I don't give a hoot about ancestors. If one of them had been a pirate or was hanged, it would be interesting.'... That outburst, in a startlingly deep almost bass voice, would be heretical in some circles, for the Scotts are to Richmond what the Pinckneys are to Charleston or the Cabots are to Boston."

Mother's strong-willed cousin never left anyone in doubt as to how she felt or what she thought. A typical example of her acid pen was her article, in the historic-preservation newsletter that she put out, entitled "Country of the Blind." "We are reluctantly forced to the conclusion," she wrote, "that large and influential sections of Richmond's population have no use of their eyes. . . . Prominent among the blind are most city officials, businessmen and social workers. . . . Perhaps we should pity rather than blame people who are blind enough to create or permit so much that is ugly." Later chapters will show the degree to which Cousin Mary Wing influenced Mother; for now it is sufficient to say that it is hard to exaggerate, from the point of view of the child that I was, sitting at that table, the contrast between the pandemonium that blew in with her arrival and the staid rhythms of breakfast in the sunroom before she came.

Cousin Mary Wingfield Scott laying bricks in her signature high-top tennis shoes
(Copyright Richmond Times-Dispatch; used with permission)

If Mother and Cousin Mary Wing decided that a lobbying luncheon was called for, Cora was often their chief weapon. It was not unusual for her to turn to and produce a business lunch four hours after the preservation crisis of the moment had been introduced into the house. At one such luncheon with the mayor and several city councilmen, one hapless participant was confused about what to do with the doily and finger bowl that came in on the dessert plate. Eventually, he decided to move the water bowl to the side, but he left the doily on the plate. When dessert was served, he put it on the doily. Mother, without skipping a beat, followed suit. If it was not the city fathers who were involved, one or two businessmen might have been lured uptown knowing that they would be asked to extend a loan or to lobby the legislature for preferential tax treatment. But while they knew they had been cornered, they also knew that Cora's soufflé was going to be high, light, and good.

If she were not entertaining, lunch would be salad and soup, served with a little dark bread and a strong cheese such as Liederkranz, or the Scandinavian goat cheese that is orange and looks like nothing so much as a cake of Octagon soap. One house guest who thought it actually was Octagon soap, found that although it didn't make suds, it worked well enough.

When I came home from school in the afternoon, I would hope to find that Mother was busy, so that I could pull a stool up to the long, marble-topped kitchen work table and put away some of Cora's cookies while hearing about her day and telling her about mine. The worst news would be that Mother was home and wanted me to change into my work clothes and come outside. Mother didn't believe in down time, not for herself and certainly not for her children. If it was daylight, it was time to work, and if she was working she particularly liked having a step-and-fetch-it handy. After working hours, I was the only likely candidate. When she pruned bushes, I carried the brush to the dog yard and piled it up; when she planted bulbs, I carried the bonemeal and the bags full of bulbs; and when she fed the shrubs, I pushed the wheelbarrow with the fertilizer in it.

My main job was sifting the compost when it was nearing the stage when it could be used as fertilizer. This was the job I hated most, and is probably the reason I'm not a gardener. It was tedious, hard work breaking up the clumps of coarse compost, and forcing them through the wire mesh. If Mother had to go inside to take a phone call, I would drop my shovel and go play with Blackie. (I was responsible for this unimaginative name for our black cocker spaniel. When we bought him as a puppy, Mother and Father told me that I could name him, and that I had a month to think about it. When they turned to me expectantly at the dinner table four weeks later and I proudly announced that the dog's name was Blackie, they must have thought that the gene pool had run dry before their youngest child came along. But after they failed to talk me into names like Liverwurst and Inky, Blackie was allowed to stand. Years later, when our four-year-old named her fox terrier R2-D2, I knew how they felt.)

Blackie was important in my life because he was the only one I could order around. It would be nice to be able to say that I spoiled Blackie with affection, but it's closer to the truth to say that I trained the bejeezus out of him. When I got fed up with taking orders myself, I would walk him up to the wide, grassy median strips that divide the two sides of Monument Avenue, and between the statues of J. E. B. Stuart and Robert E. Lee make him practice strict obedience. The poor dog must have hated these sessions, being made to heel and sit and lie down on command, getting a doggie bone on the few times that he met with my approval, and getting spanked when he disobeyed. That this punishment of Blackie was an obvious mirror of Mother's spanking me for anything less than my full obedience was lost on me then, but that's what it was. I was a smart alec and got a perverse pleasure out of answering back when Mother was giving me instructions, and punishment was usually immediate. Furious, she would take me to her bathroom, go to her closet to find a shoe tree, put me over her knee, and spank me on my bottom. Bessie and Freddie were spanked with hairbrushes or switches, but by the time I came along Mother had discovered that shoe trees did a better job. She used a metal one that was a sickly green color and had a frightful amount of spring to it. It hurt. For Mother, punishment was not a symbolic exercise. It was meted out on an "eye for an eye and a tooth for a tooth" basis, and it was meant to hurt in proportion to the severity of the crime.

Dishonesty was chief among crimes, and it was the one that brought me most frequently to her bathroom. I lied to get out of work, I cheated on my assigned duties, and worst of all I stole money from Father's bureau. I had been doing it for ages when I finally got caught, and I didn't feel badly about it because I saw it as a game.

Father, after all, was an easy hit. If I asked him for two dollars on a Saturday night to go to the Lee Street movies with a friend, he'd slip me five dollars. If I asked Mother, she would give me two hours' worth of gardening work and, after I finished it, give me the two dollars. So in my mind I didn't think Father would begrudge me the small change that I lifted. Every night he emptied his pockets onto the top of the high chest of drawers that stood just inside the door to their room. After I knew they'd be asleep, and you could tell because Father snored and Mother fell asleep the minute her head hit the pillow, I'd tiptoe through the corridor and stand in front of the chest of drawers that was outlined by the street lights on Franklin. Not tall enough to see over the top, I'd grope around with one hand until I found the pile and then finger the size of the coins until I had picked out a quarter, a couple of dimes, and a nickel or so. Careful not to destroy the shape of the pile, and careful also not to be too greedy and give myself away, I'd close my fingers over the loot and tiptoe back to bed. Father was meticulous in his personal habits, and without blowing the whistle may have known all along that this was going on. In any case, it was Mother who woke up and discovered me.

Punishment was postponed until the next day, which only served to deepen her anger. The arc of the shoe tree was as high as her fury, and I can still remember the stinging pain. The depths to which I had sunk had been explained to me: "Here you are stealing from your Father who would give you anything you wanted. How could you!" But instead of making me feel remorse, I felt that if he'd give me anything I wanted, then he wouldn't mind my game. The ethics of the issue seemed secondary to its practicalities. My friends got twice the allowance I did, and all they had to do to earn it was easy chores like taking out the trash and feeding the dogs. As far as I was concerned, this was my way of evening out the playing field. Adults, I figured, just saw things differently.

Mother definitely saw it differently. Ethics came first, and my lack of contrition and determination not to cry as she spanked me egged her on. She admitted years later that she had spanked me too hard, and it was not long after this that she substituted memorizing poetry for physical punishment. Further contests of wills between us meant that passages from Longfellow, Poe, and the Bible took up comfortable residence in my head. Once, when I had been sent to my room and took revenge by making cut-out figures using the bureau scarf, Mother assigned the Beatitudes. I took pride in learning them backwards.

* * *

The signal that Father was home from the office was the sound of the heavy iron-and-glass front door shutting on itself. He would yoo-hoo up the stairwell, and usually get one in return, before taking off his hat and overcoat and hanging them in the closet under the stairs. His routine was unvarying. First he came upstairs and traded his business jacket for a burgundy-red velvet smoking jacket with a black collar and his shoes for a comfortable pair of evening slippers. Then he would go back downstairs, just as Tinsley was appearing with the ice bucket, highball glass, soda, and Scotch. The two would exchange pleasantries while Tinsley arranged them on the butler's tray and lit the fire, and then Tinsley would retreat while Father poured himself the first of two two-ounce Scotch and sodas.

This was my time with him, while Mother was bathing and changing for dinner, and I would hover while he settled himself in the high, straight-backed armchair in the downstairs sitting room. He had had Bright's disease as a child, which Mother thought was the reason that his legs were short relative to his torso, and he used a footstool to make himself comfortable. No one else would have thought of sitting in that chair, not because it was sacrosanct, but because it was so uncomfortable. As soon as he was settled with the Scotch and soda on the table beside him, I would get in his lap and we would read. He read me the Babar and the Madeline books, and later *Heidi, Call of the*

Wild, and *White Fang.* Undemonstrative by nature, he would choke up when we got to sad passages, and I would have to read for a while, until he got control of his voice again. During funny passages, he would laugh silently, shaking me up and down on his lap. No sounds emerged, but his eyes twinkled and his face matched the color of his jacket.

Our favorite pastime came on the evening of the day the *Illustrated London News* arrived in the mail; I think it was fortnightly. In the advertising section at the back of the magazine were pictures of estates for sale in the British Isles, and under each picture was a brief description of the building, listing its number and type of rooms. Our game was to find the largest but most ill-equipped castle—the one with the most rooms and the smallest number of bathrooms. Inevitably, it would be in Ireland, and Father would shake and I would laugh out loud when we would find a drafty wreck with twenty-three bedrooms, fourteen public rooms, and one bathroom.

Mother made a conscious effort to shift gears when Father came home. While we read, she would dress for dinner—bathing, redoing her hair, and coming down in one of several full-length robes, more formal than a bathrobe, but not formal enough to be called an evening dress. When Mother made her appearance, we would go in to dinner. The downstairs sitting room had sliding doors that stayed retracted into the walls and opened onto the dining room, whose mandarin-red walls were filled with family portraits. All of them were done in the romantic style of portraiture, in formal dress. Mother, painted as a young married woman in a very low-cut gown, was over the mantel of the fireplace, directly behind where she sat at the table. Grandmother Bocock's big, square portrait was hung over the sideboard. She was seated on an Empire sofa, and with her were Bessie and Freddie, who looked like English children in a Romney portrait—unrecognizable as the brother and sister I knew. They were playing with their long-haired dachshund, Pumpernickel. On the wall opposite was a portrait of Grandfather Scott, regal and unsmiling—slightly annoyed, as if he had gotten wind of a business deal gone sour.

Dinner was a three-course meal that usually began with soup. Most of Cora's soups I loved; but oyster-crab soup, a delicacy so rare that today you never see it, I loathed. Mother's rules about eating were simple but contradictory: Eat everything on your plate that you put there. Do not refuse anything offered during the meal. In other words, there was no getting around oyster-crab soup, or anything else one did not like. Tinsley would help by barely covering the bottom of my soup dish when ladling it from the tureen. Just seeing the little pink bodies of the oyster crabs, their tiny legs swimming in the creamy base of the soup, made me want to throw up. It was Father's favorite soup, and he would be on the alert in case Mother turned her head to tell Tinsley something, and I would have ten seconds to reach from the middle of the table down to the end where he sat and pour my soup into his bowl. Sometimes I was so anxious to get it done before Mother refocused her attention that I would slosh some of it in his lap, but he never let on.

There was no such thing as saying "no, thank you" to the following course, whether it was a roast and potatoes or thin slices of calves' liver smothered in onions and served with bacon, or a poached, stuffed rockfish. Blackie lay in wait under the table, but he was no help with vegetables or potatoes. Liver he loved, but I had to be deft to sweep it off my plate and into my lap at the right moment. The onions that he turned his nose up at would lie under the table, their translucent rings blending into the patterns of the Persian rug.

Cora had some vintage cookbooks from Grandmother Scott's era, but she rarely referred to them. She had come from a big family and, being observant, had remembered the cooking she'd seen done. But her skill went far beyond reproducing what she had seen others make. She was an adventurous cook, open to new ways of doing things, and open, too, to ingredients that were totally new to her. If Mother came back from a trip raving about braised endive as a first course, Cora would order up endive from R. L. Christian's, query Mother about how it tasted, and experiment with cooking endive. She would discover for herself what Mother didn't know to tell her—that cooked endive is only as good as the stock it is braised in.

Like many creative cooks, Cora drove people crazy who came asking for her recipes. Her salad dressing was famous in Richmond: stout with mustard, pepper, and curry, and on the tart side; any salad dressed with it sat up and paid attention. All of our friends at one time or another approached Cora asking for the recipe. But there was no recipe: each time Cora made it, not only the proportions, but the ingredients themselves, would change. Capers might find their way into it one week, hickory salt the following, and chopped herbs the next. When, older and married, I realized I had a hungry husband and didn't know how to cook, Cora would come to visit a few days at a time, and she and I would work together. There was no point in asking her how to do things: I just watched and wrote down what she did, knowing that when she made the same thing next week it would be different, but if I could just begin to absorb the rhythms of her cooking it would be a start. For the last fifteen years of her life we had a grand time together whenever we managed to

Grandmother and Grandfather Scott as a young married couple

share a kitchen, she making fun of me and my dependence on whatever my vast supply of cookbooks told me, and me forever looking over her shoulder and watching the magic.

After dinner, Mother, Father, and I would go back into the sitting room, and Father would perk up the fire before settling down with his book, while I did my homework in the comfortable armchair on the other side of the fire. Often Mother would retreat to the darkened living room across the hall to "put her head down for just a few minutes." She was a night person, and often revved up for two or three hours of work, after we went to bed, by stealing an after-dinner nap. She would ask to be woken up at a certain hour, and it was like trying to raise the dead, she would be in such a sound sleep. But a demi-tasse of real coffee that Tinsley had left for her, the saucer covering the cup to keep it warm, would bring her around; and she would join us in the sitting room and sew while Father read aloud to her until he and I went to bed.

Mother in her Red Cross uniform and Father in his army uniform during World War II

2. Father

ATHER WAS A MAN OF FEW WORDS, an intensely private person, and someone I never knew adult to adult. As a child I was a star held firmly in the gravitational pull of Mother's planet, caught up in a whirlwind of physical activity: work in the garden, horseback riding, delivering flowers to friends who were in the hospital, soup to those sick at home, water to drought-parched trees newly planted on the Turnpike—all those and a myriad other things, whether planting bulbs around family graves in Hollywood Cemetery or raiding Mr. Caravati's junk yard, that were part of Mother's working day.

Life on Father's planet involved mainly the life of the mind, and when he was home he could usually be found in his high-backed armchair in the drawing room, reading. When my star crossed into his gravitational pull it was usually over books. He never made any verbal demands on me, never issued any orders or reprimands. He was there when I cared to join him, and he was there on my terms, reading what I wanted to read, stopping when I wanted to stop. He was not jealous of Mother's stronger gravitational pull; nor would he act as a refuge for me in the face of her demands. Her word was law, and he had faith in the way she brought up children.

I remember tension between Mother and Father over only one issue concerning me while I was growing up—and, typically, the arguments took place out of my presence. It concerned whether or not I was to get the Salk polio vaccine, which Collegiate School required. Mother found the incidences of faulty vaccines more worrying than the likelihood of the disease, whereas Father saw the vaccine as a miraculous scientific breakthrough. We had had a polio scare the preceding summer when we had visited Geneva, Switzerland. On arrival, Mother and I had gone swimming in the lake before dinner; when we got back to the hotel we were told that the lake was closed because of a polio outbreak. Having an overactive imagination, I resigned myself to having polio. All the rest of that trip we brushed our teeth with bottled water and I was allowed to drink beer or wine, mixed with such water, with meals. Although Mother disapproved of the school's forcing the vaccine on students, Father prevailed. I was given the vaccine.

Father was as quiet as Mother was flamboyant, as sedentary as she was active, and as steady as she was mercurial. To say that opposites attract is too simple an answer to the question of how such disparate personalities got together; the real question is how, once love's initial chemistry wore off, they forged such a peculiarly happy married life. Contrary to how it might seem on the surface, all the accommodation did not flow just one way. Father was not a doormat, and Mother was not simply a beautiful, spoiled, willful woman. Each of them held one of the two keys to their mutual happiness. In Father's case, it was his age and the patience that comes with it. Almost forty when he married and almost sixty when his youngest child was ten, he knew himself well enough to follow his own inner compass, to take pride in his wife's activities, to marvel at her energy, and to be dependent on her buoyancy.

A husband of her own age and of similar personality might well have felt himself in competition with Mother, because of both her public profile and the fact that she ran our household. But Father did not want a public profile, and he wasn't interested in running a household. He loved his children and made them feel it, but felt no need to be involved in day-to-day decisions concerning their lives. As an adult, I have sometimes wished he had been more involved. He might have overridden her decision when the orthodontist explained that straightening the jumble that passes for my front teeth would cost several thousand dollars, and Mother replied that she preferred to use those dollars to restore an old house.

Father wanted to be free to work long hours at the law, which he loved, and to look forward, when he came home, to the worlds of Dickens and Thackeray, Galsworthy and Trollope, and the worlds of intrigue created by Dorothy Sayers and Agatha Christie. Father had no commercial instincts whatsoever and did not keep up with trends in the marketplace. He was so lacking in worldly practicality that other people worried for his safety. By common consent, Uncle Billy Reed bought our cars for us, told Father when to get them serviced, and asked him at regular intervals when he last checked the brake fluid or the air in the tires. Father came from a long line of academics and clerics, and could easily have been one himself.

The key that Mother brought to their happiness was a realization, by the time she married in her late twenties, that she needed a strong counterweight. It was as if she had compared herself to a car, discovering that she had a fine engine, plenty of gas, a luxurious interior—but no brakes. This dawning realization led her to respect those qualities of mind and of personality that were at opposite ends of the pole from her own. This respect deepened every year of their marriage, until she became as dependent on his restraint, his thoughtful approach to problems, and his skeptic's view of human nature as he was on her buoyancy. On his advice, many letters that Mother wrote in the heat of battle were not sent. In the ones that did make it to the postbox at the end of our block, diatribes were softened and personal references deleted. Mother was possessed to get a letter in the mail before the ink was dry, often walking the half block to mail it late at night, carrying a hatchet for what she thought was protection. She blamed most of her worst mistakes on the fact that she had not "asked Jack," and learned the hard way to wait until Father could cast an objective eye on what she had written the next morning. I can still see the amused expression on his face as he eyed her over the top of his reading glasses, letter in hand at the breakfast table. It wasn't until after his death that it became clear to what extent he had become a necessary balance in her life.

To help me describe him as a man at the height of his vigor I am, as I write, looking at a black-and-white picture of us taken on the porch at 1107 Grove Avenue when I was a baby. Grandmother and Grandfather Bocock are in the photo, too, possibly because they had come for my christening. I'm being held by Grandfather, and everybody is laughing because, with a look of fierce concentration on my face, I'm busy twisting his ear, hard, with my right hand. "Mother Bo," as Grandmother Bocock was called, is seated right in front of the two of us and has not seen what everyone else is smiling at. A delicate, small-boned woman, her expression is serene, her white hair full around her face and fixed in a bun, her steel-rim spectacles perched on the bridge of her nose.

She and Grandfather Bocock were transplanted Virginians who lived all their adult lives in Athens, Georgia, where Grandfather was head of the Classics Department at the university. With their two children (my father and Aunt Bo), they lived in a large clapboard house on Milledge Avenue that, like its neighbors, was set well back on its own lawn. They led a pleasant, quiet existence that was governed by the rhythms of college life. They did not lack for the essentials, but there was never any extra money floating around because Grandfather Bocock ran his own unofficial scholarship service. This service ran by the Hundred Dollar Rule. Whenever the surplus in their household account exceeded a hundred dollars, he would inquire of his wife whether she had any outstanding needs. "Not that I can think of, Mr. Bocock," she would reply (they were of a generation that referred to each other formally; nevertheless, although he had a Ph.D. he never referred to himself as Doctor).

A Bocock family grouping, perhaps taken at my christening. I am in Grandfather Bocock's arms.

Within days, the surplus would be promised to a needy student who, taking the advice of others, had gone to Professor Bocock's office for help. This was their legacy to several generations of students, and it was especially crucial after the onset of the Great Depression. This unheralded generosity, as much as his academic reputation, is probably why the Bocock name is still easy to trace in Athens today.

Both Grandfather and Grandmother Bocock were exceedingly gentle people, quiet-mannered and thoughtful, with a certain Presbyterian fatalism in their outlook on life. They loved their headstrong daughter-in-law and came on long visits to Richmond at Christmastime and during spring and summer vacations. Periodically, during the 1930s Bessie and Freddie were sent alone on the train to visit their grandparents. Father was a regional general counsel to the Southern Railway, so they traveled on the Southern even though it did not have tracks through Richmond's Main Street station, nor through Athens; they boarded the Southern Pullman car at a freight siding in Shockoe Bottom.

Freddie remembers that Mother would pin tags to their coat lapels, saying who they were, where they were going, and what they were doing, written in large, clear letters in green ink. Mother tended to write identifying tags such as these in discursive style. In addition to the bare-bones information of names, addresses, and telephone numbers, a reader of the tag would also be told, for instance, that even though the children were young they should be expected to carry their own bags, or that the little girl should be reminded not to talk at the top of her voice but to use modulated tones, etc., etc. On pain of death, these tags were to stay where they had been pinned; the wearer came to feel real sympathy for Hester Prynne. Mother's writing was so large that the tag could be read from yards away. When she herself was at her busiest, she would pin her own notes to herself on her sweater, upside down, so that a quick glance downward would tell her where she was to be next.

Bessie and Freddie would be delivered personally into the hands of the train conductor, whose responsibility it was, at 5 A.M. the next morning, to get them up and put them off at a small town near Athens where the train made a whistle-stop. Bo would drive out to meet them. They did this successfully several times, then on one trip, when Bessie was about nine years old and Freddie about seven, the train made an unscheduled stop in the predawn darkness, and the conductor, thinking it was the usual whistle-stop town, put them off. "We weren't scared," Freddie later told me, "because we were together. We were just amazed to be standing there with our handbags in a cornfield."

Following the disappearing train, the children walked down the railroad tracks in the direction of some lights. They came into a small crossroads village, but nobody was up. While they were standing around waiting for people to wake up, a paperboy came by and took them to a telephone. They called Grandmother Bocock, who was able to relay a message to Bo, who was apoplectic after having been told by the conductor that he had already disembarked the Bocock children. The incident probably took several years off of the lives of the elder Bococks and Bo, who for at least a few sinking moments had to have been convinced that the children had been kidnapped or murdered. But Mother's reaction, when she heard of it, was probably that it was just the kind of satisfying adventure with a good ending that would help build Bessie's and Freddie's sense of independence and initiative.

In the Grove Avenue picture, Freddie is seated between Grandmother Bocock and Mother, a broad smile on his face, his eyes lively with amusement. He looks impossibly cute, but—truth to tell—he was genuinely adorable. He was the apple of Mother's eye, as cooperative as Bessie and I were argumentative, as smiling as we were scowling. He knew the secret that a simple "yes, ma'am," thrown into the conversation early enough, might be so soothing to Mother that she would forget what she was about to ask you to do. Bessie and I were apt to come up with ten good reasons why we couldn't do that particular mission now, which would leave us not only with the original request but also, depending on her mood, with punishment for talking back. We called Freddie Little Lord Fauntleroy and were envious of the special treatment he earned himself. But neither Bessie nor I could be mad at him for long because he was too nice. Freddie and I shared a love of horses; he taught me how to ride, play tennis, and ski, and never complained about having a ten-years-younger shadow stuck to his side. My nickname was Squeak, because I would squeak whenever I thought I was being left out of things or not given my due in adult conversations. I was preoccupied with keeping up.

In the photograph, Bessie is standing between her father and her grandfather, a twelve-year-old who has just been through a growth spurt, about to pop out of the velvet dress with the prim lace collar. Her long arm is half extended to help her grandfather with the baby, and her expression is loving, rather than amused. Her movement suggests that she has the habit of little gestures that make things easier for other people. Her features make her recognizable as the granddaughter of the older couple. From her seat, Mother is laughing at Grandfather and me, her long neck gracefully inclined toward us, Pumpernickel, the dachshund, on her lap. Her hair is waved away from her face and drawn up neatly in the back, which emphasizes the classic beauty of her features. Her simply cut white blouse is as becoming as the drapery on a fifth-century Greek sculpture.

Father is standing directly behind Mother, his attention turned to the camera, a slight smile visible underneath his mustache. In physiognomy, he is obviously the son of the older man in the picture—the same wide head, the same jug ears, the same broad nose and intelligent eyes. Father's bearing is square-shouldered; he looks healthy and fit, and his face and frame don't yet have the weight on them that I remember. His isn't a handsome face; the features are just slightly too heavy to be called handsome. But it is a face that speaks of integrity and trustworthiness. Father lived a life based on the loftiest ethical standards of anyone I have ever known, but to my knowledge he never once spoke about them, much less held them up to his children as a set of principles to live by. Just as Trollope's Warden, one of Father's favorite fictional characters, refuses to defend himself verbally against his accusers, Father felt that if one's smallest actions added up over a lifetime did not uphold one's honor, then nothing one could say could take their place. He looks happy and proud of his family, with no trace of the worries that began to have an impact on his health as he got older.

Father was a worrier. He worried about icy driving conditions as soon as he heard the winter weather advisory; he worried about being late (with good reason, since Mother almost always made him late for anything they did together); he worried that awful things would happen to his children from which he couldn't protect them. Once, his abstract worries became concrete when a freak tornado set down in Richmond, and he watched, helpless from his office window on the ninth floor of the Mutual Building, knowing that Mother and I were out riding at the old Deep Run Hunt Club on Broad Street. As it turned out, we were not in the path of the tornado, and it was eerily peaceful. The damage was done along the James River, which was what he was looking out on. The fact that we had not been touched proved to Mother the futility of worry. To Father, it just proved the infinite possibilities of disaster that any tomorrow could bring.

Our family habit of staying in close touch by telephone may have started as a way of assuaging Father's worries. However it started, it became routine that if your plans changed or if you were away from home, you phoned in daily. During her lifetime, Cora was command central; when she died and all three of us had grown up and moved out of 909, it was Mother with whom one checked in. It didn't necessarily have to be a long, drawn-out conversation, but she wanted to know physically where you were and what was going on in your life. This was part of her definition of what it is to love someone. No vague, benevolent sentiments of goodwill, here—but a sharp, concentrated, concrete attachment, like a tug on a rope.

Father must have been a very satisfactory child to his parents. Studious and hard-working in public school, he was the model son of a university professor. He worked odd jobs to make his spending money, and in his spare time played baseball. He went to Athens High School, where Bo later taught, and took the least expensive route to a college education, graduating Phi Beta Kappa from the University of Georgia at the age of twenty. After university, he taught elementary school and played semiprofessional baseball in Milledgeville, Georgia, for two years, in order to save enough money to start law school.

At this point he made a decision that was to influence the rest of his life:

with an eye to where he wanted to end up after graduate school, he came back to his roots, entering law school at the University of Virginia in 1912. The work habits of a lifetime took hold, and he applied his fine analytical mind even more diligently than before, graduating first in his class. Despite the efforts of Mary Munford, who was busy lobbying the state legislature to create a coordinate women's college, the University of Virginia was all male, and Jack Bocock was clearly popular in this setting. In those days, there was not such a clear definition between the graduate and undergraduate schools; the law school anchored the central campus at the other end of the Lawn from the Rotunda; and the number of students was considerably smaller—all of which contributed to a much more cohesive atmosphere than exists today.

Father was president of the Tilka Society—unusual for a graduate student. Since the purpose of the society is to have fun, we can know that Father stopped studying long enough to have his share of the conviviality. He had other important connections: at his funeral, a wreath in the shape of a 7 appeared. The Seven Society at the University of Virginia is so secret that no one outside the society is sure whether it is made up of seven picked each year or seven living members at any one time. The only tip-off as to who has been a member is the wreath that appears at a member's funeral. It is a society honoring outstanding young men of each generation, and bright, hard-working Jack Bocock was tapped. In 1916 he joined the ambulance service attached to the French army and served as a first lieutenant with the unit until 1919. He was decorated twice with the croix de guerre, with palm. For a person who was extremely sensitive to suffering, war service must have been an agonizing period of his life. Perhaps the surest sign that it was is that he never talked about his experiences in France, or left any written record of them.

When he returned to the States in 1919 and settled in Richmond to look for a job, he was more mature than most law-school graduates, and he was almost thirty years old. Along with other eligible bachelors like Walter Robertson, who became a close friend, he lived at Mrs. J. K. Jones's boardinghouse on Park Avenue, which backed up to the alleyway that ran by the 909 carriage house. The law, in those days, was a profession at which young associates could not expect to make good money for several years; but they could, and did, expect drudgery, long hours, and no indication of how their performance was measured. Just finding a job in a market flooded with returning vets was a feat in itself. Jack Bocock was offered a job in the law firm of McGuire & Bryan by Thomas Pinckney Bryan (later to become Jack's daughter-in-law's grandfather), but although he had work he did not have pay. He was to work for a year's probationary period without salary, and if during this period he did not bring new clients to the firm, not only would he be let go but he would be required to pay rent on the office he had occupied.

Soon after he moved to Richmond he met Elisabeth Scott, probably introduced by his friend and her brother, Buford, also just returned from the war. In 1919, Elisabeth Scott was eighteen years old, a graduate of "finishing school" at Saint Timothy's boarding school in Baltimore, recently returned home ready to kick up her heels during her debutante year. At last, young men were back to liven up the scene!

ESB's handsome, dark-haired brother was close to his spirited younger sister, and he was proud to introduce her to society. What a season it must have been! Those lucky enough to have lived through Argonne Forest and the Ardennes were home again—ready to make up for lost time and to find their brides in the crush of dinner parties and tea dances.

During his years in Charlottesville, Father had squired around a young horsewoman named Elliewood Keith, but after law school the war intervened, and when he moved to Richmond, Charlottesville was a long way away. As soon as he met ESB he fell deeply and permanently in love, but he was enough of a realist to see that he was going to have a long wait while this flighty debutante grew up, and a hard fight with a lot of competition to win her hand. It is typical of his steadfast nature that he did not take it amiss that she didn't fall head over heels in love with him. Why should she? He didn't have it in him to make small talk; he was a notoriously poor dancer; and when she insisted on wearing three-inch heels, she was taller than he was. She loved nothing more than to dance all night, and was happy to be the center of attention to a host of attractive suitors, who responded to her teasing, put up with her pranks, and generally followed her lead. A lifelong friend, Néné Fleming, remembers that when things were not lively enough for ESB, "she'd think up some terrific things to break the boredom, because she would rather die than be bored—if people got longwinded or tiresome, watch out!" Half of the fun that ESB got out of many of her shenanigans was making the opposite sex do *what* she wanted *when* she wanted. Néné Fleming told me: "We were on the way to White Sulphur Springs, going over a near precipice on a bad road, when Elisabeth told Pinckney Harrison to stop the car *right that minute*, that she had to go to the bathroom. [In those days, just mentioning such a subject to the opposite sex was shocking.] Pinckney didn't stop, so Elisabeth put her leg over the door and scared him into stopping, *on the* precipice."

Had Jack Bocock known it would take nine years of courting he might have faltered, but he took things one day at a time and began, slowly, making an impression on her consciousness by always being there. On that same trip to White Sulphur, Pinckney Harrison fell out of favor by paying too much attention to a blonde New Englander. According to Néné Fleming—I know her as Miss Néné—ESB put up with this for about six hours, then went to a telephone and called Jack. "Darned if he wasn't there by dinner!" said Miss Néné.

As 1919 gave way to the Roaring Twenties, ESB, looking for broader horizons than Richmond could offer, widened her sights to include the whole East Coast. She visited her friends from Saint Timothy's and traveled with her father and mother. Grandfather Scott had made a name for himself in national business circles by the successful reorganization of the International Mercantile Marine Company and through his work with railroads as an investor and financier. Various directorships, plus his seat on the New York Stock Exchange, caused him to spend a good deal of time in New York City.

It must have often seemed to ESB, herself in her twenties, that the looser, freer, go-go atmosphere of the century's third decade was made especially for her. Having fun was an end in itself, and higher education had been ruled out when she chose the curriculum not oriented toward attending college then favored by all but a couple of girls in her class at Saint Timothy's—girls whom no one envied since they had to study by flashlight under their bedcovers after curfew to keep up with the demanding Bryn Mawr College entrance-exam curriculum. Grandfather Scott violently disapproved of college education for women, and this did not trouble ESB since at that point in her life it was the last thing on her mind. She was much more interested in cultivating beaux.

ESB did not hesitate to string along several men at the same time. Lockhart Bemiss, Sherlocke Bronson, and Pinckney Harrison in Virginia, George Bailey and Carlton Francis in Pennsylvania, and Murray Hoffman and Tuey Kinsolving in New York City all thought, for a time, that they had the inside track. These men were all eligible suitors, but there were also other highfliers, who knew how to show this high-spirited young woman a good time, who refused to be put off by the disapproval of Grandmother and Grandfather Scott or one of their many surrogate chaperones from New Orleans to Boston. From time to time, rumors of an engagement would surface, and gifts of jewelry would be used by her parents to bribe her to her senses. In extreme emergencies, when even the jewelry was not having the desired effect, she would be sent packing—in one instance all the way to Egypt, with cousins who, luckily for Grandfather and Grandmother, were going to be away several months.

It was not only her parents who tried to impose their choice of husbands on her, as she points out in the following vignette, one of several she wrote for *The Richmond Quarterly* in the 1970s.

A PROPOSAL BEFORE WITNESSES

It was June, [and] Isabel had been happily married to Edward for some time. Young Rossie and Brother Freddie were not at home; perhaps they were with Mother at Royal Orchard.

Mrs. Juliette Gordon Lowe, founder of The Girl Scouts of America, had called from Savannah to say she was on her way back to England, where she also had a home, and wanted to see ME on her way north. Of course, I thought she wanted to get me to work for the Girl Scouts in Virginia. I was old enough.

She said she'd like to come to 909 early that Tuesday. I explained that Mother had her butler, John Fauntleroy, and his assistant, Arthur Wood, and the yard man, Harrison Hewlett, taking up every rug, scrubbing floors, waxing, and putting down straw matting. That didn't matter. "I want to talk to YOU, Elisabeth, not the rugs!" she said in her firm clear way.

Mrs. Lowe combined the charm of a warm-hearted Savannah aristocrat with the forthright approach of a London "Bobbie": courtesy without foolishness. Her clothes were London-cut-and-tailored: her shoes sensible and highly polished. Her voice was gentle and firm.

She came in mid-morning. The three good men had, by then, removed enormous rugs and were ready to clean the floors for waxing. This was not a noisy job, only smelly: turpentine was in the air.

We sat in the undressed drawing room. She—not I—chose the room when she entered. Even the draperies had been taken down. You could hear a pin drop. But, Mrs. Lowe was deaf and definite. She came immediately to the point.

"I want to talk about Bee Gordon."

I had known her entirely through her nephew, "Bee," a man of my age with whom I had become good friends playing tennis (always doubles; I was not expert enough for singles.) He was, and had been from infancy, stone deaf. She, childless and wealthy, had seen to it that he went to the best schools and learned lip reading.

I said, "How is he?"

She said, "I suppose he is well; but I came to talk about YOU."

"Ann Read," (whom I had often visited) "may have told you that I have a deep devotion to Bee and have fixed it so that he will always have plenty to live on. It would not be easy for him to make his living, and it is best if he is protected from worldly cares."

I had begun to wonder what that had to do with me.

"In short, dear child, I want you to marry Bee."

I said, "But Mrs. Lowe, he hasn't asked me."

She: "Of course not; he never would. You know that he is aware of his great handicap."

I said, "But he has never shown the slightest romantic interest in me; he only likes my foolish chit chat; he knows I'm a rotten tennis player; he never even offered to hold my hand or wanted to kiss me; in fact, the only compliment he ever paid me was when I told him I had no trouble talking to him because he reads lips so well. He said, 'Not at all, Elisabeth; it is because you have such a big mouth.'"

Under the aegis of stately John Fauntleroy, the three gentlemen polishing the floor in the hall heard every word. They may have winked but did not guffaw, at least not loud enough for us to hear it.

In the book *Historic Savannah* . . . is a photo of the lovely house into which she would have moved her nephew and me had she not struck a snag.

ESB's lack of enthusiasm for Mrs. Lowe's plan mirrored her lack of interest in marrying anybody at that point in her life. Playing the field was too enticing. In the 1960s, when Mother was a widow and would be asked to dance at a party, she would say "No, thank you," adding, with a smile, that she had danced her way through a decade and that now she was older, she would leave it to the younger generation. Unlike many of her friends, who married early, she had no midlife regrets about what she might have missed. She had ridden the roller-coaster of the F. Scott Fitzgerald era to splendid heights, and thanks to her parents had never had to face the ride's sickening lows.

One story from that era stuck with her the rest of her life, and she claimed that it happened in New Orleans. Visiting the city for Mardi Gras, like many others she was dancing the night away, in the streets, in jazz bars, and at formal balls. Her escort, she claimed, got very drunk early in the evening, but she was told by others in the party that one could drink champagne all night long if each glass of champagne was alternated with a demitasse of strong black coffee. This worked miraculously, she said—although her statement was followed by a story that suggested the coffee might not have been strong enough. On the way to the hotel in the wee hours of the following day, she got on a city bus, still in her evening clothes, and making her way to the very back lay down on the seat that went all the way across the back of the vehicle. The driver stopped the bus and ordered her to come forward and sit in the seats reserved for whites. She refused, not out of principle, but because she was sleepy and comfortable and used to having her own way. "How," she queried, "do you know I'm not black? I might have only a tiny amount of black blood and not show it." Bone tired of dealing with disorderly revelers, the bus driver would have none of it. The police were summoned and ESB was unceremoniously ushered off the bus, although the police declined to press charges.

Back in Richmond, Jack Bocock was working as hard as ESB was playing. Having survived his probationary year, he now drew a small salary. He left no record of what he thought of ESB's romances, but I imagine he felt a little like a spectator at the races, watching the horses being led around the paddock before the race begins: racehorses are thoroughbreds, so tense and energized, so aching to be let loose to run, that sometimes they rear straight up and walk on their hind legs for a few feet, their handlers helpless to do anything except wait for them to come down to earth again. At one point in the mid-1920s, Father was out of the country for long periods, sent by his firm to represent the mining interests of Averell Harriman Sr. in Soviet Georgia. How a firm in Richmond, Virginia, got this piece of business is a mystery, but it is easy to see why they sent a man of some maturity and European experience into the lawless aftermath of the Bolshevik Revolution. This is another period of his life that Father never talked about, but he must have been exposed to incredible upheaval and danger.

The contrast between how Father spent the 1920s and what ESB was up to could not have been greater, but slowly the two wildly divergent lives began to converge. Father had established himself in Richmond as an able lawyer with a bright future, which put him at rights with Grandmother and Grandfather Scott, who were adamant that their daughters marry Virginians. Mother had danced holes in the soles of her high heels, looked around, and found most of her friends deep into motherhood: she woke up to the reality that good dancers do not always make the best husbands. When and how Father's patience paid off and they got engaged I don't know, but they were married, with the help of eighteen bridesmaids and groomsmen, ring bearers, and flower girls, at high noon on May 3, 1928, in Saint Paul's Church. The reception was held at 909.

Mother and Father's trip by car to Royal Orchard for the first part of their honeymoon quickly turned into a disaster, as Mother's vignette describes:

A QUIET MOMENT

We had hardly reached Beaverdam when that horrid sound of a blowout tire stopped us, too far from town to call for help.

So poor, tired Jack took off his brand new jacket and "westcoat" (vest) and set to work. Luckily, he had had to change a tire earlier in his thirty-eight years although he and his close friend Eddie Moon had only owned one-half each of this, their first car, a year or two.

A nearby farmhouse happily allowed him to wash up and put on his fine cloth jacket and vest again.

With a sense of high relief, we set out, again, on our simple journey; daylight would be with us on that long May day for some time yet.

Nobody has ever been able to pin the blame on anybody and few people have ever believed us; but very soon another tire very quietly *leaked* air until it, too, went flat. This time a nearby farmer was noble enough to interrupt his supper, furnish small sections of rubber called "patches" and show Jack the way to apply these.

"Standing by" was all I could do, having never even seen Thornton (Mother's English chauffeur) mend a tire. In my soft apple green spring coat with wide, off-shoulder red-fox fur collar, I must have looked like an import. I certainly looked and felt useless. . . .

If you don't believe this nightmare came again near Louisa, no one can blame you. But it did.

As we drove up to the nice new Monticello Hotel across from the Albemarle County Courthouse in Charlottesville, a young "Red Cap" quickly came out to help us. He was gracious in his welcome; naturally he took for granted we had come to stay.

Jack went in ahead to clean up, and I to the telephone just off the lobby to report to Mother why we had not yet reached Royal Orchard and called her to report and thank her and Father for all the trouble they had gone to in giving that lavish luncheon and wedding reception (long, long ago) that morning.

Just as Mother's voice came through, I saw, to my horror, the kind and quick "Red Cap" was energetically bringing in all the large and small suitcases he could handle.

Simultaneously, newly washed Jack appeared across the lobby, but not facing the entrance. So, I yelled in my consternation, "Jack, the idiot is bringing in all our stuff." At which I heard Mother, in a sad, tired voice, say: "If you feel that way about him already, just come on home."

They did, finally, make it to Royal Orchard, and after a short stay they traveled to the Château Frontenac Hotel in Québec. Not to be left out, Grandmother and Grandfather Scott, Aunt Rossie, and Cousin Eda Williams appeared, driven north to Canada by Thornton so that they could wave the newlyweds off on a leisurely trip to Scandinavia, Mother still showing off her apple-green suit and matching hat. For the month of May, the couple toured Scandinavia on board a Norwegian freighter with an unsettling name—the *Drownding Maude.* It was a small freighter that pitched and yawed, but both of them loved it. Already they were setting patterns for their life together, reading to each other about the places they were to visit and, when the freighter docked, taking long walks. Mother began the chore of writing thank-you notes for their wedding presents, delighting one Richmonder with the absent-minded sentence, "The vase is so grateful and I am so beautiful." To her mother, she wrote that she thought it unfair that on their honeymoon they had to swim separately, since fencing was set up on the nude beaches to divide the male and female sections.

When they returned to Richmond, they lost no time in starting a family. Bessie was born the following May, but not before Mother had won the silver cup of the side-saddle division of the Deep Run Hunt Club Horse Show, riding over jumps and on the flat when she was eight months pregnant, the voluminous folds of her riding habit disguising her condition. Bessie, who later learned the story, told me, "The doctor told her to lead a normal life, so she did what was normal for her and continued to eat salads and jump horses. A month later I was born with rickets and jaundice. Jaundice turns you yellow and rickets turns you red, so people cried when they saw me."

Freddie was born two years later, and by this time the Great Depression was in full swing. Like many young men in Father's position who were earning little but were anxious to take advantage of the bull market of the 1920s, Father had bought stocks; he did this on a margin account, through Buford Scott at Scott and Stringfellow. When the depression knocked the bottom out of the stock market, he was left with a debit account, a considerable worry to a man brought up as he had been, and married to the Scott and Stringfellow boss's daughter. Aware of this, Grandfather Scott asked Father to come see him one day, and when he arrived told him that he was erasing Father's debit balance, and in exchange wanted a promise that he would never again willingly take on any debt, which Father had no difficulty agreeing to. In addition, Grandfather Scott suggested that Mother keep a household budget, making this seem a more acceptable idea to her by offering to increase her allowance if she did so. Aside from being a generous act, what Grandfather Scott did showed an understanding of human nature—in particular, the personalities of his son-in-law and daughter. Father was probably already easy to peg as a worrier, and Grandfather could see that starting off married life in debt was a huge personal burden to such a conscientious man. Moreover, he could see that unless his daughter's personal spending habits were reined in, the debt would only increase. Being a man of action, he dealt with both issues simultaneously.

Father was able to repay this generosity not long afterwards, not in kind, but with his own time and attention when Grandmother Scott suffered a cerebral hemorrhage from which she never recovered; she died within the year. Mother revered both her parents and knew this was a loss that would leave a huge void in her father's life. Father and Mother changed the pattern of their daily lives to incorporate a suddenly desperately lonely man, going to eat with him in the big dining room at 909, sending the children to cheer him of an afternoon, and visiting him for long spells at Royal Orchard. Father seems to have gotten along with his powerful, autocratic father-in-law very well, possibly because they were so different in personality. Billy Zimmer, a law partner of Father's, says: "To me, one of Jack Bocock's greatest accomplishments was marrying into the Scott family and still being his own man."

In his law firm, which became McGuire, Eggleston, Bocock and Woods, he had been made a partner, and was becoming well known for his legal skills. By this time, the senior partner of the firm was Mr. John Eggleston, who was so bright, eccentric, and abrupt in his manner that even his partners were scared of him. "The smartest man alive," says Billy Zimmer. Young associates found it disconcerting to be given assignments while he did crossword puzzles, never once bothering to look up. They also found, when they were stumped by a problem, that if they had the courage to go ask Mr. Eggleston, he always had the answer—again without looking up. According to Tom Gordon, a young associate at the time, no one had a clue where they stood with the boss; there were no evaluations and no way of knowing whether or not you were on the right track. After several years of this, Tom decided to use his immediate boss, Father, as a middleman. He and another associate, with some trepidation, decided to ask Father to make inquiries as to whether or not it was realistic for them to expect ever to be made partners in the firm. Far from being annoyed, Father seemed vaguely amused and agreed to take it up with Mr. Eggleston. Relatively quickly they found themselves partners, leading Tom Gordon to wonder if it ever would have happened if they hadn't asked.

Tom, a partner in the firm until he left to go on the bench in the 1960s, said of Father: "He was the greatest delegator I ever knew. It was so great to work for him because he would let you do it. He was a gentleman of the old school. I never heard him curse, and I'd never have thought of calling him by his first name." Referring to Father's dry wit, Tom added: "He had a philosophical approach to things, but with a practical bent. If he ordered lunch at the Commonwealth Club and said 'don't bring me any potatoes,' but they brought them anyway, his response was they were sent by providence and therefore it was all right to eat them."

Father was too old for active service during World War II, but he wanted to be part of the war effort. After a brief stint in Baltimore, missing his family, he was sent to help train officers in Lexington, Virginia, and we all moved west to be with him. Mother and Father loved Lexington and their life there, and Father's suitability for the work he was involved in is shown by the following vignette that Mother wrote.

IN THE ARMY NOW

Once during our busy family and army life in the Reid White House after a Sunday afternoon hard but delightful leaf-raking of the huge maple tree's multi-million leaves into double-bed sheets and thence to compost pile . . . Jack, tired but contented, said, "If I ever make it to Heaven, I'll be living in this house, in this town, with this lawn and this crowd, only I'll be Mayor of Lexington, not in the Army, because they move you to new places."

But he really liked his army work. He had a quiet, listening, ear-to-the-ground gift with men of all classes and color, though timid with women.

Once an officer-student in the School of Special Services, of which Jack was Executive Officer, came to Jack's office and said, "Major Bocock, may I have permission to have my meals in the town? I am from the South, and have never sat down at table with a Negro, and I don't like it."

Jack, remembering there was only one colored officer in the school at that time, said, "Wouldn't it be better if you trade seats with me? It was the colored boys in Athens, Georgia who taught me to play ball. I like 'em."

The exchange took place. The "Southern" officer-student sat in the Executive Officer's place, and Jack next to the colored officer whom he enjoyed and found to be also from Georgia.

This problem never came up again.

The war years must have been the divide for Father between being a young partner and coming back to find himself an elder statesman. Never talkative, he began to have the reputation formally granted to Mr. Eggleston, only without the eccentricity. Bob Patterson was a young associate working for Father in the early 1950s. On a Monday in 1953, he was assigned a brief that was coming up in a case before Judge Lamb's court. He worked hard on it all week, handing it in to Father on Friday. Saturday morning, he was paralyzed to find on his desk the brief, with two words written across the top in Father's neat script, "WON'T DO." After working on it all weekend, Bob Patterson resubmitted it Monday and was mightily relieved when it came back to him with "WILL DO" and a few minor edits the second time around. Often, when they had worked late, he would give Father a ride home. They seldom talked en route, but each time that he pulled up to the curb at 909, the same conversation took place. Getting out of the car Father would say, "Won't you come in for a drink, Mr. Patterson?" To which he would reply, "No thank you, sir, I'd better get on home." This went on for years. Another associate from those days, Carl Davis, remembered driving Father to a meeting three hours away from Richmond. He tried making small talk, which he was able to keep going only as far as the Boulevard, about a mile and a half from the office. The rest of the way there and back they rode in silence.

Freddie, who went to the University of Virginia, remembers many a trip to and from Charlottesville with Father in total silence. Yet he says Father exerted a greater influence on him than Mother, especially at a low ebb of his life, which came while he was at the university. Freddie was vice president of the Student Council his senior year, and he and two of his closest friends lived in one of the suites on Thomas Jefferson's Lawn that are particularly sought after by students. One spring weekend, another friend asked if he could use their suite that evening. They agreed. While Freddie was home for the night in Richmond, the friend snuck his date in (women were not allowed in dorm rooms in those days) and had sex with her in the empty bedroom. The next night, the young woman, who was sexually active, was again involved with several medical-school students at a different site, and took home from this encounter enough marks to arouse the suspicion of her mother. University officials were notified, and in the week following, Freddie and his roommates went to see the president of the university to tell him as much as they knew about what had happened. The president indicated to them that he needed more information, and so they got twenty-three others to testify about the incident. The next thing they knew, everyone who had stepped forward received a letter from the dean of the university informing them that they had been expelled.

At the time, Father was teaching a class in corporate law at the law school, so Freddie went over and waited for him on the steps of the building where he taught. Eventually Father emerged, and with no preparation at all Freddie handed him the letter of expulsion. Before he had heard any of the circumstances, Father said, "Well Freddie, there's bound to be a mistake here, we'll get to the bottom of this." Looking back on an event that happened forty-some years ago, Freddie analyses Father's reaction by saying, "Either he had complete faith in me or he wanted me to think he did. I think it was the former because he was not an actor. He said it in such a way that gave his child fantastic confidence in himself. On the other hand, Mother's reaction was that the university was right. We'd violated the rules knowingly; we'd made a mistake and we should be kicked out."

As a lawyer, Father has to have realized that although the punishment did not fit the crime (their error in judgment in loaning their room), they had in fact broken the rules of the university on whose Student Council two of them sat. On the surface of the matter, Mother had a point. Yet in both his initial reaction and in the steps that he took to get the university administration to reexamine its decision, Father put all his energies into showing his son that he had faith in him. The stakes involved were high, for both Freddie and his roommates. At a time when to be drafted meant to be sent immediately to Korea, all three had military commissions at stake, and one had a scholarship to graduate school dependent on graduation. Freddie remembers: "Father went to work and kept right at it until the three of us were readmitted. There were newspaper articles about it in the Paris *Herald Tribune* and the *New York Times.* We had to take our exams without having gone to classes, but our friends helped us through those. We weren't allowed to graduate with our class, but we got our diplomas in the mail in August."

The scars from this episode in Freddie's life are so deep that when his nephew, Jack Carter, graduated from medical school at the university, Freddie spent the morning pruning trees at "Redlands," the Carters' farm, to avoid sitting on the Lawn thinking bitter thoughts about the graduation he had not been allowed to participate in. What the episode showed him about Father is what he has tried to put into practice in raising his own children. As he puts it, "The essence of Mother was very physical. She delivered hugs and kisses and spankings. The relationship was very clear, not at all subtle. She was a wordy person, gifted with words and letters and notes. Father thought the fewer words the better, so it was hard for someone who didn't know him well to realize how strong an influence he could have."

* * *

When Bessie and Bobbie were first married, they lived for a brief period in the apartment Mother had made on the third floor of 909. Describing his relationship with ESB, Bobbie said, "There was a sort of standoff between us." This was brought on by Bobbie's feeling that "I saw your Father bullied and I didn't like it. It was contrary to what I thought was the way to treat a decent, fine man, and I resented your mother doing it."

Neither as a child nor as a teenager do I ever remember feeling that Mother had belittled or bullied Father—perhaps because, with the instincts of a child, I recognized the underlying acceptance, and even relief, with which Father viewed Mother's need to call the shots. But Bobbie was an in-law, a most difficult position to be in vis-à-vis Mother; and, feeling the undertow himself, he probably wished Father was more of a fighter. "He was certainly kind,"

Bobbie told me, "and as an older man to a younger man he was welcoming and always tried to put me at ease. He had a fine taste in wines, he preferred the Burgundies, and he would tell me about them. He knew that I was uneasy, and he understood my feelings of awkwardness."

What Bobbie overlooks is that Father, without much effort, could put himself in his son-in-law's shoes, and remember what it was like to be an ill-at-ease newcomer at Grandfather Scott's table. For the two tables, Grandfather and Grandmother Scott's and Mother and Father's, were similar in style and formality, despite the intervening twenty years. Bobbie remembers the black-tie midweek dinners, before the opera or the symphony, when, after they had moved to their own house, he and Bessie were summoned to 909.

We would get there around seven o'clock and go in through the back door. Bessie would go in to see Cora, and I would find your Father, and he would fix a big drink and offer me one. We would walk into the sitting room and stand around there, and he would generally tell me who was coming and something about them. Then around seven-thirty the doorbell would ring and the guests would come. Bessie would appear and Tinsley and Cora, to take people's coats, and your Father and Bessie and I would stand there. Then, when all the guests had come, your mother would come downstairs and make a grand entrance down the wide stairway into the front hall—dressed beautifully and eyes sparkling—it was very theatrical.

This sort of stage presence, and even stage management, had been not only allowed but encouraged by her parents, and I think Father probably saw no harm in it and may even have been proud of it.

* * *

In Father's new role as a senior statesman at his firm, he became counsel to the Trust Department at the First and Merchant's Bank, and also handled legal work for Scott and Stringfellow. His approach to the long meetings that this work entailed was to listen patiently, seldom intervening. After two hours or so, those who had called the meeting would turn to him and say, "Jack, what do you think?" He would tell them, they would follow his advice, and that would be that.

On the nights when he did not work late, he would walk home, sometimes stopping for a little sociability in the basement of the Commonwealth Club en route. This usually involved bourbon, bridge, and politics, and was, of course, all male. Father was at home in this atmosphere, although he traded in the bourbon for Scotch. A drink was named after him: "a Bocock" was a stiff three fingers of Scotch. Father took his turn at the presidency of the Commonwealth Club, but he was not truly an organization man. Serving on vestries, charities, or corporate boards did not interest him. He was happiest left with the law and his books.

When he was walking down to his office with Bill Frazier, or playing golf with his good friends Zach Toms or Andrew Christian, he did not have to say a word if he didn't feel like it, and neither man took it amiss. Cocktail and dinner parties were another matter, and Father was continually being up-braided by Mother for letting his end of the conversation down. Their friend Walter Robertson was assistant secretary of state for the Far East, and once, when they were at the Robertsons' for a party in honor of John Foster Dulles and his wife, Father sat next to Mrs. Dulles. Try as she might, poor Mrs. Dulles could not keep a conversation going, all of which Mother took note of from the other side of the table. Driving home, she lit into him, saying "Jack, why didn't you make more effort with Mrs. Dulles? I was talking my head off to Secretary Dulles, saying all the wrong things, I don't know any-thing about politics . . ." Father let her go on for a while, and then said in a quiet voice, "Would it have made things better if there'd been two of us do-ing that?"

Despite his refusal to compromise on small talk and his unwillingness to fill the airwaves with noise purely for the sake of propriety, he rose to the oc-casion when he realized the importance of putting someone at ease. Berta Bo-cock, Freddie's wife, remembers being brought into Father's hospital room to meet him the year that he died. It was understood by the family that she and Freddie were going to be married, although their engagement wasn't public. Father, knowing how much this young woman meant to his son, greeted her with a cheery, "Where have you been hiding yourself?"

His wit was subtle, dry, and never at the expense of anyone else, although he did favor a gentle tease when he knew the person was up to it. Aunt Rossie, coming to lunch at 909 one day, was late arriving. On arrival, she apologized, saying she had stopped by the hairdresser's on the way. Father said he was sor-ry it had been closed. Mother loved his comment to her one night when he watched skeptically as she got into bed with cold cream on her face, a band around her hair, and gloves to protect the lotion on her hands. From the oth-er side of the bed came the growl, "Don'cha want ya sou'wester?"

Exercise, for fun and for his losing battle with weight, he got by walking to the office, splitting wood that Garrett stored up for him in the dog yard, and playing golf (those were the days before golf carts). He also loved to duck hunt at Church Point and to go on fly-fishing trips to northern Canada with Pinckney Harrison, or on family vacations at the R Lazy S Ranch on the

Snake River near Jackson Hole, Wyoming. He and Mother seemed to have worked out a compromise on travel, because every other year (the "odd" years) we went to Europe, with heavy emphasis on France and the British Isles, and "even" years we went out West to Lake Tahoe, or Pebble Beach in California, or to Jackson Hole.

It is easy to understand why Father favored the golfing and fishing summers out West: the European trips were logistical nightmares. First of all, the travel party was seldom made up of just our family of five. Inevitably, cousins of the same age were sent with us, another family joined us, or friends who needed a pick-me-up were taken along. Mother did not know how to travel light. On one trip to Ireland and England, we had nine travelers and thirty-six pieces of baggage. Mother could be counted on to have an upright steamer trunk, complete with fold-out compartments for evening dresses, shoes, day clothes, and so forth. A hatbox, a big suitcase, and a small toiletries case made of alligator leather always went along, plus a carton full of guide books and maps, so that on long train trips the children could read out loud to her about our next destination. There was also a food box that carried Virginia specialties for the friends we were to visit, and oranges, rotting bananas, and chocolate bars for snacks.

One reason British trains are so punctual is that they do not stop for long in the smaller provincial stations, and so whenever we got where we were going, it was nip and tuck to see if we and our luggage could exit the train in the ninety seconds before it began to pull out again. We all had our assigned roles in this effort. Long before we got to the town, Freddie would stack the luggage in the space between the facing rows of seats; then he would roll down the windows of the compartments we occupied. As soon as the lampposts on the outer fringes of the station platform appeared, the men in our party would begin hurling suitcases out the window, so that by the time we emerged from the train, there would be a trail of luggage all along the platform. My job was to leap out before the train had come to a complete stop and start counting pieces of luggage, all the time trying to imagine in my mind's eye which ones I hadn't seen. Someone would stay on the train until the very last second to search for luggage that was unaccounted for, leaping off when a message was relayed that the hatbox had been located where it had rolled into the shrubbery. Recovery from an arrival took most of an hour.

On these trips, country stays near golf courses like St. Andrews in Scotland alternated with Mother's whirlwind compulsory visits to museums and cathedrals in cities. One summer we bicycled around Ireland while Father followed us by train with the luggage; another year we hiked in England's Lake District.

But the summers Father lived for were those spent fishing at the R Lazy S Ranch in Jackson Hole. Tennant Bryan, the Richmond newspaper publisher and lifelong family friend who vacationed with us, remembered Mother's approach to the rigors of western riding: "Elisabeth wore a pair of overalls big enough for her to fit in a styrofoam pillow pushed down to protect her seat on horseback. She rode with a parasol over her head for the sun, and took along a book of poetry to read while your father fly-fished." Some of the attributes that made Father a good lawyer also made him good at golf, fishing, and hunting. His patience and discipline were qualities that paid off particularly well when he was putting, casting, and shooting.

At home, whenever Father had free time, he spent it reading: biographies or Victorian novelists if he was reading out loud to Mother, which was nearly every evening, histories or whodunits when he was reading for himself. Bookshelves encircled the piano room on the opposite side of the hall from where we sat after dinner, and that room was floor-to-ceiling in books. Churchill's volumes on World War II, Douglas Southall Freeman on Southern history, Lytton Strachey, and countless biographies and autobiographies appealed to him. Well-written nonfiction was probably his favorite form of literature, in part because emotional expression was foreign territory to him, and partly because at heart he was such a realist.

But before books, certainly before sports, and before the law, even, came his family. For twenty years of his adult life he had lived as a bachelor, and it was not a state he missed. His family was a cocoon of security to him; the orderliness and cohesion that it represented was fundamental to his happiness, and his deepest urge was to protect and nourish it in every way that was open to him. "In some ways," says Miss Néné, "your Father never got over his happiness that your Mother married him. He had been in love with her forever. Everything else fell into place after that, and nothing else that happened really rocked him. He always felt, deep down, that he was lucky." And somewhere along the way, Mother came to realize that she was lucky, too.

ESB's Suffolk Punches on a drive-around by Saint John's Church on Church Hill

3. A Passion for Preservation

*M*OTHER ACCOMPLISHED a great deal in her life that materially and visually affected both the city of Richmond and the state of Virginia, and the level of public appreciation of her work was brought home to me one day when I was working on this book. I was returning research files on ESB to Virginia Commonwealth University Library when Ray Bonis, who helped me get the files up to the Special Collections Department, told me that a fifth grader had recently appeared at their door saying she wanted to research the life of Elisabeth Scott Bocock. When asked what had interested her in this, she said her teacher had given her a list of Richmond heroines from which she was to choose one to write a paper on; she had chosen ESB.

Mother did, indeed, belong on that list. She hit her stride as an activist gradually, having frolicked her twenties away and having spent most of the 1930s looking after her widowed father and concentrating on raising a family. When Bessie and Freddie were growing up she was, in their words, "a typical Grove Avenue Mom," the kind whose children volunteered her for any job that needed doing. Bessie remembers meeting some resistance when she came home from school one day and told Mother that the teacher had asked for a volunteer to produce a piano for a school recital, and she had told the teacher Mother would be happy to oblige. The resistance surprised Bessie, because it had never occurred to her that Mother could not have produced the Moon— the real Moon, that is—if it had been necessary for the performance.

Grandmother Scott died in 1932, and 1107 Grove Avenue, where Mother, Father, Bessie, and Freddie lived, was right around the corner from 909. Even before the gas rationing of World War II, her friends remember Mother careening around the corner from Harrison Street onto Franklin on her bicycle, the foxpaws of her fur tippet flying out behind her and her long-haired dachshund, Pumpernickel, racing on his short legs to keep up. Mother went around the block to 909 on a daily basis, seeing that Grandfather's household ran smoothly and acting as his hostess both in Richmond and at Royal Orchard.

From my perspective, looking back on that part of her life, she looks like the model—if, even then, unconventional—daughter and wife. But a note in her files, in her handwriting (undated, but almost certainly written after Father's death), is a brief, poignant glimpse of her that suggests what she felt were her failings on this score. Labeled "As You Desire Me (With Apologies to Pirandello)," it reads: "Had I wanted to be the kind of wife my husband wanted instead of wanting him to want the kind of wife I wanted to be, it would have been easy."

She did not do justice to her efforts. For at least the first twenty years of their marriage, she saw to it that the balance tipped in Father's, and her children's, favor. She certainly wanted to be a good parent, but I am convinced that the real motivation for consciously holding herself in check was her knowledge that she was married to someone very different from herself, and that she needed to adjust the pace of her life to his. In the 1930s, the efforts she made for charitable causes followed predictable patterns for the society she was born into, and also were a response to family expectations. She was a founding member of the Junior League of Richmond, a member of the James River Garden Club, and followed in her mother's footsteps on the board of the Memorial Home for Girls. But even as early as the 1930s, Mother's interest in historic preservation began to grow.

Richmond had been built on the steep hills near the center of commerce, the James River, as the city grew from east to west. Riverborne seventeenth-century newcomers established the city at the last navigable section before the falls of the James, as the river dropped from the piedmont region into the tidewater section of Virginia. The prospering city became the state capital, and as barge traffic grew in the eighteenth century, merchants built warehouses along the river in Shockoe Bottom and comfortable houses on Church Hill, above the bottom, where they could keep an eye on their businesses.

The burning of Richmond at the end of the Civil War had left little in the way of colonial or federal architecture. However, much of the charming, individualistic architecture of the High Victorian period that replaced it was not seen as particularly valuable or worth saving. Business buildings began to surround the next hill to the west that was home to Jefferson's Capitol building and its square, and as the automobile took over the streets, requiring parking lots, more and more of these interesting examples of domestic architecture fell to bulldozers.

In a *News Leader* article about ESB the day after she died, she was described as "the preservation conscience of Richmond." Her cousin Mary Wingfield Scott, Richmond's first serious preservationist, was responsible for the awakening of that conscience. Cousin Mary Wing determined early on that she could turn this young matron into another serious preservationist. Both women were members of the Association for the Preservation of Virginia Antiquities—the APVA—a statewide organization dedicated to maintaining and interpreting Virginia's historic sites. By the mid-1930s, Cousin Mary Wing was worried that the APVA was unable to cope with preservation crises, like the threatened demolition of the Adam Craig House in Shockoe Bottom. Adam Craig's daughter, Jane, was the subject of Edgar Allan Poe's poem "Helen." Mary Wing could not get the board of the APVA, timid from the adverse effects of the Great Depression on fundraising, to concentrate on this close-to-home threat. The solution was to found a branch of the APVA dedicated to salvaging properties of historic or architectural value in Richmond, which she did in 1935, naming it the William Byrd Branch of the APVA. She remained president of the new branch for twelve years, until, in 1947, she moved out of the presidency so that she could rouse the membership to greater militancy through the newsletter that she began.

One member whom she was gradually transforming into a militant was ESB, though at first ESB's role was as a society hostess for preservation causes, often in tandem with her sister, Rossie Reed. The 1930s were the beginning of a pattern that saw the sisters' names linked in many preservation initiatives, first as hostesses and later as partners in raising quick cash in last-minute house-rescue operations on Church Hill. In 1972, they won an award together, the Barbara Ransome Andrews Award, for their contributions to restoration, preservation, and conservation, given by the Junior League.

Wartime displacement to Lexington put a temporary hold on ESB's Richmond interests, but not before she served as Richmond's Salvation Army Christmas Mother of 1942, a job that, through public appearances and publicity, involved getting others to give to the campaign. The year 1945 found us back at 1107 Grove Avenue, and the next big preservation battle involved the Glasgow House, where the Virginia writer Ellen Glasgow had lived and worked. Through the efforts of ESB, Miss Glasgow's brother, Arthur Glasgow, gave it to the APVA and left money in his will to preserve the house. The APVA sold it to the William Byrd Branch at a low figure. At this point, 1947, ESB was finance chairman of the William Byrd Branch; she wrote more than two hundred letters to raise funds for the purchase. A *News Leader* article from December 10, 1947, titled "Saving by Using," takes note of the continuing partnership between Cousin Mary Wing and Mother: "Mrs. John H. Bocock and Miss Mary Wingfield Scott, who preserved the lovely old Barrett House at Fifth and Cary, have employed the same device to assure the future of the Glasgow House: they have leased it to tenants who will respect it at the same time that they pay enough to keep it in good order. To save a historical structure, find a use for it. That is the 'secret.'"

Louise Catterall's handwritten minutes of the William Byrd Branch in the 1940s show ESB by this time deeply involved, working hard, giving money, making motions, and hosting meetings. As she and Cousin Mary Wing took on more projects in tandem, ESB proved that she could hold her own in frankness. Referring to some disagreement, ESB wrote her cousin, "I would excuse your bad taste because of your good brain."

In April 1949, ESB spoke before the planning board at City Hall about old houses in Richmond that were used commercially, as well as for civic and cultural appreciation, hammering home the point that historic structures not only deserve protection but are also useable. That July, there was a marvelous picture in the *News Leader* of ESB lobbying Governor Tuck about preserving the interior woodworking in an old house that the state must have owned. ESB has on a hat that rises at least six inches above her head and French high heels; she faces him with erect carriage and a beaming smile, in a dress with considerable décolletage, which is contributing to Governor Tuck's obvious problem in concentrating on the interior woodwork of the house.

In the 1950s, when Cousin Mary Wing was increasingly absorbed in scholarly research for her books, ESB and several members of the William Byrd Branch of the APVA were fomenting a revolution. This was the point at which Cousin Mary Wing and ESB reversed their roles as commander in chief and loyal foot soldier. This was satisfactory to both of them, as part of a letter from Cousin Mary Wing to ESB shows: "I have had to take too much initiative in my day and am now content to sit back and help other people's enterprises in so far as I am able."

The Historic Richmond Foundation, or the HRF, was founded in 1956 to address the need to move quickly when a historic property was threatened, a necessary bypass around the APVA's requirement that it hold the title to any property purchased. There was no room—and more importantly, no time—for this process in ESB's Early Warning System. If the bulldozers were parked out front, the purchase sometimes had to be completed in a matter of hours, not days or weeks. Sometimes Mother would put up the down payment herself, and then, in a flurry of phone calls, raise promises of help from friends, from civic-minded businessmen like Doug Fleet or Morton Thalhimer, and often from Aunt Rossie. Louise Catterall, writing the history of the HRF, describes the five pioneers who were granted a state charter in 1956; she refers to Mother, one of those five, as the person "who had the initial vision." But Mother was also the convener, for the initial meeting of fifty business and government leaders was held at 909. Typically, ESB was a trustee but not an officeholder on the board, a situation that left the details to others and left her free to do what she did best—a genteel form of arm-twisting.

Tom Gordon once said of ESB, "She was the most inconsiderate considerate person I ever knew." What he meant by this, and what countless other people refer to in interviews, was that if you were sick, or in any way in need, Mother was usually the first, most generous, and most consistent source of help that came your way. But if she needed you to do something, forget your business schedule and your home routine, most especially in the early hours of the morning. Judge Gordon said that if he saw an envelope with the tell-tale green ink shoved under his door as he sat at his breakfast table, his heart would sink: he could predict that the legal opinion she was after was needed by later that morning, and that if it wasn't forthcoming her phone calls would follow him to the office. Jim Whiting, who was president of Historic Richmond in the 1980s and a great admirer of Mother's, describes a typical ESB predawn raid. "She would call up, always about quarter of seven in the morning. She never called me 'Jim,' it was always 'Jim Whiting'; she'd say, this is Elisabeth Bocock. I have been thinking about this and I want you to do thus and so, or I need your advice, or I want you to meet me at such and such a place."

The city council and the Richmond newspapers were the first groups on the receiving end of ESB's persuasive powers in the push to build momentum for the Historic Richmond Foundation. The first order of business was to get the council to enact a historic zoning ordinance; the focus then turned to Saint John's Church, in the heart of Church Hill, where Patrick Henry roused his fellow colonials against the British with his famous words "Give me liberty or give me death." The church is arguably the most historic structure in Richmond, but the neighborhood surrounding it had been going downhill since the nineteenth century, as white merchants moved their residences west and the centers of commerce did likewise. By the 1950s, Church Hill was poor and black, with deteriorating housing. Revitalization of the whole neighborhood, not just of individual buildings, was the initial goal of HRF. Once the zoning ordinance was passed, a pilot block immediately to the west of Saint John's Church was chosen.

Part of ESB's vision was that the pilot block would be enhanced by a landscaped mews running the length of the alleyway in the middle of the block.

The Garden Club of Virginia made this a restoration project using funds it raises yearly during Historic Garden Week. Different pieces of decorative wrought iron delineate the center section, and the whole, shaded by trees in the adjacent gardens, is an oasis of quiet and beauty on Church Hill. ESB imported from England the idea of turning an alleyway into a series of gardens, and the transformation it produced is magical. Another example of her farsightedness was the idea of having an architectural survey made of Richmond buildings. Many city organizations joined in this effort. The Valentine Museum gave office space for the project and it resulted in the publication of *The Architecture of Historic Richmond.*

Despite the loftiness of her goals, ESB was not above trench warfare. Jim Whiting remembers: "When I first came back to Richmond and went on the Board of Historic Richmond, I got calls from both your Aunt Rossie and Aunt Isabel saying, 'We want to warn you about Elisabeth. . . . She has been quoting you, and it doesn't sound like something you would have said.' I said, 'Well, I guess I said something similar, but it was taken out of context.' And they said, 'Just be careful what you tell Elisabeth, because she will use any means she has to get to her goals.'"

Jim and ESB shared a common background. It was the absence of a common background that was at the root of the disconnect between ESB and Mike Gold, a self-described "Jew from Brooklyn" who held the job of managing director of HRF from 1974 until the mid 1980s. At that point, he was, as he put it, "fired, more or less." In my interview with Mike Gold for this memoir, he spoke bluntly, unlike others among my interviewees. Working on the book, I soon developed antennae that helped me sense, as I talked to people, a course correction in the conversation, just as the person was about to say something critical. This was less of a problem with family members, who knew that anyone as powerful as Mother sometimes stirred up dust storms when she whirled into their lives. Mainly the problem arose as friends and professional associates swerved away from criticism of someone whose death had put her in the unassailable niche of Great Richmond Character. Not so Mike Gold.

In its early years, the HRF office was run by executive secretaries who were there to carry out orders—at first the orders of the founders and later those of the executive committee of the board. Mike Gold came from the Landmarks Commission of New York, and neither his view of what the organization should be doing nor his way of operating were compatible with ESB's. Until his appointment, she had been acting both as a strong voice within the organization and as a free agent in her own projects on Church Hill. Cerebral, curious, and blunt, Mike began our interview by stating in a matter-of-fact manner: "I don't think she liked me very much, I didn't like her very much. She was still on the board, and my feeling was, quite frankly, that she was more trouble than she was worth." When I asked if she used the power of her position or her purse to get her way, it became clear from his answer that he did not see her as powerful, just as spoiled and troublesome. It was almost as if we were talking about two different people. The difference was that Mike had walked, cold, into her culture in the last ten years of her life, whereas I brought to my questions the knowledge that prior to his arrival ESB had, whether one approved of her way of operating or not, established her credentials as a bulwark of the preservation movement in Richmond.

As Mike explained it, he could not find for ESB the motivation that he could for other older ladies, for whom he had great respect. Cousin Mary Wing, he pointed out, had her own serious scholarship to buttress the role that she played; and Mrs. Catterall felt that everything that made life charming and attractive had been trampled by modern life, which made her angry and bitter, so her fury and obstreperousness were easier to put up with. ESB was different; he was annoyed not only by her but also by those who gave her free rein and would say, "Oh that's just Mrs. Bocock." He remembers wondering "why were they making allowances for her, especially when she wasn't giving us any (big) money. There may have been projects which she funded not through the establishment books, because she didn't want to be bothered with me. That's very possible."

I tried to explain to Mike Gold that while Mrs. Catterall's bitterness sprang from a sense that almost all that was worth saving had been lost, in manners and mores as well as in architecture, ESB's frame of reference was the opposite. While she valued the past she was not nostalgic for it. She lived in the present so optimistically that plans for a future that did not include her presented no terrors for her. The source of her phenomenal energy was her belief that the work she and others were doing to preserve the best of the past would be lived in, added to, and appreciated by future generations. Long before she died, she gave her children and grandchildren houses that she had restored on Church Hill, not just for tax reasons but to try to tighten the ties of her offspring's interest early on.

Mike was correct in thinking that she had taken her marbles and gone elsewhere. Although still on the executive committee of the board, she had preservation projects going on all through this period; and since Richmond was her cultural bailiwick, she was often as productive as Mike, who sometimes seemed to be operating in a cultural vacuum. ESB's great strengths were that she knew how to work the system and she had the energy and perseverance to get what she needed—whether it was permits from city bureaucrats or financial backing from downtown businessmen. She also had the personal charm to make the majority of people she worked with delighted to be associated with her.

Freddie and ESB were on the HRF executive committee together for several years. Susan Williams, whose tenure on the board of HRF also overlapped Mother's, remembers ESB's antics. "One day," she said, "we were the only women at a meeting upstairs in what is now Jack Zehmer's office. Elisabeth was called to the telephone, and on the way hit her head on the newel post. The blood was streaming. I wanted to take her home then, but she said 'no,' and lay down on the floor of the room we were meeting in. Sometime later she raised her hand and said, 'Would the chair entertain a motion from the floor?'" The meeting, of course, dissolved in laughter. To this day nobody remembers the motion, but everyone remembers how, and from where, it was made.

Freddie, years after ESB had died, was walking down the street one day when an elderly black man stopped him, saying, "You're Mr. Bocock, right?" When Freddie responded that he was, the man continued, "I just want to give you a hug, if you don't mind. I loved your Mother, and I miss her so much; it would make me feel better if I could hug you." So the two men had a long hug, and then both went their ways. He happened to be a waiter at the Commonwealth Club, but the same could have been said by many, many others who worked more with her than for her. She had a natural charisma that is infrequently seen.

Her independent means allowed her to be a sort of mirror organization to HRF, but from Richmond's point of view they got two for the price of one. Marguerite Crumbley, in analyzing ESB's contribution to HRF, said, "Principally she was the founder, but she also did everything she could to interest other people, foundations and companies that could help by buying houses and doing them over. . . . I don't think she gave as much cash to HRF as other people did, but she bought properties and rented them—which to me was the main object of the whole thing." In her projects she often teamed up with Douglas Fleet, a North Carolinian who had made his fortune in a bottling company. ESB and Douglas Fleet saw eye to eye, and ended up buying properties together during several preservation crises. Both of them shared a passion for preservation, and, more importantly, had confidence in each other. They were also co-conspirators, plotting together to keep the extent of their financial involvement in preservation from being known. Doug, in a letter to ESB, makes the rueful request, "My family, in some ways, thinks I am crazy, so I would rather have this between you and me." A letter from ESB to Doug, about a contractor she thought was taking them for a ride, shows the same familiarity, "You are a generous, noble-hearted sucker, and I should be ashamed to be less noble-hearted, less generous; but I ain't no sucker by nature no how."

Her first experience actually moving a building in order to save it came in the 1960s, when the city was going to tear down a row of nineteenth-century houses to make way for the expansion of the main library at Second and Franklin Streets. Two of these substantial brick houses ESB and Doug moved to the 2600 block of East Franklin Street on Church Hill; and the third, which ESB called "the Little Chintz Shop," because it was the workshop of her friend Miss Myra Stone, she reconstructed at 2515 E. Grace Street. It is a jewel of a small house, with an arched doorway, a lovely balcony, and stepped gables, and has the dates of its construction included in the brickwork of the east gable. When Jack Zehmer, who retired as director of HRF in 1999, is conducting a walking tour of the area, he enjoys pointing out that ESB never asked permission of the Architectural Review Commission to have the mason install the two dates so prominently in the gable. When it was drawn to their attention, there was talk about having the gables dismantled and rebuilt without the dates, but fortunately good sense prevailed. One of ESB's standard operating procedures was never to ask permission, especially when she calculated that the answer would be no.

Jack's second favorite ESB story is about the house that President Tyler's widow had lived in. This became a cause célèbre to Mother. The house, which originally stood on Grace Street, was dismantled and put in storage, where it stayed for many years. During the storage period, ESB exercised her most persuasive powers to try to talk various people into reerecting the house. As the years went by and no one took the bait, builders began to pilfer—an iron railing here, a mantel there. My cousin Strother Scott, who moved to Richmond in the 1970s, remembers Mother taking him down to where the house was in storage, sure that he would see the possibilities, and triumphantly opening the doors on what looked like a mammoth, jumbled pile of firewood.

Failing to inspire anyone else to rebuild it, she decided that she would have to do it herself, and that the perfect place for it was the side yard of the Elmira Shelton House, headquarters of the HRF. She was nearly the only person who saw the rationale for this location, but the adverse reaction of the board did not sway her thinking. She nearly drove the board crazy with her requests, and was told no any number of times as they stuck to their determination to keep open space around the Shelton House. After being voted down repeatedly, ESB finally bought a vacant lot on Church Hill in order to resurrect what was left of the Widow Tyler House. There was, however, a problem: the lot turned out to be too narrow for the house. Eventually, after other restorations had taken up her time and interest, she gave the "pile of firewood" to HRF, and many years later a considerably smaller scrap pile was sold for parts.

Some of ESB's fellow preservationists, most notably Cousin Mary Wing, disapproved of ESB's penchant for moving houses. They found the cost extravagant and thought the money would be better spent restoring dilapidated housing that did not need to be moved. Others, although sympathetic with moving structures that were otherwise condemned, balked at the idiosyncratic way that ESB restored the house interiors.

As a child, I spent a lot of time on Church Hill with Mother, sorting bricks, tidying backyards, delivering material to workmen—doing whatever she was doing. As we drove around, she would pepper me with the history of streets and houses, down to and including the ghosts of houses no longer there, like the home of the Civil War spy Mrs. Van Lew, set on the bluff overlooking the river, which was torn down by myopic city authorities to make way for the Bellevue School. Most of this lore was lost on a child's deaf ears, but now, when I walk Church Hill as an adult, trying to reconstruct ESB's efforts there, I find overwhelming reminders of her presence. Certain houses speak to me. To see why, I have to refer to the Church Hill Historic District book—and when I look up a site reference, I find that there is indeed a reason for the feeling that particular house gives me. A glance at a certain facade will bring back a memory of the layout behind the facade; the detailed ironwork of a gate will jog my mind, and I flash back to holding it upright in the Mercedes for the drive from Caravati's junkyard to Church Hill; or a glimpse of the St. John's Mews will remind me of picking up litter in the alley of that block in the fading light of a winter evening, before there was a mews.

Looking at the houses that she either moved herself or helped in moving to Church Hill, I find myself cheering both for the structures themselves and for her effort of stubborn will. That effort saved the delicate tracery of the Pulliam House's ironwork from the Expressway bulldozers; it saved the hospitable archway of the Little Chintz House from oblivion. No doubt three houses could have been restored for the cost of moving one, but an important layer of city history would have been lost beyond retrieval. I give Mother enormous credit for recognizing, even in the 1950s, that much too much of Richmond's history had already been rubbed out.

Freddie, with his chronic good humor and imperturbability, spent an enormous amount of time at ESB's beck and call in this period. He was often asked for advice that he knew was not worth the effort of engaging his vocal chords. One cold, rainy, winter's day, he was working at his office when the telephone rang. "Freddie," sang out ESB's voice, with an edge of excitement in it, "You have *got* to come down here right now and see this marvelous house that I can get at the bargain price of seven thousand dollars." "Where are you, Mother?" said Freddie, trying to disguise the weariness that came over him at the thought of a morning's work being shot. "I'm down in Shockoe Bottom," answered ESB, and gave him the precise address. Freddie reluctantly kicked back from his desk, wishing he had followed his instincts, early that morning, to wear a warmer raincoat. At that point, Shockoe Bottom was a slum, and Freddie was not surprised, when he drove up, to find a rundown wreck of a house. The only clue that it might have seen better days was a rusty, cast-iron front porch.

Freddie went inside and yoo-hooed until he traced ESB and Garrett to the basement, which was open to the outside and littered with rat droppings and odds and ends that belonged to the homeless people who took shelter there. "Freddie!" ESB exclaimed as she kissed him. "Isn't this an incredible bargain?" Before answering, he tallied, in his mind, the cost of what she was clearly about to embark on, with or without his "advice." She would buy it for $7,000, move it for $50,000, and then spend what was left of $100,000 restoring its interior. After a long pause, he looked her in the eye and said, "Mother, I'll give you $7,000 right now if I can go back to my nice, warm office." After she absorbed the shock, she dressed him down smartly. "You may be my son," she said, "but you are a no-count, unimaginative young man." He was summarily dismissed, much to Garrett's amusement. Needless to say, the house was bought, moved, and restored. Freddie's prediction was wrong only in his estimate of total cost, which more than doubled.

When Freddie and Mother were on the HRF board together, Mother was in her mid-seventies, which might have been the time to give Freddie a little breathing room and support from the sidelines. But ESB did not know the protocol for life on the sidelines, and had she tried it she probably would have paced up and down like a frustrated coach, barely masking her desire to take over the play on the field. This is the ESB that Mike Gold found when he took the job at HRF, but the woman he describes is a stranger to me. When she first asked Mike and his wife to 909 for a drink, he was nonplussed when she offered them John Jameson Irish whiskey and nothing else, not so much as a peanut. Mother had a sentimental spot for Irish whiskey because it was her father's favorite drink, but I never, ever remember her offering whiskey without also offering something weaker, like sherry, tomato juice, or ginger ale. She also felt strongly about serving something to eat whenever serving alcohol, even if it was just crackers, or an ancient piece of cheese that her refrigerator had coughed up.

It occurred to me, listening to Mike's description of groping to figure out what he was dealing with, that Mother's totally atypical behavior was a signal that she, too, was dealing with an unknown quantity. In our conversation, Mike had referred to various forms of anti-Semitism, but when I asked him if he thought ESB's response to him was driven by it, he answered, "No, I just thought she hadn't had many dealings with Jews. I think she felt, 'Mike Gold sort of looks like a regular person, talks and walks like a regular person, but can't really be one.'"

It was a fair analysis. Despite the fact that Dr. Edward Calisch, rabbi of Temple Beth Ahabah, was one of Richmond's most beloved citizens in the first half of this century, the world that Mother knew was overwhelmingly Anglo-Saxon Protestant. Virginius Dabney's book *Richmond, the Story of a City,* refers to many instances in the nineteenth century of Gentile and Jewish intermarriages among the merchant class that predominated in the city; but by the twentieth century, Jews, Gentiles, and blacks lived in airtight compartments. In the 1950s, the exception to this was the Thalhimer family, who owned one of the city's two big department stores and whom the city came to depend on for civic leadership. Morton and Ruth Thalhimer were among Mother's close friends. In the last thirty years, Sidney and Frances Lewis, who founded Best Products, are probably among the best known of many Jewish families whose success has made them prominent in the city. They have been incredibly generous to Richmond institutions, in particular to the Virginia Museum of Fine Arts. But it is still fair to say that Mother could have counted her Jewish friends on her fingers.

Mike's motivation to take the job at HRF was an expanded opportunity for him to preserve old and historic structures. He admits, "I never cared about revitalizing Richmond." As far as ESB was concerned, that was a missing link. Revitalizing the city of Richmond was certainly as high a priority for her as preservation for its own sake. She had always lived in Richmond, as she always would, and the health of its schools, its retailing, its museums, symphony, and ballet, as well as its housing stock, were all of a piece in making up a city that attracts and holds people. This difference in motivation, plus a dislike, on ESB's part, of being made to feel marginalized, guaranteed their incompatibility. I think that had he known her better—and, more importantly, earlier in her life—they would have found more to appreciate in each other.

Jack Zehmer, who took over from Mike, was affable and relaxed when I interviewed him—his edges as rounded as Mike's were sharp. Jack became director the year before ESB died, inheriting the confusion over the multiple forms of partnership between HRF and ESB. As he pointed out, "On more than one occasion she would buy something or she would lend the Foundation the money to buy it without them having to pay interest on it. And it got very involved as to who actually owned what, because it was easier to say 'yes m'am' when she said she wanted it done than to argue with her. It seems so silly—that people didn't know who owned what or who was responsible for what."

One of those cases was the house in Shockoe Bottom that ESB had looked at with Freddie. Once it was torn down, the bricks were stacked for "temporary" storage in the yard of the Elmira Shelton House. The two people who helped ESB piece the bricks back into a house on the site found for it at 1103 Grove Avenue were Jim Whiting and Evie Massie Scott. Evie, married to ESB's nephew Strother Scott, was the architect for the project; Jim, president of HRF at the time, acted as negotiator, general handyman, and ambassador to the HRF board. Both of them stuck with a roller-coaster ride of a project because they loved Mother, remembered they were dealing with an eighty-four-year-old, and were able to laugh at her illogical reasoning, the frequent changes, and the daily drills.

ESB, not enthusiastic about modern techniques of construction, wanted the house to go up all brick. And she did not like looking at the concrete walls with brick veneer. She kept saying to Evie, "but we have the brick." This was not actually true, although Evie, by buying pressed bricks from another old house, managed to get the house up (much of the original brick was unusable). Unfortunately for Evie, ESB took a trip to Charleston that spring and came back determined to recreate a third-floor back porch that ran the length of the house. With the third floor already up, Evie patiently explained that, had she known Mother's plan earlier, she could have run the joists the opposite way from the direction they now ran in, making it possible to cantilever them out for a nice porch. Predictably, ESB said, "Find a way," and somehow, with the aid of a structural engineer, they jury-rigged a porch. Evie's nightmare was that it would fall on somebody, but so far it is still up there.

ESB wanted Evie to use old lumber she had at 909 on the porch floor, the cast-iron porch being the whole reason for the huge investment involved in reconstructing the house. To do so, Evie studied the dim little photographs and horrible xeroxes of what it used to look like. Mother also "paneled" a basement room with old doors collected from Caravati's junk yard. Sometimes ESB and Evie would go to lunch at the Commonwealth Club to argue these issues. Evie would order something normal, like an omelet. ESB would say to the waitress, "I'll have the soups, please." This was no surprise to the waitress, who would say, "What order would you like them in?" ESB's answer was, "Any order, as long as the curry soup is last." Then she would have a bowl of each of four soups, soups being easier on what she called her "ancient teeth." Evie loved the fact that nobody else thought this was the slightest bit odd.

Evie, realizing at the time that this project was unique, saved all of ESB's correspondence, of which there was a great deal. As Evie puts it, "Every time I tried to save a little money and do things less expensively, it always backfired." One of ESB's letters to Evie explains her theory of cost analysis: "If your aim is for something of distinction, you have to give 'economic feasibility' less priority." That, in a nutshell, was her philosophy of either building or rebuilding. At one point, says Evie, she was halfway fired in a deliciously worded letter from ESB dated March 9, 1985. "What would you think of trusting me and getting yourself off the hook for as many months as you and I feel would be safe for Jim Gregory, contractor, to turn to me only in event of any decisions which would hold up the job? . . . I would like to reserve the right to call you when architectural advice seems to be essential, and you would thus charge for that specific occasion. . . . Hope to catch you Monday for a briefing, dear Evie. Love, Elisabeth S. Bocock." Evie did not allow herself to be fired.

Evie kept a list of the materials that went into the house—a list that would have pleased ESB, the recycler, enormously. Many pieces came from Caravati's junkyard, but my favorite is MARBLE SLAB IN NORTH BASEMENT ENTRY—SOMEONE'S TOMBSTONE.

* * *

Jim Whiting's relationship with ESB was part professional, through HRF, and part social: they were good friends. They enjoyed each other tremendously despite there being thirty years' difference in their ages. He felt comfortable with her, and never felt that she would talk down to him, or that he had to talk up to her. In a period of his life when he had recently divorced, ESB asked him to be her escort for the Symphony Ball. He agreed, and they had a lovely evening at a table right down at the front. She wanted to leave before the event was over, and Jim agreed. When they got outside, she grabbed his arm and said, "Jim, I've lost my bridge." "Your bridge?" he said. "What the hell is that?" "It's a bridge hooking two teeth together," she explained, "I took it out to eat the steak, and I think I left it on the table. You go back and get it." He went back in, all the way down to the front, and by that time they had lowered the lights and somebody was getting ready to sing. So he sat down at the table and felt around on the tablecloth, unsuccessfully. Everyone was saying, "What are you doing?" He said, "I'm looking for Mrs. Bocock's bridge for her teeth." The entire table doubled over in laughter, watching Jim crawling under the table, feeling around in the dark. He still couldn't find it. When he went back outside, he found ESB standing there calmly. "Oh, Jim," she explained, unconcerned, "I've found it in my purse!"

When Jim lost a brother, Mother called him up and gave him the choice of either receiving a condolence note or being taken out to dinner. When he chose the latter, they went to a dinner-theater in Ashland. Mother could not hear well, so they left and returned to 909. ESB sent Jim up to the mezzanine to fetch the whiskey (Irish, naturally) and they sat, talking about every subject under the sun, from philosophy to politics. Says Jim, "I guess we talked until about midnight. If anybody had the joy of life—she reeked of it. She could relate to anybody."

It was this store of friendship that ESB called on when she gave 1103 Grove to HRF, for them to finish and, hopefully, to sell. Jim was the liaison between HRF and ESB, and he quietly saw to taking the doors off the walls, putting in plaster, and finishing what was needed to make the house habitable. Eventually the house did sell, although not for anywhere near the amount that ESB had put into it.

Jack Zehmer remembers that others in HRF minded the fact that, despite her never wanting to be an officer, she still considered herself a spokesperson for the organization. As he puts it, "We would be out there on a limb, and she would still speak [for us] although that wasn't what we were saying." At the other end of the spectrum from the showmanship was what he considers her biggest contribution, the quiet financial things that she and her sister, Rossie, did that did not get attention because people did not know about them. He cites as an example the leadership they showed in the first major HRF project that was not on Church Hill. It involved the 200 block of West Franklin Street: eight mansions, four on each side, were put up for sale, and the block was advertised as perfect for high-rise apartments. This was a watershed for HRF. The foundation put up $50,000 of option money to buy the block for $900,000, although it had nothing like that kind of money. HRF commissioned a feasibility study, and ESB and Aunt Rossie paid for it. ESB and Aunt Rossie also used their influence to persuade the Junior League to buy one of the mansions for their headquarters, and ESB helped furnish it with ornate Victorian pieces from 909.

There were other instances of ESB giving HRF the financial means to do the planning that sound preservation is based on. She gave the special funding for a study of the historic Broad Street district, an area that in the nineteenth century was the retail and entertainment heart of Richmond. In the twentieth century, the area became a seedy, down-at-heel strip of girlie bars and pornographic movie houses, yet behind many of the hurriedly constructed facades are interesting old buildings. A copy of the study was given to the owner of every single building in the district, to alert them to what they could accomplish if they worked together.

Broad Street is just two blocks north of 909, and Mother knew it well. Her car-repair shop was there. And she and Garrett would also go over to Broad when they needed practical help with a restoration project in progress: Harrison Higgins, whose talent for making and mending furniture she admired, had his shop around the corner on Broad; and Fred Odell, at Pleasants Hardware right down the street, was usually willing to be her personal shopper. Harrison describes the whirlwind it caused when ESB appeared at Pleasants. "One day," he says, "I was standing behind the aisle talking to Fred and I looked away, distracted. When I looked back, Fred wasn't there. I was looking around, and then I noticed something at my feet. Fred was literally on his hands and knees crawling away down the aisle. I said, 'Fred, what are you doing, are you all right?' He said, 'Shhh,' and pointed down the aisle to where your mother had come in. Apparently she, like me, would make a beeline for Fred and just latch on to him." Before Fred persuaded Mother to call in her orders in advance, she would race in the door, collect the things she needed, and pile them on the counter; then she was ready to leave. He had no time to write up tickets for her; she didn't want to be held up by that.

* * *

In ESB's mind, closely associated with the preservation of old houses was the preservation of aspects of nineteenth-century existence that would help people understand the style and pace of life that had been lived in those houses. She was particularly concerned that schoolchildren would have no idea of what life was like before cars; plus, she had a garage and carriage house full of pony carts, carriages, sleighs, and mildewed harness equipment inherited from her parents. Early on, her interest in putting them to use involved transporting a few of them, first to Royal Orchard and then to Goose Chase, a property adjacent to Royal Orchard that she had bought in 1959. A pair of Suffolk Punches (huge draft horses) and two wickedly bad mini-mules were purchased and occasionally hitched up for drive-arounds in the mountains for family and a few intrepid friends. I say intrepid with good reason: one never knew when harness that had been stored, unoiled, for several decades would break; when wooden wheels that were not used to the rocky, precipitous mountain trails would splinter; or when the pullers would take it into their heads to run away, leaving the pullees to decide for themselves whether the coachman was going to get things under control or whether to jump for their lives.

These drive-arounds so fired her imagination that in 1966 ESB founded the Early Virginia Vehicular Museum and hired as its director a soft-spoken, easygoing young man named Bill White whom she had first known when he rented her apartment over the carriage house at 909 while he was an undergraduate at Virginia Commonwealth University. His personality made him one of the few people who could have signed on for the long haul. He had mastered the art of "not reasoning why" before he ran into her illogical (sometimes *uniquely* illogical) form of decision making—a mastery that her children, who knew her better and loved her more, found amazing. He was a hard worker, and one who was obviously happiest when he was working out of doors or with his hands. But what endeared him most to Mother then, and to everyone who knows him now, is a deep-rooted desire to please.

ESB and Bill discovered that carriages of all sorts were for sale at the Martin Brothers Auctions in Intercourse, in the Amish area of Pennsylvania, and she and Bill raided these auctions, bringing home their booty in her pick-up truck. They also discovered that a man named Mr. Lapp could put in mint condition the dilapidated vehicles they dropped off at his shop, although it always took him months, and sometimes years, to complete a restoration. Never one to return home with an empty truck, Mother once bought a handsome Pennsylvania pie chest with a beaten-copper front that she had noticed in the back of the pick-up truck waiting in front of her at a stoplight in Amish country. Acting on impulse, she jumped out of her truck and ran up to the other driver's window to say how much she admired the piece, and to ask if it was for sale. Now it lives in our house, one piece of an eclectic furniture collection of canopied beds, bentwood rockers, and standing lamps and bedside tables made from the limbs of apple trees, all of which came our way through Mother.

Once the Early Virginia Vehicular Museum—the EVVM—had evolved from a dream to a reality, an invitation to its first public-welcoming drive-around read as follows:

"Miss Virginia" and "Sweet Afton" invite you to
Preview a Dream
ON
Sunday afternoon, October 16th, 1966
OR
Sunday afternoon, October 23rd, 1966
OR
Sunday afternoon, Oct. 30th, 1966
AT
"Wild Goose Chase"—Afton Mountain
Between 3:30 and 6:30 P.M.
tea and Brunswick stew
on their feet with you
Please note: Horse-riding clothes, heavy
walking shoes, blue jeans, or full skirt
NECESSARY
Directions for leaving your car will be given
at entrance to Royal Orchard drive from
Route 250 turn-off.
Please reply on enclosed post card.

Logistics later forced the removal of the EVVM to Richmond. Whenever she got a chance, ESB delighted in combining, in any form her imagination could come up with, two of her pet projects. So it was no surprise that the EVVM's new home was in the basement and courtyard of the Ligon House on Church Hill, which she and Doug Fleet were restoring. Her vision for the museum was to make it possible for tourists visiting the historic section of Church Hill to be able to do so by carriage ride. Some of the carriages went back to the 909 carriage house, and the horses and mules lived in the large dog yard that adjoined it.

On Easter Sunday, 1970, the EVVM held a drive-around on Church Hill, despite rain and freezing cold weather. Five little boys showed up. Here is ESB's description of the afternoon:

Having promised on the WRVA newscast at 9:10 Easter Sunday morning that, though the big vehicle parade was called off, should the rain let up, there would be three or four small animals pulling small vehicles at the Ligon House just the same, for those who might want to brave the weather. . . .

Before we were thoroughly hooked up, Bill White came to help, and we got the High Picnic Cart, pictured here in the *News Leader,* with Frosty ready to go. But, luckily, we had put no children in it and Mike was supposed to be driving up the slight incline from the Ligon House courtyard to East Franklin when Frosty decided she'd rather go backwards; and Mike, having no whip, was helpless to make her go forward, and, having no brake, was helpless to prevent her pushing the vehicle over something of a precipice toward the hand railing of the steps that take the place of the street on 26th Street down to Main. But, with several energetic taps on the backside, Frosty was persuaded to pull up again and Mike, no whit discouraged, took all the little boys aboard. You never saw such happy faces!

After he had given them a nice twenty-minute drive, they refused to get out; and Sue King, having arrived, gave Lindsay Nolting, "Ticket Taker," $5.00 with which to pay for them to ride the rest of the day.

Now I ask you, is this how any other sixty-nine-year-old widow spends her Easter Sundays?

The Big Vehicle Parade that ESB called off Easter Sunday took place the following Sunday, and big crowds appeared. ESB took a ride herself, on the topmost perch of a magnificent four-in-hand coach. She spent the ride clinging to the small iron railing, trying to forget that, despite all the work that had been done to the rooftop seats, they had been patched together from dozens of loose pieces found in an old C&O freight building. As she put it in her EVVM report:

You couldn't be asked to believe it: my dream for EVVM come true! At least for one glorious day, April 5th, when the weather (no wind, no heat, no bitter cold) and peeps of sunshine in the late afternoon combined to make ten horse, pony, mule (Equine) drawn *authentic* vehicles of the late 19th and earliest 20th century possible.

The number of people who had the treat of riding in any one of them could not be counted. Several generous-hearted people stood on various corners, giving out tickets which they bought in blocks of $10.00 (i.e. 40 children's tickets at a time). . . . Many of the children would go back and stand in line in front of these nice philanthropists.

The unsung hero in many of these drive-arounds was Freddie, whose devotion to ESB and sense of loyalty meant that he came early, stayed late, and helped deal with the inevitable crises of balking mules, crowd control, and loose horses. His very presence was reassurance for her, and his knowledge of horses and personable nature meant that he was permanently on call as a driver.

By 1971, ESB was beginning to realize that she was exhausting herself, others, and her exchequer by staging major drive-arounds, sometimes as part of civic functions and sometimes for the benefit of the HRF. As the following report shows, she was beginning to cast around for a saner way to manage the EVVM.

Freddie Bocock and Alfred Scott trying to slow down Sweet Afton, who has escaped from the dogyard
(Copyright Richmond Times-Dispatch; *used with permission*)

Mike Bulls trying to keep Frosty from backing off the precipice at a drive-around, ESB giving advice
(Copyright Richmond Times-Dispatch; *used with permission)*

Red Letter Day! I am persuaded that keeping EVVM vehicles with one or two pair of animals to drive and, of course, harness to use with them oiled and in shape is far more feasible than trying to keep *enough* horses, mules or ponies to make it worthwhile putting on a drive-around just through my own sheer optimism and extravagance.

Also, red letter because yesterday, late-ish, Mr. Merle Luck called to ask if I'd like to have about 15,000 cobblestones all covered and hidden by cudsu vine between his office and A.C.L. RR main line tracks to Florida because Richmond Metropolitan Authority link, which is now in tentative building/bulldozing right there on the Luck Quarry, would push them all over into a ravine if he didn't get them moved before Monday, April 26th.

The catch in it was that he was giving them to me if I would get them moved. So, of course I said "yes!" and he said, "I thought they'd be useful in some of your historic preservation work." To shorten the story, good, kind Bobby Carter came to my rescue, found a man who'd rent his heavy pick-up and dump truck today with a driver; so, I showed him where they were to be dumped and he made 10, 12 or 15 loads (variously estimated) and ⅔ of them are now in E. Bocock–Sue Cecil pasture, no where near any trees which might be killed by the weight on the little feeder roots near the surface. The other ⅓ is down at the bottom of FSB's own horse-pasture ready "for the children to stack," which may never happen.

By 1975, the carriage house and the Ligon house were bursting at the seams. ESB had her lawyer, Tom Word, who had taken over that role when Tom Gordon went on the bench, looking into whether or not the EVVM, in exchange for tax deductibility, could operate at Maymont (a museum on the beautiful grounds of a Victorian mansion built by the tobacco fortune of Major Dooley, situated on a knoll overlooking a bend in the James River as it approaches downtown Richmond). The removal to Maymont did take place, initially with the vehicles on loan to the foundation. The foundation agreed to a peripatetic museum with a curator who was to arrange special events, including carriage drives for schoolchildren, with the proceeds going to Maymont. ESB agreed to fund what obviously was going to be an ongoing operational deficit.

ESB was happiest over the regular visits of schoolchildren during the spring and fall. Well before her death, she began giving vehicles, harness, and proper coachman's attire to Maymont, saving only a few carriages at 909. The latter were given away after her death to five of her nieces and nephews who were driving enthusiasts. Her will also specified that the carriage museum be endowed for fifteen years after her death.

* * *

As soon as the Historic Richmond Foundation had begun to make a real impact on Church Hill, and people who had the resources to care for the houses and the interest to appreciate them moved into the Saint John's Church area and the pilot blocks adjacent to it, it became clear that there was a real need for a restaurant or a club for dining, social events, and meetings. ESB chose a club, not a restaurant, because in those days buying liquor by the drink was not allowed in Virginia. As a result, there were few restaurants but many clubs, since you could wrap your bottle in a brown bag and take it with you to a club. In 1963, ESB set about creating the 2300 Club, so called because she sited it at the Caitlin House (ca. 1850) at 2300 E. Broad Street, which she bought for this purpose.

As usual, ESB had very strong opinions about how she wanted things run. She thought the club should hire an experienced hostess, use lots of candles, have continually burning open fires, and concentrate on three special dishes that would make the club famous. Evidently, by 1965 friction was already developing between ESB and the board about the allocation of expenses. In addition to buying the house, ESB had paid to have it transformed into a club, then rented it to the club for $200 a month, with the club responsible for taxes and insurance fees. This does not seem excessive, even for 1964, but it was not long before the 2300 Club was in serious financial trouble.

That trouble arose is not surprising. Because of someone's catchy but naive suggestion (it may have been ESB's), both the initiation fee and the monthly membership fee were set at $23. It would have made more economic sense, if the number 2300 had been used, to have kept the two zeros, at least in the case of the initiation fee. Initially ESB was the landlord and the board the lessee, but by early 1966 ESB had turned over doing business with the board of directors to her agent in a real-estate firm. It wasn't long before she was being asked to bail the club out of its financial difficulties. She must have thought she had done enough, as her answer was to suggest that it move to a different location. Others, too, were in favor of this, and eventually that is what happened. The 2300 Club moved to more congenial quarters closer to the core area of the HRF, set itself up on more realistic operating principles, and is a Church Hill fixture today.

Another need that ESB saw for Church Hill, in the early 1960s, was a craft shop that would both provide classes in handwork for local residents, especially children, and a place for tourists to browse, not to mention spend their money. Usefulness was a family ethic, and ESB, knowing that handwork was dying out, thought that if Church Hill children learned to weave, sculpt, or make pots, they might discover their future profession. In 1963 she swung into her familiar role of catalyst, bringing together seven supporters to found the Hand Workshop. It ran on an informal basis until 1974, when it was incorporated. By this time it had a well-developed program of adult and children's classes in pottery, art, sewing, and sculpture. As usual, ESB was not an officer, but she was on the board and sat on the executive committee. She bought the lovely, frame, nineteenth-century Whitlock House at 316 North 24th Street, which the Hand Workshop was to use rent free while paying for upkeep, insurance, utilities, and taxes. She also formed the Bocock Trust, which gave the organization a reported $175,000 in operating funds over its first ten years. In 1975, the Bocock Trust funds ran out, and there was a deficit crunch. The board was split between those, led by ESB, who wanted the Hand Workshop to stick to what they saw as its primary purpose, providing classes for children on Church Hill, and those who wanted to see it become a regional craft center, on a larger scale.

With the creation of the HRF, gentrification came to Church Hill. The area began attracting faculty and students from the nearby Medical College of Virginia. ESB was keenly aware of the displacement problems, and this was a major reason behind her wanting to preserve the Hand Workshop Education Program on Church Hill. This was perhaps a naive, idealistic vision, but displacement was of genuine concern to her. In March 1976, the Hand Workshop opened a branch on West Cary Street in the West End. Richmond's more affluent citizens live in the West End, both in more distant suburbs and in the Fan district, and in ESB's view, these people already had access to handwork classes in the arts programs at the University of Richmond and the Virginia Museum. But those on the board who favored the Cary Street location felt a need to broaden the classes, improve their finances, and take advantage of a better neighborhood. They probably also saw it as a way to get out from under ESB.

Concern grew that the Church Hill operation was holding back the growth of what was an essentially viable, and more broadly based, craft center, and that what went on at Church Hill was more baby-sitting than teaching. Over the objections of the board, who wanted to move the whole education program to the West End, Mother insisted on just the opposite: she said she would fund the deficit for four months. The move back to Church Hill occurred in February 1977, and by late that year board meetings began with a prayer—a sign of dire financial straits. There was urgent need for repairs. The kiln—an *indoor* kiln—stood in four inches of water after a rain. At a special meeting of the board in May 1978, a group of nine board members, including ESB, threatened to resign unless the Hand Workshop was put into receivership, its debts paid, and its manager fired. The management asked that the lease be extended through August 1978. In a move reminiscent of her tussles with the management of the 2300 Club, ESB declined to extend the lease. The issue was forced, eight board members, including ESB, resigned, and the Hand Workshop, eventually, moved back to West Cary Street. In time, it became a thriving arts center, going in many new directions but still involved in teaching crafts.

* * *

The battle that ESB would most like to have won, and that she came tantalizingly close to winning, she fought from 1975 to 1985, the last ten years of her life. She had always loved the electric trolleys of her childhood, and, she reasoned, what better city to restore trolleys than Richmond? In 1888, it had been the first city in the United States to install a trolley system—the brainchild of Frank Sprague, an inventor who earlier had worked for Thomas Edison and who bankrupted himself making his system work in Richmond.

Egged on by a trolley enthusiast in New York City whose company specialized in connecting cities in the United States who wanted old trolley cars with European sources for them, she founded Hop-on-Trolley, a lobbying organization and public-consciousness-raising vehicle, aimed at developing a core group of enthusiasts. She had no trouble finding helpers and supporters, but city officials were conspicuously absent from this group. So she began relentlessly peppering city officials with information about Detroit, Pittsburgh, Portland, and all the other cities that had successfully brought back trolleys, either downtown or on special tourist routes.

Manuel Deese, a courtly African-American who was city manager at the time, remembers that ESB's green-ink letters followed him relentlessly. "Oh, she brought them by sometimes, sometimes she would drop them in the mail, sometimes I'd come back to my office and they'd be on my desk. You know, they were everywhere." What stuck in the craw of Deese and all the other city officials that she encountered was the cost. Depending on the route, the estimate was for at least $3 million to get up and running, with yearly operating expenses projected at $125,000. Instead of cost, ESB focused on the pollution-control benefits of trolleys. Reverting to poetry in one of her early fliers, she wrote:

> Trolleys are chocked with glamour
> Gasoline buses choke us and stammer.

ESB delighted in the concept that a trolley, stopping to pick up a passenger, does not pollute, unlike a car held up in traffic. However, Bobbie Carter, in a letter written in 1978, politely pointed out to his nonscientific mother-in-law that even though a stopped trolley does not pollute, the energy is being wasted at the power station, and if the station is using coal or oil, it is polluting.

But not all the feedback she received from city officials was negative. At one of the public hearings at which trolleys were on the agenda, Mother sat on the floor in the aisle because there were no seats left. When she got up to make her statement, she was greeted by a heavy round of applause. Mayor Henry Marsh banged away with the gavel and when quiet was restored said, "It is against the rules to applaud at city council meetings, but because of what a remarkable person Mrs. Bocock is, and the wonderful things she has

ESB on the trolley she imported from Oporto, Portugal

done for this city, I would like to lead the applause." In appreciation, ESB sent him the following thank-you note:

Thank you! Mr. Marsh, for your surprise morale boost . . . to *all* of us electric trolley promoters: especially me.

Over the past nine years I have, as you proved you know, tried to wake up our conservative old Richmond to the fact that we allowed our historic importance to be forgotten and sold out a big asset; while younger, more wide-awake towns like Portland, Oregon (one of the newest) were building the "new thing." Like you I care deeply about our town, and I value your opinion.

ESB determined early on that what Hop-on-Trolley needed to excite people was an actual trolley car. She imported one from Oporto, Portugal, and it was put on display in front of the Science Museum. (One of the route options that the city had considered in the 1970s had been to use the old railroad tracks behind the Science Museum, which formerly had been Broad Street Station, whose construction Grandfather Scott had masterminded.) She also realized that unless she got the city's business leaders on her side, city officials would never come around. So in February 1981 she hosted an "All Pull Together" luncheon that attracted several civic leaders as sponsors. ESB was right that involving business leaders would make the difference: she managed to turn over leadership of the Task Force to Restore Electric Trolleys (the successor organization to Hop-on-Trolley) at this meeting. Then she watched with satisfaction as a well-organized study of the possibilities took place. Guy Friddell, ESB's most loyal supporter in the press, makes it clear, in an article in the *News Leader* of December 3, 1984, that trolleys were almost a done deal. "Elisabeth S. Bocock's 10-year dream of bringing a system of electric trolleys to Richmond is well on the way to becoming a reality."

The business leaders and the city were proceeding with a plan that combined public and private financing when, in the mid-1980s, federal funding for cities dried up, and the city council was unable to find money for the project—a reversal that was a real blow to ESB. But she never let her failures dim her vision. Currently, the Science Museum is working to create a small trolley loop, and ESB's children are seeing to the restoration of the Oporto car to run on those tracks, so some part of her vision is yet aborning.

* * *

In the fifty years that ESB was involved in saving buildings and fighting civic battles, her major role was as a visionary. For her, it was easy to see things as they might be, rather than as they were; and as with other visionaries, her frustration with those who could not make that jump was huge. People could, and did, quarrel with the concept of moving houses, and with her unique, and sometimes bizarre, restorations. But no one would quarrel with the conclusion that she helped transform Richmond's attitude toward historic preservation. In her years of her civic activism, at first her weapons were feminine guile and an instinct to start out with a diplomatic approach. In the second half of this activist period, she came to share the conclusion of Cousin Mary Wing: that unless one throws occasional fits, no one will pay attention. In the last part of her life, dramatic action and melodramatic prose became the norm rather than the exception. As some wise person once said, "As we get older we just get more so."

She was never much interested in details. When she was involved in implementation, it mirrored her charm and eccentricity as well as her need for power. She was very interested in power—in one of her files is a list of the books she had read that year, and every one of them was about a woman of note. She thought she had to keep control of things to achieve success, and it is ironic that when control was wrestled from her, as in the 2300 Club and the Hand Workshop, success—for the organization if not for her initial vision—often followed. As she got older, her vision usually involved taking the side of people who had few means and no political clout, and who were the losers in the civic battles she was involved in. Often her visions for them and for the neighborhoods they lived in were idealistic in the extreme, but her motivation was genuine.

There is no discounting the fact that ESB's metabolism pushed her into a state of perpetual motion. Crises seemed to arrive in bunches, and she was usually way over her head in her commitments of time, energy, and money. Her energy level, instead of decreasing with age, stayed high, although this took a toll on the rationality of her decisions because she was often physically exhausted. Age put no crimp in her faith in what she could get done in the course of a day, but it did put a crimp in her stamina.

The greatest proof of her impact on her city, and to a lesser extent, her state, is that she left a more graceful environment than the one she found. One can look around Richmond and see the things that she affected and the people whose lives she changed. Saint Pinckney, a family friend, expressed it well in a letter written after her death. "Walking down Grace Street today I saw many of the things that your mother saved for me, and for many others still to come. Into this provincial southern town she brought an inquisitiveness, an excitement of exploration, and an enjoyment of life."

What Saint Pinckney put in personal terms, a joint resolution by the Virginia House of Delegates put in formal terms after her death. After "Where-as-ing" its way through most of the initiatives described in this chapter, it ends with the statement that her death "creates a distinct void in the City of Richmond and in this Commonwealth, but the enduring evidence of the best of the past, preserved at her insistence, assures that her indomitable spirit will always be remembered." Mary Wingfield Scott, ESB, and many other preservationists helped save Richmond from itself. ESB would be proud of that legacy.

The Big House at Royal Orchard

4. Heaven Has Nothing on Royal Orchard

As a child, I measured time according to how soon I would be back at
Royal Orchard. If we were leaving there in the predawn darkness to
drive to Richmond for school and work, I grieved for the days that
stretched ahead before we would return the next weekend. If we were on a
glamorous trip, and I was asked what I thought of my first view of the Mat-
terhorn, or the Grand Tetons, or the Pyrenees, my answer was always the
same: "It doesn't compare to Royal Orchard." Mother's retort, too, was always
the same: "If that's the way you feel about it we should have left you there."
But no matter how hard I begged for her to do just that—to leave me with
my cousins when the next trip was planned—she never gave up trying to open
my mind to the world.

Today the trip from Richmond to Royal Orchard is accomplished in an
effortless ninety minutes on Interstate 64. In the 1950s, it involved at least another hour on a hilly, dangerous road that went through downtown Charlottesville. The first hour was spent freeing ourselves from the monotonous
pine barrens west of Richmond. Mother would be behind the wheel. In order
to pass other vehicles, she would bide her time until we came to a three-lane
section and then would hurtle us out into the passing lane, overtaking as
many trucks and slow cars as possible before the road shrank back to two
lanes. I held my breath, not knowing when we might meet up with another
car doing the same thing from the opposite direction. Mother was a good
driver, but aggressive, and there were many times I wondered if we were going
to make it.

Depending on the clarity of the atmosphere, we generally got our first
peek of the mountains around Zion Crossroads, so this was where my spirits
got their first lift. Sometimes, if it were a particularly hot day, we would stop
for a ginger ale (Coca-Cola and television were the twin devils of American
culture, from Mother's point of view, jointly responsible for rotten teeth,
worse morals, and the general decline of the work ethic). Before we set off
again, we would stretch our legs by walking around the old station wagon,
wood-sided and high-topped and with 1107 marked on the door, still with us
after the move to 909.

Twenty miles or so further on we came to Charlottesville. Skirting the north bank of the Rivanna River, we would stop at the house of two old-maid sisters who sold homemade orange cupcakes, moist and delectably full of both rind and juice. They had a long, steep flight of steps to their front door, and usually I would be sent running up them, money in hand, to collect these delicacies. The cupcakes oozed so much orange that the box bottom was soggy and had to be supported from underneath. Heading toward the center of town, our next stop was at the Early Dawn Dairy, where we pulled into its semicircular drive just long enough to run in and buy milk, butter, and ice cream. At the dairy, the trick was to make sure that Mother stayed in the car, in order to avoid the fifteen-minute conversation that would follow if she came inside. If we had not stopped at Zion Crossroads, an ice cream bar was now negotiable. There were days that were so oppressively muggy that I would lean over and stick my whole upper torso into the cooler, letting the frosty air swirl around my head before I chose my snack.

After the dairy, when we were leaving Charlottesville, I would let myself get really excited. The landscape unfolds into the hilly country of the Piedmont Valley, which runs east to west and is bound to the north by the gentle, ancient outlines of the Blue Ridge Mountains and to the south by the Ragged Mountains, which are little more than hills. Each ridge top gained gives a still more pleasing view than the one before—of roll-away pastures with Hereford cows standing belly-deep in ponds to keep cool; of miles of white fencing and neatly stacked hay; of corn growing in the fertile lowlands around Mechum's River, where the road turns hard left under the railroad overpass; of simple clapboard houses with wrap-around porches and elegant houses of brick made from the red clay of Albemarle County soil.

If I had a friend with me who had not been to Royal Orchard before, Mother would embarrass me by pointing out to her that she could locate where she was going by looking just off the crest of the twin mountains straight ahead that resembled "gently rising bosoms." As a ten-year-old, I thought this description was neither apt nor funny. As soon as I outgrew my prudishness, I realized that that was exactly what they looked like—nothing voluptuous, not Dolly Parton specials, but the virginal breasts of a young girl.

The last straight stretch across the valley floor is close enough for one to see the layout of the place outlined on the mountain in miniature. The upper and lower horse pastures break the forests of hardwoods that cover the mountainside, as do the east and west apple orchards for which the place is named. Clover Cottage and California Cottage appear as small dots in the heartland, overshadowed by the massive structures of the barn/garage and the Big

House, both built of mountain stone. The Royal Orchard entrance road cuts back across the southern face of the mountain for more than a mile, climbing at one point at a 9 percent grade. The inside curves cross gullies that in the springtime run with water from underground springs, and after each hairpin turn, more and more of the valley is laid out below. Two-thirds of the way up, there is suddenly a vista of the Big House, appearing either forlorn or welcoming, depending on the season.

Mother drove the Royal Orchard entrance road with the sure hand and foot of someone who knew it by heart—who had memorized it as a child on the agonizingly slow trips in the mule wagon that hauled the family up the mountain from the train station at Afton when they came from Richmond for the summer. She would get a running start on the relatively slight incline at the bottom, and then charge up the steepest part of the slope, knowing exactly when third gear could no longer carry us and shifting quickly down to second, taking the worst turn with her outside wheel riding the outside edge of the road in case she met someone on the way down. At each curve, one of her gloved hands would come off the wheel to blow the horn with the signature pattern that meant this is family coming—*hep, hep, keep good step.* She did not lessen her speed for curves for that would have meant shifting down to first, but took the whole mountain at a steady clip, the motor in the high whine that sets up when second gear is pushed as far as it will go.

My heart would be in my throat as we careened up the mountainside, not out of fear, but from the sheer pleasure of it. I was back where I wanted to be, and if I leaned out of the window of the car I could feel the air get cooler with the altitude we gained around each curve. When we reached the Big House vista, I would usually hear a sharp intake of breath from anyone who was a newcomer: the sight is wildly dramatic. There is the house, which is a cross between a Newport mansion, an Italian villa, and a Scottish castle, still a half-mile off and still above you, dominating a promontory that juts out over the pasture that falls away below it, overlooking the whole of the Piedmont and Rockfish Valleys and the folds of mountains that stretch south toward the plain of the James River. The last few turns lead to the beginning of the lawns, which slope up the hill toward the children's swings and the flower garden, and down, below the entrance road, into Pool Hollow. The swimming pool, one of the first in Virginia, follows the contours of the farm pond it once was, curving gracefully around an old oak tree.

Heated these days to a sissy's 72 degrees, in my childhood the water temperature reached only 70 on the hottest days of the summer, starting off

Memorial Day at 58 degrees, which was the frigid temperature of its mountain spring feed. It was so cold that when we were swimming, adults would interrupt our play at regular intervals, check our lips to see if they had turned blue, and make us run up and down the steep hill to the pump house before we were allowed to get back in the pool. Bluestone, which was used to keep pools clean before chlorine, kept it a pretty blue-green and dyed the blond hair of my Reed cousins to a greenish hue. The water was murky, and we all knew that water moccasins lived beneath the rickety wooden baby pool near the steps; they could sometimes be seen sunning themselves on the partially submerged rock in the deep end. There was a diving board at one end of the long part of the pool, and when I was very young there was also a wonderful, twisting, water slide at the end nearest the road.

Just past the pool the road divides, and you can either swing around the front of the Big House to unload at the porte cochere on the vegetable-garden side, or go straight up a last steep incline that levels off in the asphalt parking outside the barn/garage. The road then shoots up again, going through stone pillars and past the old tennis court and Clover Cottage to become a mountain road after it swings right and passes California Cottage at the end of the lawn. What is left of the straight lines of the old Albemarle Pippin apple orchard are laid out on the mountainside above the lawn and the houses.

Although it was Grandfather Scott's success in business that built the Royal Orchard that all of his descendants cherish, it was his wife's bold move in bidding on a bankrupt apple orchard without his knowledge and with very little spare cash that gave him that opportunity. In 1893, as a young, newly married man, he had taken a big risk in order to go into the investment-banking business in Richmond with his friend Charles Stringfellow. Working overtime to make Scott and Stringfellow a success and to build a client base, he periodically worked himself into a nervous collapse. One of these bouts followed the banking panic of 1903, and to recuperate he had gone for an extended stay at a spa in New York State. Back home, his wife, Elise, was looking for a summer house in order to get their young children away from the dangerous fevers that struck in the heat of Richmond summers. She read in an advertisement that an apple orchard on the side of Afton Mountain was to be auctioned. Unable to leave home, she asked their friend Chiswell Dabney Langhorne (the father of Nancy Astor, the British peeress) to ride up from Mirador, his house in the Piedmont Valley, to inspect the property for her, giving him leeway to spend most of the Scotts' nest egg to bid on the property if the price was right.

Royal Orchard originally had been an agricultural experiment by University of Virginia professors trying to grow Albemarle Pippins, a tart, green, cooking apple much sought after in the nineteenth century. By the time it came into the hands of Grandmother and Grandfather Scott, it was clear that the temperature extremes on the mountain kept the orchard from living up to the success of the orchards in the valley below. The name Royal Orchard came from a story about a U.S. ambassador to the Court of Saint James's who, it was said, had given Queen Victoria a Christmas present of a bushel of Albemarle Pippins, delivered in a silver bushel basket. The queen loved not only the apples but the basket, choosing to keep it, and asking in subsequent years for more Albemarle Pippins, some of which came from Afton Mountain.

On the property was what appears in pictures to be a sturdy, two-story clapboard farmhouse. The Scotts lived in the farmhouse for enough summers for Grandfather Scott to decide that he had spent too much time waiting in line with visiting cousins and spinster aunts to use its one bathroom. In 1910, the farmhouse was torn down, and Grandfather's business success allowed them to build the Big House over the next several years. As many as a hundred men worked on it, paid a dollar a day to walk up from the valley each morning and work extracting the gray stone from the mountainside, coaxing it into position using a manual and horse-drawn block/tackle/pulley system.

The Big House is built in the shape of an L. The short part of the L forms a servants' wing that overlooks the terraced vegetable garden, and the long part faces the breathtaking view. The dining room and living room are cavernously large and high-ceilinged. In the dining room, the fireplace of walk-in size dominates the room. Around the tops of the walls are raised, hand-painted friezes with scenes from Arthurian legend. The friezes in the living room and the small, round music room off of it were painted by German artisans who, in the years of World War I, had to be kept away from the Italian artisans working at the same time on the raised hunting friezes in the dining room. In the living room, one knight on horseback looks suspiciously like Mother. He is riding up a roadway toward a far-off castle that looks somewhat like the Big House. The wall opposite is dominated by Saint George, dressed in elegant white robes that flow down the sides of his horse and onto the ground. As a child, I thought anyone foolish enough to dress so impractically deserved to be pawed off his horse by the dragon.

An intricate ironwork screen separates the front from the back hall, with its sports closets and powder-room doors flush with the dark oak paneling of the walls. One closet has rows and rows of hooks for tennis shoes of all sizes for loaning to guests; another is full of props for parlor games. An oak chest houses tennis balls and rackets. Another paneled door leads through to the huge pantry, the children's dining room, the kitchen, the servants' dining room, and the laundry. Above these are the bedrooms of what used to be the servants' wing, and over the main part of the house, two corridors of bedrooms, all opening off a central hall with stained-glass windows, Aubusson tapestries on the walls, and Persian rugs on the floor.

All the bedrooms are named. One is the Florentine Room, another the Boys' Sleeping Porch, another Grandmother's Room, and so on. Each is furnished with English and continental antiques that blend with the medieval and Renaissance motifs that were so popular with the Victorians. It takes a running start to get into the heavy, carved-oak canopy bed in Grandmother's Room. The hardwood seats in the hallway are choir benches. The walls are covered with family photographs, of picnic outings in pony carts on the Richmond streets and of family brides in ornate frames. All the rooms are interconnected through their shared bathrooms—a layout that has led to a least one pots-and-pans marching band Tour de Chambres in the wee hours of the morning.

The main staircase has carved gargoyle posts, each representing one of the Allied powers of World War I. Few parties have lasted more than six hours before the animal gargoyles get funny hats on their heads and cigars or cigarettes in their mouths. A long, columned porch runs the length of the house on the first floor, turning the two corners to include views to the east of the Italianate, terraced vegetable garden dropping away to the lower horse pasture, and to the west of the lawn sloping up to the flower garden and down to the arbor steps leading to the swimming pool. In good weather, the porch is an outdoor living room, everyone naturally gravitating to its wicker sofas, rocking chairs, and tables arranged around jute rugs. Stone flower boxes run the length of the porch, the blooms of geraniums and nasturtiums brightening the massed gray stone.

In the middle of the porch are wide front steps leading up to an enormous main entrance. When I was a child, these steps were the site for the annual family picture taken during Old Home Week, when we were all there together. Both Grandmother and Grandfather Scott had died by the time I was born in 1941, but their five children, Uncle Buford, Aunt Isabel, Mother, Aunt Rossie, and Uncle Freddie, sat in a row, each in a chair at the top of the stairs. Below them sat their wife or husband, followed in descending order of age by their children, each with arms resting on the legs of the person behind them. There were nineteen of us in the third generation.

Patriarchal lineup at the swimming pool, ca. 1935

In the 1930s, the earlier versions of these family photographs were taken in a similarly formal lineup under the big oak tree by the pool. These were arranged by height, Grandfather being the tallest. In front of him came the men, positioned by height, followed by the women. Children came last, arranged by height only, not by sex, down to the latest baby, clutched tightly by the youngest child able to stand on its own. In one of these pictures, Grandfather, looking debonair in his white linen suit and white bucks, has one hand resting on his ivory-handled cane, his hat at a jaunty angle. He is looking over his brood with proprietary pleasure, and it is easy to read into the scene the pride he must also have felt at the domain he had created for them.

It is significant, as well as symbolic, that while Grandfather was alive the annual pictures were not divided by family branch. His children married and produced offspring, but it was still one family, and he was very much its patriarch. This was a natural dominion Mother had no trouble accepting, whereas after his death she was quick to rebuff her elder brother, Buford, when he moved to step into his father's shoes. The strict order in the photograph is a mirror of the hierarchy of life at Royal Orchard. Grandfather had created a veritable Garden of Eden, and whether one was born into it or married into it, the price for staying to enjoy it was obedience to his will. He had an analytical mind, a quick temper, strong opinions, and an autocratic way of delivering them. He controlled the flow of conversation and of events for his offspring, in-laws, grandchildren, and the flow of kinsfolk and guests that always seemed to be in residence.

He did not, however, control his wife, who seems to have been the one person who could reduce him to rubble. She never did this in public—it was always behind closed doors and often done in letters—but it was clear that her wrath was the one force he could not overcome. She was as short as he was tall, but she was vivacious, passionately in love with him, and deeply intuitive about how to prod, support, punish, and encourage her volatile, high-strung husband. The chain of command descended from Grandmother Scott to Miss Jane Thornton, a plump, diminutive Englishwoman much beloved by everybody, the wife of Grandfather's chauffeur. Orphaned at an early age, she had raised her brothers and sisters, and she used these same skills to run the households and manage the servants at 909 and Royal Orchard.

The children's world was run by governesses, but intersected with the lives of the adults at regular points during the day, for prayers, for meals, and for horseback rides and swims. Jackie McElroy, who started visiting Freddie at Royal Orchard when he was seven in 1938, has vivid memories of life there and of the way Grandfather loomed large in it. He told me:

It was wonderful, going to Royal Orchard. There was nothing like it then and there's really nothing like it now, either. The place is an institution. Thornton, in his very formal chauffeur's outfit, and Freddie picked me up at home. We got to Royal Orchard around lunch time and met "mad'moiselle." Lunch was on the corner of the porch overlooking the vegetable garden, and we had onion soup, which I had never had before, and salad served in a separate salad bowl.

I remember Freddie and mad'moiselle and I were sitting at the table on the porch, and Grandfather Scott came down in his riding clothes. I was three feet tall and he was about six feet five inches. He had put on his riding boots and he was the tallest man I had ever seen in my life—a most imposing figure in his well-shined boots and with his riding crop, which he was twacking on the side of his boot.

There was the routine of daily work, which in the morning involved picking potato bugs in the garden and taking them up to Grandfather, called "Popo," as he read the paper over his breakfast tray, in bed. He paid a nickel per one hundred bugs, which would be counted out on the tray, but would come up with a nickel even if they were short a few bugs.

Work usually had a whole lot of fun attached to it, like going down in the pasture with bushel baskets and pitchforks in the green pony cart to pick up manure to put on the rose bushes. We would get precious little manure—it was hard to handle with the pitchfork. The pony would run away, and we would cut a corner too close coming around one of those great stone gateposts and break the wheel off the pony cart.

Sometimes they were sent blackberry picking on ponies. When they got bored with picking they would pile up brush and make little jumps on the trail and spill most of their blackberries. A swim, followed by lunch and a nap, came after their morning work, and a horseback ride was usually the highlight of the afternoon. Jackie remembered one particular ride:

Grandfather was on Dodo, a big black horse, regarded as one who had to be carefully handled. Your mother and Freddie and Bessie were riding, too. We went through the tunnel underneath the Skyline Drive on the other side of the mountain, and were on the trails below there. Freddie was tired and he and your mother turned back. I felt as if we were ten miles away from home and as if we were in the absolute wilderness on a great expedition.

There was a soggy place across the path where there was an underground spring, and when your grandfather's horse came to it he put in a leap. Your grandfather—I can see him right now—sort of toppled off to the right and hit the ground like a great oak tree falling out of the sky. Dodo ran on down the path and your grandfather just lay there. I looked at Bessie. Bessie had a little brown felt derby on her head, and she was in her jodhpurs and little jacket. She was sitting up on her horse, crying, and said "What's happened to grandfather?"

I remember my instincts right now—this man is in trouble, that bad horse got him and he's going to come back and get me, too. I got off Polly and went up the side of the bank and climbed six feet up in a tree. Dodo came back up the path with his reins dangling. Dodo didn't run away, and about that time your grandfather started stirring and climbed up the bank so he could get back on. Bessie and I rode in complete silence behind him back to Royal Orchard.

Dinner was about as formal as anything I've seen before or since. There'd be a couple of butlers in tuxedo jackets bringing in the food. Your mother would wear a long dress to dinner. There'd be lots of courses—I'd never seen courses before—whatever I got at home always came out on one plate. They were wonderful meals, using lots of vegetables from the garden.

After dinner we'd go out and play baseball with Thornton. Freddie and I would play Bessie and her friends while it was still daylight. Then we'd go in and your mother would read out loud to us before bed.

The difference between the grand style of life at Royal Orchard that Jack-ie McElroy describes and the one that I grew up in came about as a result of the death of Grandfather, the disruption of World War II, and the greater in-formality that came in its wake. While there was always a manager and one or two workmen, and while the "five little Scotts" usually brought a cook if they were in the Big House, by and large we children had replaced the servants that peopled Jackie's memories.

World War II turned Mother into a farmer, and when she ran out of space in Richmond, Royal Orchard was there to expand into, as shown in the fol-lowing paper that Mother wrote for a college English class in 1959.

MURDER FOR MONEY

In the effort to find enough meat for my husband and our family of growing chil-dren in the second year after Pearl Harbor, I hit upon the easy-sounding scheme of raising turkeys at home.

The war-time meat ration tickets were eternally insufficient for people spoiled as we had always been with bacon and sausage for breakfast, cheese or seafood for lunch, and a roast of some sort for dinner. Turkeys seemed so simple.

There was no trouble buying the baby turks. The farmers brought their turkey eggs to town to be hatched out in the electrically heated brooder house, whence am-bitious poultry people (like me) could pick them up in cardboard boxes—fifty to a box. You could not believe when looking with loving eyes at those tiny creatures how quickly they can grow into giants, gentle, timid, cowardly giants.

All the children, ours and our neighbor's were pleased pink when I brought them home, complete with electrically controlled thermostatic heater, and installed them in our sunny, if small, pantry just over the furnace room. Our darling old Lucy James was entirely on our team. She thought it would be fine to be able to cook fat young turkeys, in a few months. We were all for the turks and the turks were all for us.

Pretty soon it became clear that the whole family would *have* to be all for the turks, as cleaning, watering, feeding them, as well as keeping the temperature even, became a dreadful, time-consuming duty. The pantry got smaller and smaller (and smellier and smellier) before school let out in June.

By Chesapeake and Ohio Railroad, I set forth with my brood to travel to the Blue Ridge Mountains, a blessed change for our now heavy-to-handle (nearly) one hun-dred turks. (We had grieved over, and buried, several in our little city garden, earlier.)

On the splendid "Sportsman" we took a drawing room, ostensibly so that my youngest child could have a nap, but really to smuggle the turks, for the C & O Rail-road authorities did not look favorably upon live stock in their swank Pullman cars, nor understand the danger to young turks from violent changes of temperature in the freight car. They had no idea how happy our livestock could be in their luxurious Pullman drawing room.

All of our luggage, even small suitcases, was checked so that each child could carry his or her weight in turks, all concealed with cleverness (we hoped) in boxes of different sizes and shapes. My own children each had a child guest, so that we made quite a mob. I had to carry the baby, but even she clutched tightly, in her little fists, a boot-sized box of turks. Dear old Lucy, delicately built and skinny, had much more than her own share of turks in many different cartons, some slung around her shoulders. By bribery and corruption we eased all of our burdens into that drawing room (small family size) without the conductor knowing a thing about our poorly hidden poultry. At any moment, one of the children might have dropped a box with disastrous results, but they all hung on heroically, perhaps in terror of me!

Not a turkey peeped from the time the covers to their boxes were put on, at home, until we stealthily uncovered them in our stylish quarters.

Once on the mountain the turks came into their own. They had a heavenly-happy time, safe from weather and weasels up on a rat-wire balcony, swung across the big, horse stable box-stall with a lovely window on the south to soothe their pent up emotions, and in which to sun themselves in that champagne and cherries climate.

Miracle of miracles, we raised over seventy-five of them. There was one cripple, a touchingly brave little creature on whom the bigger, tougher turkeys liked to *sit*. So we never counted on our "crip" as market material, only as a dear, but humble, poor relation, in need of special pity, protection and provision.

So the summer sped on, relatives related rumors of evil odors from the horse barn, but we who worked there had learned to live with, if not to love, this fragrance.

In 1946, when I was five, the work ethic was still applied, but it was less an ethic and more a necessity. If we were going to have wild strawberries with our rhubarb, or if Cora was going to cook peas or green beans for dinner, somebody had to do the picking and the shelling and the snapping.

Every Royal Orchard–raised generation had its version of tricking the adults into thinking a great deal of work had been done. When we were set to weeding the lawn, Mother would supervise us, in a distracted fashion, from the windows of the second floor of the Big House, where she was working. Between checks, we would sneak up to the pasture and fill the bottoms of our bushel baskets with the huge leaves of cabbage weeds, making sure that we looked to be hard at work with our weeding knives when she next looked out of the window. She would remind us to "Get all the way down under the *root*, children, don't just grab at the leaves above ground." After a suitable amount of time had passed, we would show her our baskets, brimming over with two inches of lawn weeds and ten inches of pasture weeds, which, from the second floor, all looked alike.

The miles and miles of beautifully graded horse trails that had been built by Grandfather's workmen had to be cleared—of trees that had fallen during winter ice storms and of vines, blackberry and wild grape, that overtook them in the heady growth of early June. This was done in half-day work parties on foot, the lead two people clearing logs from the path, the middle two using machetes to hack down the overgrowth, and the two bringing up the rear wielding long-handled clippers to take out the overhead branches that would get in the way of a rider or walker. This was exhausting, sweaty, and sometimes dangerous work, because those who worked with the machetes (or today with the weed-eater) not infrequently disturbed bees' nests; when you heard the cry *"Bees!"* you ran for dear life. Sweat trickled out from my gloved hands and down through the bandanna on my forehead. Gnats found their way into eyes, ears, and noses. The worst heat of summer would often be broken by a thunderstorm, which would wash over us, stuck as we were, miles deep in the woods, like a squall flattening sailboats.

Children were needed to hold the head of the horse when Jake Hicks built a fire in the forge under the archway below Blighty and shod each horse in its turn. The flag needed to be put up and taken down, and the Big House cried out for endless flower arrangements. Mother and Aunt Rossie, who were both partial to wildflowers, were liable to send us up the mountain in search of feathery stems of Queen Anne's lace or the splotchy orange of tickweed, to brighten the dark interior of the Big House. Tinsley Truslow, the gardener, needed help weeding and mulching the raspberries if they were to bear twice a season. Mother and Tinsley always had at least one major project per summer: building retaining walls, as vegetables like okra and simlins were added and new terraces claimed the hillside; experimenting with flowers planted in the midst of the vegetables to hold down the aphid population; throwing up barricades of chicken wire to keep out the deer and the groundhogs.

Mother was violently opposed to killing snakes, even poisonous ones, because of their ecological contribution in eating insects. The workmen were willing to humor her by moving blacksnakes, usually wound around a pitchfork, when they came upon them. But rattlers they killed, no matter how many lectures they got, skinning them and nailing the skin up on the door of the barn.

* * *

When it was ESB's turn to run Royal Orchard, she put her radical horticultural theories to work. She banned pesticides in the vegetable garden and on the apple trees, grew mushrooms in the dark, dank, rock-walled corridors in the basement of the Big House, built water-storage tanks to catch the rainfall from the downspouts off the roof, raised pigs and chickens for our consumption, and bought a jackass to breed with horses to produce mules.

Never a consensus builder, Mother would get an idea and move immediately to make it a reality. Aunt Rossie probably had the most sympathy for Mother's experimentation, if not for the high-handed way she carried out her ideas before checking with her brothers and sisters. The basis of most of their battles over how to run Royal Orchard grew out of their fundamentally different view of the place. To Mother's brothers and sisters, it had long ago ceased being a working farm: what they were looking for when they came to visit was a smoothly run country retreat. Instead, they were awakened by the rooster crowing at the first hint of dawn, and, if they managed to sleep through that, pretty soon the jackass would set to, sending long-drawn-out, defiant brays up the hollow above the shed in the lower pasture, the last hee-haaa coming long after his listeners were sure he had run out of breath. Guests eating at the porch table overlooking the vegetable garden got unwelcome sniffs of the horse manure that had been spread around as fertilizer, and squeamish city folk did not like walking by a hog-scalding or dealing with their children's nightmares after watching Jake Hicks wait for a headless chicken to stop its death dance. Mother, on the other hand, required her children and later her grandchildren not only to watch the chicken being killed but to hold the neck for Jake. Squeamishness in the face of unpleasant jobs was unacceptable, as was what she considered misplaced sentimentality over animals. Where she got this zealously realistic approach to natural processes I don't know. Perhaps it was a reaction to her sheltered childhood.

Just as her sisters and brothers reacted to her latest horticultural enthusiasms, she would become incensed over unilateral action on their part. She would fret to find that someone had removed English box bushes near a cottage porch for fear they might be a haven for snakes, or pruned the lower branches of the enormous hemlock tree that blocked the view of Humpback Mountain from the Big House porch. The incident that upset her most was the discovery that, while she was away on a trip, the asparagus patch in the vegetable garden had been cut down. It took up a sizable space between the currants and grapes and the spinach, and was a favorite spot for games of hide and seek. Again the fear had been of snakes, and since threats of punishment had not kept us out of the cool, green canopy it provided, one day the whole patch was cut down. Asparagus takes years to establish itself, and Mother was heartsick over its disappearance.

* * *

Despite their differing philosophies, there was a great deal of love and civility between the brothers and sisters, and most of all an incredibly strong family bond. No one ever said it to me outright, but I grew up knowing, the way you know the most fundamental truths, that my family was my strength. My aunts and uncles and first cousins were the context for my life, largely because Royal Orchard made them so. I know my first cousins the way other people know their sisters and brothers, because my aunts and uncles made a conscious choice to raise each other's children as well as their own.

Mother did not play tennis and so was unconcerned about my learning to play properly, figuring that if I wanted to do so badly enough I could learn by playing with others who had had lessons. This did not wash with Aunt Rossie, who stuck me in the car with her own children and took us down to lessons with Mike Dolan, the pro at Farmington Country Club outside of Charlottesville.

Aunt Isabel took the news smiling one evening when I dragged myself into the living room at the Big House to tell her that I had fallen through the top of her convertible, having picked the car roof to hide on for a game of hide-and-seek. The Fred Scotts would arrange for me to go for extended visits to Bundoran, their farm twelve miles south of Royal Orchard, and I had a second home at the Buford Scotts whenever Mother's discipline got too intense.

For Leezee Scott Porter, the youngest of Uncle Buford's three daughters and the cousin that I am closest to, Mother was aunt, godmother, and what Leezee describes as "partial mother." "You have to remember that my mother wasn't really around," says Leezee,

so I think your mother took an extra role with me. My sense of it was that she felt she needed to teach me the things that mothers are supposed to teach daughters. She balanced out her loving support with huge criticism.

She, like my father, could bring me to tears when she would see me at Royal Orchard and say, "Can you go back to the same people that you went to to get your hair that color, and tell them to take it away." Or, "You know, people your size shouldn't wear bathing suits like that." And she'd say this in front of my boyfriend. She seemed unafraid of being disappointed in someone, or expressing her pride, or being sad about something. She just seemed bigger than life, with her willingness to get hurt, or get laughed at, or make people angry, or shred things up, or love people up . . . letting the chips fall where they may.

Happier memories for Leezee involve listening to Mother charm the policeman who had pulled her over on a fast trip from Richmond to Royal Orchard. When told how many miles an hour she was going, Mother's response was a wide-eyed, "I was? My husband will be so pleased to hear that this car can still go that fast." She contrasts that with a later image of Mother, in her eighties, "blasting off to church in her yellow pickup truck with her bonnet

The five little Scotts—happy times at Royal Orchard in the late 1940s

and gloves on." Leezee also recalled Mother's sense of feeling at ease, no matter where she was. She described Mother stopping, on trips, and going into the simplest kind of diner and saying to the waitress, "May I please have some tea, and would you possibly have a cot in the back where I could take a nap?" "It was wonderful," said Leezee, "that sense that either she created in herself or someone gave her as a child, that the world would take her in."

Whoever was staying in the Big House just accepted the fact that the house they were in was open to all. Children raced through the upstairs hall to raid the costume closet; adults wandered in to borrow a tennis racket or to dig the baseball bat out of the sports closet; and everyone just naturally gathered in the Big House living room after they had finished dinner. Aunt Isabel Anderson would gravitate toward the music room, and as soon as she got out the sheet music she would be surrounded by singers. As children, we spent the twilight hours playing sardines in the flower garden, jostling the peonies as we scrunched down under their tall, leafy cover, checking out the dark corners behind the love seats in the middle of the garden, or trying not to giggle when the person hiding with us started tickling. When we tired of playing sardines, we would collect fireflies in jars with holes in the top, but as soon as we heard the first notes of "A Bullfrog Sat" we would race down the lawn that sloped gently toward the Big House and burst through the screen door from the porch into the living room. Wedged between the windowsill and the piano we would take turns turning the pages for Aunt Isabel. Whenever she finished one song, arguments would erupt about what she should play next, hands thrusting music in front of her from all directions.

She had the sheet music from all the major musicals of the forties and fifties, and we sang them so often that we can sing most of them by heart to this day. The girls could be counted on to cut loose on the duet in "I Hear Singing and There's No One There," singing with our fingers in our ears so as not to be thrown off by someone next to us singing the competing melody. Either George Wayne Anderson or Fred or Bill Reed could raise the hairs on the back of your neck when they sang "Old Man River." Another favorite was "Gotta Wash that Man Right Outta My Hair," vigorously pantomimed. Songs we never failed to sing were the World War II rouser "They All Called Him Johnny Zero" and "The Hokey Pokey," with chairs and sofas moved back so that everyone could "get their right leg in and shake it all about."

We children knew it was time to go up the hill to the cottages or upstairs to bed when Aunt Isabel began to play "Good Night Ladies." After we were pried away from the piano, we would race through the dark up the hill, avoiding the shadowy threat of the flower garden, not stopping until we came within the reassuring circle of brightness cast by the back-porch light of Clover or California Cottages.

The nineteen first cousins included three age groups: an elder group, a middle group, and a younger group. I was smack in the middle of the middle group, and had six or seven cousins either exactly my age or within a few years of it. Each age group moved as a pack and preyed on the one younger than it.

Freddie and Elisabeth and the cousins who were their age called the shots, and used us as conscripted laborers. We were their lackeys, meant to do their chores, run their errands, and loyally submit to their command. If we told on them, we were taken to the bottom of the barn for the dreaded Treatment. They would roll the big, black barn door shut so no grownups would hear our screams, then taking us one at a time they would hold us down on an ironing board, twist our noses, give us cauliflower ears by rubbing them with both hands until they were an angry red and felt like they would fall off, and tickle us on our sides and feet until we begged for mercy.

We, in our turn, tried to boss around Rossie, George Ross, Strother, and Alfred in the youngest group, but we never were able to pull it off. Instead, we got punished for picking on the young and defenseless. One common punishment was to be sent on foot down to Afton for the mail. Afton was two miles downhill, and even though we could spend our Sunday allowances on candy on arrival, the trek back up on a humid summer's afternoon was a killer. Hot and resentful, we would tease plump Leezee, lugging the big leather mailbag, when she burst into tears of self-pity. Fred Reed and Fred Scott would trade candies while I blew bubbles with my bubble gum, or tried to mimic Fred Reed, who could burp the alphabet. In all things I tried to model myself on Fred Reed, who in addition to having this unique talent was also a fearless horseman and had a deep, beautiful, singing voice. When we got back, we would head for our secret meeting place on the henhouse roof, which we could jump down onto from the retaining wall at the top of the vegetable garden. This was where we kept our stash of "tobacco"—corn silk cut from the tasseled corn on the bottom terrace of the garden and laid out on the henhouse roof to dry. Using the cigarette papers we had just bought, we would roll cigarettes and sit cross-legged with our backs to the retaining wall, puffing on our cigarettes that burned down so fast that they burned our fingers.

Because we moved in groups, we were allowed a lot of freedom, and since several of us rode, the horses and ponies available extended our range. We could play tag bareback on ponies in the orchard, using a halter with the lead line tied on like the reins of a bridle, or canter under the limbs of the old apple trees, grab a branch, and swing clear off the pony's back.

One of our best expeditions, that took most of the day, was a ride that took us up and over our own mountain and down to Rockfish Gap on the old Appalachian Trail. We crossed over Route 250 on the Skyline Drive overpass and rode right up to the door of Howard Johnson's. Somebody would hold the horses while we went in and bought Coke floats (Mother not being around) or ice-cream cones, which we ate on the next part of the journey up the mountain that rose behind the restaurant, en route to Swananoah. Built by Major Dooley, the Richmond tobacco millionaire mentioned earlier, about the same time as Royal Orchard, Swananoah was a marble palace set in formal gardens. In the 1950s, it was owned by Walter Russell and his wife, Lao, who claimed that they ran, on the premises, the University of the World and wanted to build a 250-foot statue of Christ of the Blue Ridge in their garden. They both seemed to us a little dippy, and since so far as we could tell they never had any students in their university, they welcomed us when we arrived, hot and tired, bearing a squished container of raspberries from our garden, which was our excuse for visiting.

Mrs. Russell would greet us in a long, flowing dress and give us something cool to drink. Dr. Russell would sit us down in one of the rows of funeral chairs at the foot of the wide staircase and then walk up the stairs to the landing where there was a huge pipe organ. He would play for us, losing himself in the music, the tempo and volume steadily rising until organ music filled our heads and the whole, vast space that rose up to the second floor. He would forget we were there, and when the novelty had worn off we would tiptoe outdoors, untie our ponies, and head back on the three-hour ride to Royal Orchard.

Sometimes, with one of the older boys such as Buford, Bill, Freddie, or George Wayne at the wheel, we would all pile into the back of the huge, slat-sided farm truck and go down to Afton to watch the passenger train to Chicago whoosh into the Crozet Tunnel, fascinated by the frozen images of passengers, one fluffing a napkin in the dining car, or others letting their bed down from the wall in their compartment before the train shot into the tunnel that carried it through to the Shenandoah Valley. This never failed to produce a spasm of terror in me; the train seemed to be so horrifyingly powerful and the people in it so unaware of being catapulted into the heart of darkness. On trips to the Skyline Drive-in open-air movies, fifteen or twenty of us in the back of the truck were covered with hay before we left Royal Orchard. Freddie or whoever was driving would pay only for the cousins who were in the cab of the truck with him. Those of us in the back were threatened with "the Treatment" if the straw moved or a giggle was heard, and since we knew we would not get taken if they had to pay for us, we cooperated.

Most of our entertainment, however, was self-produced, and it was on the mountain. The adults occasionally put on play weddings in the flower garden.

They would dress in their Sunday best, with hats and gloves, and be the congregation. The bride and groom would be chosen from the eldest batch of cousins, the bridesmaids and groomsmen from our ranks, and the flower girls and ring bearers from the youngest children. Margery would "marry" Bill or Isabel would "marry" Buford, with Mary Denny and Alice as their bridesmaids and Rossie and Alfred as flower children, strewing rose petals between the boxwood that formed an aisle. The ceremony would be followed by an elaborate reception, the whole affair being orchestrated down to the most minute detail.

Every Saturday night, the sound of the Big House bell being rung meant that the hay wagon pulled by Queen and Nell, the two white mules, was about to leave the barnyard headed for Round-the-World Rock, and if you didn't want to walk up you had better hustle. Each family took their own picnic food, but in the crush of bodies around the flatbed table that held the food, I could usually avoid Mother's cheese and black bread, leftover salad, and rotten bananas and put away some of the Scotts' or the Reeds' hot dogs, Cokes, and some-mores. There was another picnic spot, on a little knoll up the hill from Pool Hollow, where we were allowed to go as fairly young children, without the adults. Camp Buford has a small log cabin and an outdoor fireplace, and we felt very independent trudging up the steep hill behind the pump house carrying our own supplies and making our own fire when we got there. Sometimes, at the Big House cocktail hour, we could hear their voices out on the corner of the porch that faces west toward Humpback Mountain. In symbolic defiance of their authority, we would chant—first softly, then louder, and finally yelling so hard our faces turned red—"Who put the underpants in Mrs. Murphy's chowder, nobody answers so I'll shout a little louder!" As a child, the only time that I remember wishing I was a boy was when the boys made a big show of putting out the campfire by peeing on it.

Bad weather in the mountains invariably meant fog, sometimes so thick that driving up or down the mountain was dangerous. Mother's reaction was to double the amount of out-loud reading required each day, but at some point word would spread that parlor games were being played in the Big House, and I would be excused to race down the hill to join in. A whole closet under the stairs was full of supplies needed for parlor games: hats for a hat version of musical chairs and toilet brushes attached to rope that were tied around the waist and used to propel a tennis ball forward to the finish line in the toilet-brush race.

A play wedding in the flower garden. Freddie is "marrying" Margery

My favorite game, and one that I became good at, required an elaborate setup. Old wicker laundry baskets were brought into the living room and suspended in the air by running a broom handle through the basket handles and balancing the broom at each end on a chair seat. Four handkerchiefs were placed on each corner of the backs of the chairs. Two people competed against each other. Someone helped each competitor to sit on their broom handle, with feet resting, on either side, in the suspended basket. Each was given a stick, which was used to keep balance by touching the floor. The object of the game was to raise the stick from the floor four separate times to knock the handkerchiefs off the chair corners, and to do it faster than the other person. Either it would be done in a coordinated millisecond, the stick gotten back down to the floor, or the tippy laundry basket would whirl on the broom handle and deposit the player in a heap on the oriental rug. The faster the competitors tried to do it, the more they spilled, and the more the hilarity mounted. To win, the player had to get all four handkerchiefs with no spills between, and each person had a cheering squad and helpers to get them back in the basket. Whether doing it or watching, the tears were streaming down our faces, especially if one of the aunts or uncles was trying it.

Pass the Orange also caused an uproar, because the fastest way to pass the orange down the line was to lie down and have the person next in line lean over you and grip it with their chin and shoulder. In no time, the floor was a writhing mass of prone, giggling bodies. The very earnestness of the competition in a very competitive family was funny. I can remember being so convulsed with laughter that I couldn't command my muscles to move, or my voice to speak. No one present was allowed to sit out, and as the evening went on a kind of manic glee gripped not just the children but the adults, too.

Manic glee by the younger generation, gotten away with in a context of strict decorum imposed by the older generation, seems to have been a family trait long before the parlor games that I remember. Uncle Freddie's wife, Aunt Elizabeth Pinkerton Scott, says of her husband and his sisters and brother: "They all had that Irish kind of a sense of humor—you know, undisciplined, throwing butter balls on the ceiling, suddenly shouting out with something quite bad."

After I went to boarding school, I began to realize that in other families people didn't do the things we did—like walking fully clothed into the swimming pool, twirling a parasol, or coming down to breakfast dressed in six veils and a strange hat, just for the fun of it. Aunt Rossie was a genuine comic, gifted as a mimic and always able to make people laugh at what she did, either by her unpredictability or by her clowning. Mother was not a comic, but she had an innate sense of drama and delighted in the unconventional pose or the pointed remark that reshuffled a conversation even as it was taking place. She was also aware that for Father, a little hilarity went a long way. When the mindless joy set in for the evening, he would drift quietly out of the scene, and on our return we would find him deep in his book on the porch of the cottage. But for all five sisters and brothers, high spirits were always the entrance ticket to the party. As they got older, the line between manic tendencies and simply having fun began to blur.

The part that alcohol played in all this was typically Virginian. It was always there, the before-dinner drink and the after-church whiskey sour punctuating the rituals of daily and weekly life. The drinks were rituals in themselves: the mint julep of high summer had to be served in frosted silver goblets, couldn't be too sweet, and had to be poured over crushed ice from which emerged a single stalk of mint. The code was strict. Women could drink, but never to excess. Men could get drunk, but only in male company, after the ladies had retired or in the basement of a men's club or at a fraternity at the university. People who did not drink, especially men, were suspect and presumed to have "a problem." Mother and Father were both contemptuous of the custom that was popular at the time of offering a teenage child a reward of $1,000 if they made a pledge not to drink until they turned twenty-one. They thought the goal was unrealistic, and that the concept assumed irresponsibility on the part of the teenager and encouraged an orgy of drinking when the pledge period ended. Instead, we were always allowed wine with meals, mixed with water when we were young, and when in college were offered wine and beer as a matter of course. However, I do remember Mother being livid at Uncle Buford, one summer Sunday when I was seventeen, when he gave me a whiskey sour on the porch of the Big House.

Mother's favorite drink was wine, and her favorite wine was champagne. In her seventies, she started drinking a beer at night before she went to bed, and by her eighties the bedtime drink had become a toddy of Irish whiskey, which she carried with her in a little flask when she came to visit; she drank it with water and no ice. She was apt to bring her host a bottle of Bushmill's or Jameson's, so that, if the spirit struck, there would be something to have a conversation over late at night. Even though in her old age she took to Irish whiskey, for most of her life she was leery of hard liquor, which had been the downfall of several of her uncles. She kept it under fairly tight control at her parties.

* * *

Royal Orchard is still enjoyed by Grandfather and Grandmother's descendants, who, when in-laws and children of the fifth generation are added, number more than 140, and counting. Its use has changed, in that long vacations are a thing of the past and few people can stay a month at a time, as Mother and Father and my aunts and uncles did. The Big House is more apt to be used for house parties, weddings, baptisms, anniversaries, and graduations. As our numbers have grown, and as the patterns of modern-day lives have changed the ways in which Royal Orchard is used, the intimacy of our generation has been diluted. Our children could not possibly know each other as well as we, the "new" older generation, do. But they do care as much about the place, and are willing to do the work to keep it in the family, all the while laying down their own traditions and making sure that their children cherish the place as well. Their great- and great-great-grandparents would be pleased.

Aunt Isabel, ESB, and Aunt Rossie, ca. 1930

5. Theirs Not to Reason Why

NOBODY WHO EVER DEALT with Mother, whether they were family members, friends, or professional acquaintances, would question the statement that she had a will of iron. No other element of her character was as central to who she was. As a young person, Mother instinctively understood that, as a female in a society where a woman's role was largely ornamental, she often needed to adopt disguises to get her way. The social expectation just made the game a little tougher and more fun, and as had countless women before her, she used her considerable charm both to get what she wanted and to make that fact unobjectionable.

As she got older she dropped the disguises, although she seldom failed to use those natural persuasive powers that come with beauty, a sense of humor, and innate self-confidence. Her father had been the undisputed autocrat of their family, and as a child she had been on the receiving end of a chain of command that started with him and descended through Grandmother Scott and a strict German governess, Fräulein Hennis. Long before her father died in 1939, she was raising her own children the same way, finding that giving orders came as naturally to her as it did to him. Later in her life, so far did she get from disguises that when she was in her early sixties, and my fiancé, Fred Hitz, brought his mother to visit for the first time, Mother looked her straight in the eye and greeted her with, "Liz! you and I will get along splendidly if you do *exactly* as I say." Luckily, Liz Hitz, an individualist herself, laughed and went right on doing as she pleased.

It is significant, I think, that two of Mother's close friends—both spirited, naturally imperious women—did not live in Richmond. Oxie d'Eprémesnil lived in Paris, Isabella Gilpin in Millwood, Virginia, and carrying on these friendships by telephone and by letter suited Mother perfectly. Her style in letters was as natural as her conversation. She tended to idealize those she loved when they were not physically proximate to her—children away from home and friends across the ocean became close to perfect—and this allowed these two friendships to stay untarnished by the inevitable battles of will that broke out when her Richmond friends or her sisters objected to being dictated to. Néné Fleming was unquestionably her longest-standing Richmond friend and someone that Mother was devoted to, but Miss Néné, with a mind as independent and strong-willed as Mother's, simply removed herself when Mother refused to compromise; she left the trip, got out of the car, walked away—whatever it took to hold her own. Margaret McElroy, Eda Williams, Mary Robertson, Aunt Rossie, and Aunt Isabel all would have felt closer to ESB had she been willing to compromise. She may have thought she believed in compromise, but in fact it was entirely foreign to her.

Miss Néné probably had the most experience dealing with ESB's arbitrary decisions. In 1965, when they were both widowed, they took a trip to France together. The trouble started on the transatlantic crossing, when ESB blithely announced that they would eat meals at different tables because each of them would make new friends. There was nothing wrong with the logic behind this announcement, but Miss Néné thought she already had a friend. Once they got to France, ESB enrolled in classes at the University of Rennes that were held in the coastal town of Saint-Malo, Normandy, depriving Miss Néné of a traveling companion. In ESB's plan, Miss Néné was to play golf at the nearby golf course; but as Miss Néné put it, she could play a lot better golf on the course at home. So she threw her hands up in despair and returned home early.

Perhaps Mother's stubborn streak went all the way back to County Donegal, Ireland, because it was from there that the Scotts emigrated in 1850, during the potato famine. They were Protestant merchants in the small port town of Ballyshannon, a town where even today the Protestant church dominates the highest hill. They first settled in Brooklyn, New York, but before the Civil War they moved to Petersburg, Virginia, and the turn of the century found them in Richmond.

Whether or not her stubbornness was Irish, it was definitely legendary, and the best instance of it is the story of the owl. Church Point Farm was a haven for wildlife, and in the 1940s Father got a great deal of enjoyment out of the bird hunting there. On one such trip, Mother, by mistake, shot an owl. Piqued by the general hilarity this caused, she announced that since the family rule was that we ate whatever was shot, this owl was going to be eaten. Informed by those who seemed to know that owls were inedible, Mother countered that the owls they were talking about had not been cooked right: the owl made the one-hour trip back to Richmond in a car that still rang with laughter. Sensing rebellion in the kitchen, Mother plucked the bird herself. On Monday night it was presented as a whole baked fowl, just as if it had been a duck. No one got as far as establishing that it was inedible because there was no knife capable of carving it. This might have proved the point for most people, but not for ESB.

Tuesday night, Tinsley bore into the dining room a strong-smelling casse-role—the owl, floating in herbs and juices. Cora, attacking it with a French cleaver, had managed to cut it up, but it still could not be penetrated by human teeth. On Wednesday night, the same strong smell as Tuesday's rose from the soup tureen as the owl made its third and final appearance. Depending on perspective, you could say that Mother learned that owl was truly inedible, or, if you had been around the dinner table those three nights, you could say that he who laughs first does not necessarily laugh last.

When dictating policy Mother usually knew better than to ask for sugges-tions, but if she did ask, and then did not like the suggestions, it seldom slowed her down. Jackie McElroy, visiting Freddie at Royal Orchard at age seven, wrote home to his mother, "The second day we went to church. [After church] Mrs. Bocock wanted us to go calling on Mrs. Massie and all of us said we didn't want to go. So we went." Mother, who could laugh at her own willfulness, wrote on the bottom of the note, "Read between the lines the bullying dictatorial hostess! Nothing could condemn me more innocently than these succinct lines of my beloved Jackie."

There was a positive side to her stubbornness, and this emerged as perse-verance. Mother didn't get discouraged when told something could not be done; in fact it was usually the catalyst for turning a hazy idea into a concrete project. Some of these projects, like the crewel-work quilt, stretched into an adult lifetime of perseverance. Mother had been taught needlework by Grandmother Scott, both the practical applications like darning and hem-ming and the exquisite embroidery stitches of crewel work, petit point, monogramming, and cross-stitching. In the evenings, when Father read aloud to her, she would be at work darning sweaters or socks (she even darned stockings), monogramming an umbrella, decorating a linen sheet with beauti-ful feather stitching, or monogramming one of literally hundreds of linen kitchen towels that she gave away for birthdays and at Christmas. These usu-ally had on them the recipient's name, the date they were given, and the place the recipient was living at the time. At first she did them in formal cross-stitching, using the webbed canvas of small squares that is tacked over the ma-terial being worked on to keep the letters neat and consistent. Later she gave up this cumbersome process in favor of the simpler, handsomer pattern of writing directly on the towel in her own elegant script and then backstitching over her writing. We have perhaps twenty of these in a kitchen drawer, and every week when I get out a clean one, I am reminded of the particular seg-ment of my life that that towel represents.

Along with the everyday mending and the never-ending sewing of gifts, the quilt project got intense but infrequent attention. The crewel-work quilt lived in a blue suitcase, and traveled back and forth to Royal Orchard. A nineteenth-century antique, by the 1940s it was in such poor shape that most people would have thrown it away. There was very little wrong with the crewel work on the old double-bed quilt, although the colors of some of the flowers had faded with time and exposure to sunlight. It was the material of the quilt itself that had disintegrated. Mother is the only person I can imagine who would have thought that quilt could be salvaged, and even she must have recognized it as a half-century project, which is nearly what it turned out to be. She bought tough Irish linen as new backing and, cutting away the disintegrated material, painstakingly sewed each crewel-worked flower and stem onto the new backing, in many instances going over the crewel work itself to renew the colors.

I can see her in my mind's eye, sitting on the front porch of the Big House at Royal Orchard, the suitcase open at her feet and the section of the quilt she was working on pulled up from the suitcase and draped over her lap. Houseguests, wandering out to the porch with the morning paper, would be conscripted as out-loud readers, and many women found themselves given a needle, with some of the silk thread that Cousin Oxie sent from Paris, and put to work while their husbands read from "News of the Week in Review."

For several years before she finished work on the quilt in the early 1980s, she threatened to give it to the American Wing of the Metropolitan Museum in New York. Bessie and I both thought that was a poor idea, and told her so. We thought it ought to go either to Royal Orchard or to Redlands, the late eighteenth-century house, south of Charlottesville, belonging to Bessie's husband Bobbie Carter—a house that has never been outside of the Carter family. Mother relented, and today the quilt looks as if it had always been on the four-poster bed in the downstairs bedroom at Redlands, a room whose sixteen-foot ceilings and beautiful square proportions make it the perfect home for the born-again quilt.

* * *

Some of the disguises that ESB used, at least initially, to camouflage her willpower, she also used to hide her quick mind. Her lawyer, Tom Word, remembers: "She had a great understanding of human nature; nothing surprised her about the way that people reacted to things. She had a very, very keen mind; but consciously or unconsciously she tried to make people think she didn't—she tried to play down her insights." Judge Gordon takes it one step further: "Your Mother," he told me, "was not just a determined character, she was a very powerful, brilliant person, and I mean mentally brilliant. I've heard people say she was crazy—she was crazy, all right, crazy like a fox. Representing her was fun. She'd take completely untenable positions and get away with it."

Judge Gordon used the battle of Cousin Arthur Glasgow's will as an example. Cousin Arthur was a millionaire-businessman with Richmond roots who in his will had left a good deal of money to Saint Paul's Church to endow a library. Mother, at some point after his death, had become concerned that the library was not being kept open for enough hours, so she summoned the church authorities and her lawyer at that point, Tom Gordon, to 909. Cousin Arthur had told her of his wishes concerning the library in walks they had taken together, she informed them, and it was the responsibility of the church to fulfill those wishes (for *those wishes*, read *her wishes*). Tom Gordon pointed out that though that might well have been Mr. Glasgow's intent, he had never gotten around to putting his desires concerning the hours of the library's operation into his will.

Tom left the meeting thinking that she would see the futility of trying to use Cousin Arthur's will to twist the church's arm. Instead, under his door that night came a green-ink letter in which ESB had changed tactics completely. Not the will itself, but lawyers were the culprits, by being borderline unethical about intent when drawing up a will. When he called Freddie Bocock to get his advice on how to proceed over a molehill that had just become a mountain, Freddie's reaction was, "Oh, you never want to win an argument with Mother. That's the worst possible position to be in." Any of Mother's three children could have told both the church authorities and the lawyers that the church library *would* be expanding its hours in the future, and if the church was not embarrassed enough to pay for it, then ESB would.

Mary Tyler Cheek McClenahan, a fellow civic activist and a good friend of ESB's despite being several years her junior, recalls the power plays between her husband, Leslie Cheek, director of the Virginia Museum of Fine Arts, and ESB, who was on the museum's accessions committee. Leslie was as accustomed to getting his way as ESB was, and as cheerful in the face of a good fight. Their clashes generally had to do with which paintings the museum should move to acquire. Mary Tyler says of ESB's fighting weapons, "She had weapons that Leslie didn't have. She always spoke in that soft voice and never, never raised her voice; and then her habit of sitting on the floor at a meeting or a cocktail party or whatever was immensely effective . . . so she knew how to disarm people wonderfully. But when she made up her mind, she was absolutely relentless in carrying it through." She remembered Mother saying, in some battle they were in together: "It's time now to turn ourselves into a swarm of hornets."

* * *

At the other end of the spectrum from the all-out power play, Mother was not above exercising her natural cunning when the situation demanded it. Hunting and fishing were two sports she would never have been involved in had Father not loved them, but if she was on the trip she made a game of it. In 1939, Mother and Father went on a pheasant-shooting trip to Hungary with their friends the Gilpins from Boyce, Virginia. Each guest was assigned a guide, who was not allowed to shoot unless the guest had wounded a pheasant but failed to bring it down. Father had given her a side-by-side, twenty-gauge shotgun, a beautiful Belgian weapon, and although she got no pleasure out of shooting pheasants with it, she still liked to come in after the shoot with the most birds. So when pheasants came over, she would bang away with her gun into the air, yell *"Krank gewesen"* ("It's wounded") to the guide, and he would bring down a bird. Naturally, the guide never missed, and every evening, between them, they had the most birds. On fishing trips to northern Canada, she would fly-fish from the canoe as long as people were watching. After a while, she and her guide would slip away and portage to the next lake, where he would fish and she would read poetry. Their catch at the end of the day never failed to make Pinckney Harrison furious.

Mother's approach to horseback riding, her own sport, was so competitive that early in their marriage Father gave up trying to ride with her. For part of the year, she kept our horses at Aunt Rossie and Uncle Billy Reed's beautiful Goochland County farm, Sabot Hill, overlooking the James River. On the weekends the sisters and brothers-in-law would ride together, Mother on her horse, a handsome, white-stockinged chestnut named Shamrock. The Reed's son, Bill, remembered riding with them as a small boy and described it. "Aunt Elisabeth was a beautiful rider and horsewoman. She was elegant, always immaculately dressed with an extra pair of knit gloves and a clean kerchief neatly tucked into the off side of her sidesaddle, and carrying a shoo-fly crop. Shamrock carried herself erect, as did her mistress, and both knew that eyes would turn when they passed."

Aunt Rossie and ESB were more interested in speed than were the men, and they egged each other on to try for a record time over a known distance. ESB, when riding fast, switched from a sidesaddle to a regular English saddle.

Mother holding me in her lap on Shamrock; Bessie and Freddie are also mounted, with Lucy James look-ing on in disapproval and Mr. Cotman holding the horse. The Brook Run Stable, 1941

One Sunday, with husbands and young Bill Reed riding behind to pick up the pieces, they took a ride that convinced their husbands to give up the sport. Bill remembers:

Out of the Sabot barn flew Aunt Elisabeth and my Mother, down the hard-surfaced Sabot driveway at a full gallop, never stopping to see if there was traffic on route 6; then they flew across the lowlands to the bridge leading to Sabot Island. Down the island they rode like two hyenas, only to gallop across the high Ben Dover bridge.

The bridge was old. The planking had holes in it. The bridge was at least one hundred feet off the ground, and I think they were the only people ever to ride across it without dismounting. Through Ben Dover and into Joe Brook they charged, gallop-ing the Big Woods and back to the Sabot barn. Their time was fifty-two minutes. The previously established record time was over an hour.

Part of Mother's electrifying effect on people, when she wanted to have her way, was that she would come up with the most unconventional tactics, and then carry them out with a complete lack of self-consciousness. When we were living in Lexington, Bessie went to the local high school and had a group of friends that liked to hang around our house. One night, when suggestions that they all go home had repeatedly fallen on deaf ears, ESB put a bandanna on her head, tied an apron around her waist, got out a dustpan and a broom and went around the room in silent pantomime, sweeping the guests, one by one, out the door. Being fourteen, Bessie was unamused, and accused Mother of being funny at her expense, but Mother continued until every last teenager went home.

It had been assumed that Bessie would go to Saint Timothy's for the last three years of high school, but she was so happy in Lexington High School that she was allowed to stay there through the tenth grade despite the warning from Miss Watkins, the headmistress of Saint Timothy's and a bit of a strict constructionist, that the school would not accept students for just two years. After tenth grade, Mother sent Bessie's application to Saint Timothy's, and heard back shortly that for all the reasons given the year before, they could not accept her. Mother did not let this worry her, and when September came she packed up Bessie's steamer trunk and put the trunk and the daughter on the train for Baltimore. Some girls came by car and some by train; but Mother, who knew that Miss Watkins might ban Bessie if she herself arrived with her and it became a head-on confrontation, knew also that Miss Watkins would not be mean enough to put Bessie back on the train.

Miss Watkins realized when she was licked, and bided her time in getting back at Mother for her effrontery. Her time came a year later when Bessie was nominated for the school's chief leadership position in her senior year. Word came home via Bessie that Miss Watkins had decreed that no student who had been at Saint Timothy's only one year could run for head of school. This was something Miss Watkins had complete control over, and so, as Bessie describes it, "I got all the glory because she wouldn't let me run for it and everyone felt sorry for me, I didn't have to do any of the work it involved and Miss Watkins was the villain." In addition to being the villain, Miss Watkins also made things harder for herself—because when Bessie organizes people (and this was true then as well as now), her funny, self-deprecatory style gets them happily moving in the right direction without feeling coerced. She would have been a marvelous head of school.

The toughest aspect of Mother's willpower to deal with was its arbitrary quality. Sometimes her commands made sense; at other times they didn't. But either way, you were expected to have the attitude of the soldiers in Tennyson's poem, "The Charge of the Light Brigade": "Theirs not to reason why, theirs but to do and die." Not surprisingly, males were better about this than females; and, specifically, Freddie was better about it than Bessie and I were. Unlike us, he did not waste an instant trying to figure out why she wanted something or what possible use it could serve, he just immediately obeyed and then went on with what he was doing.

One hot summer day, Mother and Cousin Mary Wingfield were sitting on the porch of Clover Cottage at Royal Orchard, talking and occasionally looking over to the tennis court, only a few yards away, to watch Freddie and his cousins playing tennis. Mother asked Cousin Mary Wing if she would like some buttermilk, and she allowed as how that would taste good. From the Clover porch, Mother called to Freddie, interrupting his tennis game, and told him to go down to the ice chest on the back porch of the Big House and get a glass of buttermilk. Mother then fell back into conversation with her cousin. An hour went by before she suddenly recollected that Freddie had not brought the buttermilk. "Freddie, Bo!" Mother's annoyed voice rang out. "Where in the State of Virginia is the buttermilk?" "Oh," said Freddie, in confusion as he dove for a ball, "I drank it." Being stopped in the middle of a tennis game in order to down a glass of buttermilk seemed no more odd to him than many of Mother's requests. He had run downhill to the Big House, drunk the buttermilk, and returned to the game in approximately the same time that Bessie and I (had it been us) would have taken to register our complaint about the interruption.

Cousin Eda also recollects Mother's reaction once when Bessie was trying to be excused from reading aloud because she had a terrible headache. "Read on," said Mother, "it will help your headache." The requirement of absolute obedience in the face of arbitrary demands was one, according to Eda Williams, that "could have had a bad effect on certain children." Margaret McElroy agrees, adding, "A lot of children would have buckled under it." But not only did we not buckle under it, all three of us remember our childhood as happy, and perhaps Miss Néné comes closest to being able to explain why.

To Miss Néné, Mother's approach to child rearing clearly had two sides. "She gave you so much—so much pleasure, so much excitement, so many trips, and so on. Nobody's gonna have fun just having all the pleasure, and she knew that. She wasn't the kind to sap your vitality. She wanted you to have initiative, but also to obey her without question."

It is said that consistency is the secret to bringing up children, and Mother was at least consistently arbitrary. How arbitrary depended primarily on how tired or rested she was; or, to put it another way, how long it had been since she took a nap. Since she went to bed late and got up early, her naps operated on her exactly like a battery charger, and she could not do without them. She had the real talent of being able to sleep anywhere, on anything, under any conditions. I have never heard of anyone else taking a nap during a daughter's wedding reception, but Mother did. Bessie and Bobbie Carter were married on a Saturday early in October 1951, a date that was picked because it should have been safely past the humid heat of summer. Virginia weather is famous for playing tricks, especially when the season is changing, and on that Saturday we regressed into August. The reception was held at 909, and the long receiving line seemed to go on forever. The humidity was particularly enervating, and halfway through the reception, Mother wilted. The party was clearly going well, so she disappeared upstairs for twenty minutes and came back recharged and ready for the cake-cutting and the sendoff.

She had read of Benjamin Franklin's belief about napping—that the complete relaxation involved in the act of falling asleep was itself a sufficient restorative. When he napped, he put his waistcoat chain in his hand and hung his hand over the edge of the bed, so that the sound of the chain falling from his loosened grip would wake him up. Mother's version of this was that if you had a half hour, you slept a half hour, but if you had only ten minutes, that would do it. She called it her "drop dead time," and truly, she slept the sleep of the dead. No chain dropping to the floor was going to wake her up; it took a freshly brewed pot of tea to get her going again.

Mother thought napping was an acquired habit—that I should have been able to learn to nap if I closed my eyes and lay still. Napping comes naturally to Freddie and Bessie, but I have to be totally exhausted in order to go to sleep. Once, when Mother caught me reading during naptime, she made me lie down next to her on her bed, putting an arm over me so that she would know if I moved. Seconds later, she was asleep, and I lay there, paralyzed, trying not to move a muscle, knowing that it meant the difference between an afternoon playing with my cousins or an afternoon weeding raspberry bushes. But Mother would curl up for a nap with her sweater as a pillow, on a pew in the small chapel of a cathedral, under a tree in a park on a walking tour, or on the floor of a rest room. Having occasionally frightened people who came upon her prone in unlikely places, she would sometimes leave an explanatory note pinned to herself, or stuck on the door of the room where she had "dropped dead."

In her seventies, ESB began having trouble with a fibrillating heart. In addition to taking the required medicine, she used her common sense and added another nap to her daily routine. The timing of it depended on what was on her schedule. ESB's naps have to have been the secret of her phenomenal energy, because she seldom slept more than six hours a night. Aside from restoring her energy, a nap also restored her emotional equilibrium. A nap was her first reaction to bad news or discouragement of any kind, and invariably she rose from her rest with a positive attitude and a plan of action. She would have loved Colin Powell's dictum, "Optimism is a force multiplier." And she would have added that optimism comes naturally after a nap.

As children, we learned never to ask for special dispensations before her nap, nor before tea had fully restored her. We knew that confronting her head-on on any issue was a sure road to defeat, because—as Freddie had pointed out to Tom Gordon—it was not a good idea to win an argument with Mother. So we became expert at end runs ("Mother, I'm taking the bus out to Maggie's for the day and on the way I'll stop off at the Virginia Museum and see the George Stubbs exhibit") and at doing things first and asking permission later, if at all. This tactic worked surprisingly often, because Mother gave us an unusual amount of latitude compared with our friends' parents. Long before I was a teenager, I had the freedom of the city via my bike and the bus system. Working on my side, however, more than on Bessie's and Freddie's, was the fact that as she got older and became more deeply involved in civic affairs, she was often too busy to know exactly where I was or what I was doing. In fact, I was either in school or in the back alleys, but either place I was getting into trouble with my friends.

Agnes Cutchins, who lived only a block away, was a soul mate: the way we looked at it, we bore several crosses in common. First of all, we were the children of older parents, and both of us were raised as only children. Agnes actually was an only child; it only seemed as if I was one because Freddie and Bessie were so much older and were gone much of the time. Worse, we were stuck in the Fan, whereas most of our classmates lived in the western suburbs, with acres of green lawn and houses that had rec rooms in the basement and kitchens you could eat in. Many of the houses around us were boardinghouses, and next door to 909 was Richmond Polytechnic Institute, which later became Virginia Commonwealth University; RPI had not yet begun buying up the boardinghouses and converting them to offices. I came down the 909 driveway one morning on the way to school and stood transfixed as I watched paramedics remove the body of a man who had been murdered in the house just opposite us, the shape of the body identifiable under the sheet that was draped over him. Agnes, too, had a boardinghouse opposite her house, and in her spare time she kept binoculars trained on its windows from her third floor, tracking its unusual characters, hoping to catch them in one of their raunchy parties.

Agnes was not embarrassed by Mother's eccentricities. She found them very entertaining. When we got to the dancing-class stage, Mother got carried away in "decorating" me for the Christmas Holly Ball. She bought me a red jumper and pinned holly all over it. I don't imagine any of my partners tried dancing cheek-to-cheek with me that evening. I was a head higher than the boys at age twelve, anyway, so even if I had not had on an environmental hazard of a dress, none of them would have tried it.

Another good friend who also lived in the Fan was Deane Hotchkiss, a talkative, impertinent, funny soul with a saucy tongue and a boundless imagination when it came to getting into trouble. Together, our energy quickly turned into hyperactivity, and by first grade we were already the scourge of our teachers at Collegiate. Deane, Agnes, and I all went to Collegiate, an all-girls private school on Monument Avenue, in the block between the monuments to Robert E. Lee and J. E. B. Stuart. Proper decorum and manners were taken at least as seriously as academics at Collegiate, and from the start we saw ourselves as enemies of the school system. The demure older ladies who for the most part made up the teaching staff were fairly easy to fluster, a situation we caught on to early on.

My only memory of Miss Hattie Scott's first grade is of being hot. This was because in her classroom the radiator was by the entrance door, and her preferred punishment was to put the miscreant by the radiator and then open the door all the way so you were pinned there for the duration. In the fifth or sixth grade, Deane and I developed the nasty habit of terrorizing the new girls. We promised them special privileges if they obeyed us by doing things like giving up their place in the lunch line, or if they were uncooperative we would see that at recess they did not get on the swings on our concrete playground between the two buildings of the school, or get in the game of Red Rover that we played in the vacant lot across the back alley. Looking back, Deane explains her behavior quite straightforwardly. "I always wanted to be the one who did all the talking and the teaching and the telling. I wanted to be the head—the chief—not the Indian." It is equally obvious that my own career at Collegiate was in compensation, in my own mind, for the strict discipline of life at 909.

Periodically we were called on the carpet in the headmistress's office. Mrs.

Flippen was a genteel, soft-spoken woman with a beatific smile, who, when she saw it was us again, would look at us with a sorrowful expression on her face and ask us what she needed to do to appeal to our better selves. "I know," she would say, "that you both have better selves, coming as you do from families that are doing their best to bring you up properly." We would promise to mend our ways, which she always seemed to take heart at, despite evidence to the contrary that the frequency of our visits should have given her.

Agnes speaks for all three of us when she says, "I had a wonderful time on my way through Collegiate." I don't think, however, that Collegiate would return the compliment. I wonder, looking back, why Mrs. Flippen did not involve Mother more often. The reason, I think, is that by the 1950s Mother was increasingly involved in one civic project or another, and therefore home very little. Luckily for us, there were no faxes, or telephone answering machines. We were out of school at 2:30 every afternoon, and we didn't stop being bad when we walked out of its doors. We took to the web of alleyways in the Fan on our bicycles, cruising, on the lookout for mischief. It was not hard to find.

Taking down people's laundry and decorating the bushes of their yard with it was fun, but first it was necessary to do some sophisticated detective work, to make sure they weren't home. Throwing pebbles in open windows was so entertaining that we graduated to water bombs, and Agnes and I found a perfect target in the Music Department practice rooms of RPI. They were around the corner from us, on Shafer Street, but they were a dangerous target because they opened onto the street, not the alley, which made getting caught more likely. To decrease the likelihood of this, one of us was appointed bomb thrower and the other was on the lookout for passersby—potential witnesses. The target was just too tempting because the practice rooms were in an English basement with an iron railing between the window and the pavement. We were able to ride up to the window, steady ourselves with one hand on the railing, and with the free hand lob the water bomb in onto the unsuspecting singer dutifully doing her scales in front of a mirror. Then we would hightail it around the corner, pedaling furiously past the Roman Catholic cathedral and onto the leafy walkways of Monroe Park.

Probably our bikes were taken away from us and we were forbidden to play together for a certain amount of time, because the next trouble I got into was on foot, and with Deane. She and I both wanted to be in the Girl Scouts, but we wanted to start at the top and not go through all the Mickey Mouse training involved in getting there. This meant that we would have to join a troop that had never heard of either one of us. We lit on what we thought was a brilliant plan. Halfway up Franklin Street between 909 and Collegiate School, on the block before Saint James's Episcopal Church, was the Jewish congregation of Temple Beth El. A little sleuthing revealed that they had a Girl Scout troop. We got hold of Scout uniforms and bribed Deane's older sister and my cousin to lend us their shoulder sashes. The sash was all-important because a sash crammed with badges was the sign of a bigwig in the Scouts, and our two elders had many earned badges sewn on their sashes. Decorated to the hilt, we presented ourselves one afternoon, running down the side steps to the basement door and asking if we could join the troop, having, we said, recently moved to Richmond and wanting to continue our illustrious careers in the Scouts.

Our hoax lasted longer than might have been expected. We were welcomed into the troop and, when our multiple competencies were noted, we were asked to lead classes in such scouting standbys as sewing and fire building. We could sew buttons on ribbons and stack sticks as well as the next person, so these activities did not trip us up. What revealed us as interlopers was the first Jewish holiday that came along. Since it had been presumed that we were Jewish, it struck the adult leaders as odd that we did not have a clue as to what was going on. One of them checked on us through Collegiate, and that was the end of our days as Girl Scouts.

Eventually the bikes must have been returned because Deane and I were on bikes when we got caught in the prank that—as far as Mother was concerned—was the straw that broke the camel's back. It involved a woman whom Deane and I were afraid of because she was on to our bad habits and would shake her fist at us if she saw us cruising the alleyways. Her house faced Harrison Street, which meant that her backyard backed up to the 909 backyard. We thought of her as very old, although she was probably in her fifties—about the same age Deane and I are today. Thinking that she was not at home, one afternoon we leaned our bikes up against her garage door and used sticks to write the worst words we could think of—FUCK and SHIT—in big, bold letters in the gravel in front of her garage. She must have been watching the whole time because just as we were finishing she materialized out of nowhere and grabbed hold of both of us. I knew in my bones that this time we had gone too far. Our mothers and the police were summoned. Deane was released to go home with Mrs. Hotchkiss, but not before both mothers had agreed that we should be separated. I was taken in a cruise car to the police station, a trip probably arranged by Mother. An ice-cold terror descended, in the few blocks between 909 and the police station, at the thought of being sent to jail. After she thought I had been scared enough, Mother came to pick me up.

This was the spring that Freddie had run into trouble at the University of Virginia, and Bessie had just lost another pregnancy near to full term due to an Rh-negative blood factor. "I can do nothing about Bessie's and Bobbie's sorrows," she said to me on the way back to 909. "All I can do is lend comfort. The president of the University of Virginia will determine what happens to Freddie. But *you*, on the other hand, I can do something about. *You* are going to go to boarding school." It took a couple of years, but in the fall of 1956 I entered Saint Timothy's, in Baltimore, where they kept us much too busy to get into trouble.

* * *

Mother was always trying to combine learning and fun, which was how we found ourselves on an overnight road trip to Williamsburg, with bicycles in the back of the station wagon, to celebrate what was probably my tenth or eleventh birthday. We were driving down Route 5, Mother, Deane, Flossie Bryan, and I, pulling off the road to read all the historical markers along that stretch of road that is so extraordinarily rich in history.

Route 5 passes most of the great colonial plantations built along the eighteenth century's major highway, the James River, so it has an overdose of historical markers. I often think how much easier travel would have been, when I was a child, if Mother had had available to her something I got as a Christmas present several years ago—a book made up of all the historical markers in the State of Virginia, organized by highways. In any event, whenever she saw a marker, she would slam on the brakes, we would skid off the road and up to the sign, and she would turn off the engine (a must in the battle against both noise and air pollution). Then she would say, to each of us in turn, "Deane [or whoever was first in line], read the sign out loud, please. Keep reminding yourself to read slowly, enunciate clearly, and pause after each sentence. Pay close attention, Flossie, because after we've driven away I'm going to ask you to summarize the contents of the sign." We held up fairly well for the first four or five markers, but by the dozenth we were beginning to wonder if we would have any daylight left for bicycling around Williamsburg.

Deane, who even as a child was beginning to show signs of chronic sinus trouble, had an unconscious snort, which was her way of dealing with a perpetual postnasal drip. "Deane," said Mother, "that is a repulsive, unladylike sound, and I don't want to hear you make it again." "But Mrs. Bocock," replied Deane, "I can't help it, and I don't even know when I'm going to do it. It's a nervous habit." This was the worst possible excuse; for, as far as Mother was concerned, any habit could be broken. Deane's out-loud reading was punctuated by snorts, until finally Mother dealt her an ultimatum. "Deane Hotchkiss," she said, "if you snort one more time I will stop this car, put you and your bicycle out, and you will have to bike the rest of the way to Williamsburg." After that threat, there was silence in the car, because all three of us knew Mother meant it. Several minutes went by, and I was just beginning to relax when a snort that I can hear to this day broke the silence in the car, like a thunderclap on a sultry afternoon. Flossie and I sat frozen to our seats as, wordlessly, Mother stopped the car, opened the door for Deane, got out her bike, got back in, and drove off without a backward glance.

After that Flossie and I kept a lookout for mile markers, and the next one said six miles to Williamsburg. Wide-eyed in the backseat, we felt sure Mother had meant to scare Deane and would stop a mile or two down the road and wait for her to catch up. Not at all. On we drove, right up to the door of the Williamsburg Lodge. My birthday dinner was set for a late hour in order to give Deane time to pedal in. At dinnertime, there she was, hot and tired, but pleased with her independence and ready to celebrate.

* * *

How daring my escapades were depended on how physically proximate Mother was. My imagination knew no bounds when she was an ocean away. In July 1958, Bo and I were traveling to Europe on the *Parthia*, with another close friend, Maggie Chase, and her mother and sister. A long way from Mother's disciplinary influence, late one night Maggie and I hatched a scheme to throw the whole boat into confusion the next day. That was the era when people left their shoes outside their doors for the stewards to polish early in the morning. Coming back to our cabin late one evening, we noticed the shoes neatly aligned down the long corridor. Maggie and I came up with the mean trick of taking all of the shoes from A deck and putting them in front of the exact same room on B deck. For the next several hours, we were like two galley rats, scurrying up and down the steps and along the corridors while the unsuspecting passengers slept. Finally, we went to bed and slept soundly. Next morning there was a ruckus out in the hallway. Mama Chase suspected us as soon as she heard from the stewards that everyone had strange shoes in front of their doors. The purser was not amused, and public apologies were part of the punishment.

As to how she affected my life with my friends, Mother was both a magnet and a deterrent. When I was young, my hunger for normalcy made me see her eccentricities as more of a deterrent, as I often seemed to be an unwitting actor in her pranks. Jane Bryan, a friend I knew only slightly when I was young, remembers being on a summer trip with her parents and arriving at a hotel in San Sebastian, Spain. In the lobby they ran into Mother, who told Jane excitedly that she had a surprise for her and invited all three of them to tea on the lawn at four o'clock. When they arrived, Mother and Father rose to greet them, and Jane noticed a large rug rolled up next to the chairs they had been sitting in. Mother stepped forward, charged with her usual bolt of energy, saying, "Jane, here's the surprise—go see what's in the rug!" Jane unrolled the rug and—there I was!

Twelve years later, Jane remembers another singular visit from Mother. She had been married a year when, one day, looking out the window of her house, which was at least eight miles from 909, she saw Mother getting off her bike, onto the back of which was tied another rug (a smaller one, this time). "Jane," said Mother, when the door was opened for her, "I've brought you a wedding present. You mustn't think I'm tardy with it. The timing is deliberate. So many of my friends' children are getting divorced that I decided to wait a year before I give wedding presents, to see if the marriage will stick."

I think our unorthodox life was easier for Bessie and Freddie than for me, primarily because they had each other and shared the brunt of her extraordinary energy, but also because life in our household, when they were young, was more orthodox. As soon as I was not directly under Mother's care, when I left for boarding school and, later, college, Mother became more of a magnet for me as well as for my friends. Her visits were exhilarating and her knack for turning an ordinary outing into an adventure was legendary. If she was taking a bunch of us out to dinner, we might leave early to tour the historic section of Baltimore on foot, find an unusual, off-the-beaten-track restaurant to eat in, and careen, late because we had stopped off for an ice-cream cone, through the gate of Saint Timothy's after the curfew. Not to worry: Mother could always charm the lady on duty. No other parent's arrival caused such a stir of excitement. And I always knew she was going home.

* * *

As we approached adulthood, even Bessie and I were won over to Freddie's way of reacting to Mother's willpower by becoming experts at conflict avoidance. We became so expert, in fact, that what we do least well is distinguish quickly when we need to stand and fight. Our natural reaction to disharmony is to move instantly to head it off. Part of this is a southern upbringing; part is Bocock genes; and part is experience—the years negotiated knowing that it was easier on everyone if Mother had her way. Any psychologist, hearing our version of life with Mother, would know that the moment of truth would come when we fell in love. Long before we reached the age of marriage, Mother had picked out for us not only the general attributes of what we should be looking for in a spouse, but also someone who personified those attributes.

It would be incorrect to call Mother a social snob, because her appreciation of people reached into every echelon of society, but she was a genealogical snob, as so many Virginians are. For her, family defined both place and, for a young person, expectation: who their forebears were, and the land they had grown up on, in Mother's view put a stamp on them that outweighed in importance even their education. Mother traveled widely in the United States, as well as Europe and the Middle East, but the thought of living—of actually pouring one's life's energies—into any place other than Virginia was unimaginable to her. Her parents had felt the same tie, and in some only vaguely defined way, this attachment seemed to have roots in the defeated Confederacy. People that lived in the rest of the South were southerners, but Virginians were Virginians. They had sacrificed their state as the heart of the Confederacy, Richmond was its capital and paid for it with its destruction, and more battles had been fought on Virginia soil than that of any other state. The war had been lost, but four generations later the hurt still smarted, and, more than an American or a southerner, Mother considered herself a Virginian.

Feeling this way, it was not surprising that she decided I should marry someone from the landed gentry of the state. She even had someone particular in mind, a young man whose family owned one of the most beautiful of all the James River plantations. We enjoyed each other on the infrequent occasions when holiday parties threw us together, but there was not one iota of romantic attachment between us. This did not dampen Mother's enthusiasm for the match, since she had not immediately fallen in love with Father. But by my sophomore year in college, I had fallen, once and for all, in love, and had begun to bring home with me for vacations a non-Virginian whom even Mother had to admit was bright and engaging, even as she noted his Germanic name and the fact that he had been raised in Boston.

For a year or so after Fred Hitz came into my life, Mother continued to play the Richmond theme at every opportunity, widening the circle outwards

Mother not resisting the urge to tell us how to cut the cake

to include other well-mannered young men. Finally, after my junior year at Smith, ("That's the trouble with sending them out of state for college! They go and marry a Yankee") she bowed to the realization that she was no longer in control. She found solace in the fact that Fred cared deeply about a particular piece of family property, even though it was in the Penobscot Bay; and in the knowledge that his distinguished forebears included the first Swiss consul to the United States, and a grandfather who was a highly regarded federal judge. And as soon as she gave up on the proposition that I would marry a Virginian, she determined her new goal—making sure that, once married, we would settle in Richmond.

* * *

One aspect of her strong will was her fearlessness. Mother had always been as nearly fearless as a human can be, but in 1965 an event occurred that would have broken a lesser will. At this point, she was living in the apartment she had made in the back of 909—an apartment with an entrance from the backyard. On the day this event occurred, she was well into the big, beautiful room that she used for everything but sleeping before she realized she had interrupted a burglar. Moving quickly to summon help from the student living in the carriage-house apartment, she broke a pane of glass in the French doors that gave onto the garden. This scared the burglar, and he attacked her with a knife. She must still have been struggling for she was cut deeply in her thigh. To immobilize her the intruder wrapped her in an oriental rug and then, with her golden retriever cowering behind the sofa, made his escape.

With enormous effort, ESB was able to untangle herself and get help from the front of the house. She recovered reasonably quickly from the physical wounds, but the psychic damage was acute and long-lasting. Freddie and Berta moved into 909 and stayed with her for three months. ESB bought a trained German shepherd for protection, which was not the perfect solution because the pace of Mother's life precluded pets, trained or untrained. Whenever the subject of the attack came up, she would begin to stutter so badly that it would end the conversation. Perhaps 90 percent of women her age, had that happened to them, would no longer have been able to go on living alone; but Mother was determined to do so, even after a bizarre coincidence meant that she relived her own horror within the year.

She was making an overnight visit to her Saint Timothy's schoolfriend Harriet Phipps, at the Phipps's house on Long Island, when burglars broke in. Mother barricaded herself in her bedroom but could hear the burglars pistol-whipping the elderly Mr. Phipps, who was bedridden, in order to get him to say where the family's collection of jade jewelry was kept. At that moment, she must have understood the reaction of her golden retriever, those few months earlier when her own home was broken into: wanting to help, but paralyzed by fear. The next morning, Mother was spirited out of the house and onto the train to New York and Richmond so that she would not have to deal with the press; but these ugly scenes marked her permanently. For a number of years, when she went to visit other people she had to take her German shepherd with her, and any talk of violence would set off her stammering.

Only her phenomenal willpower kept her from being a hostage to her fears, which were very real. They came on every night at twilight, when she would rise from what she was doing and draw the curtains tightly shut at every window, whether she was in her own house or someone else's. She could not sit in a well-lit room after dark, with the curtains open, even in the country. But this was the only concession that she made to her demons.

Mother and Cora and their brood in the early 1960s

6. When the Wheels Came Off

*I*N HIS BOOK *The Pattons: A Personal History of an American Family,* Robert H. Patton describes the "manic élan" with which his grandfather, Gen. George S. Patton Jr., led his troops in the final, successful drive against Germany in World War II, and how poorly this leadership style translated when he had to confront "the horrors of peace." He had played too large a role on the stage of history to make the confines of domestic life comfortable for him, or for those who shared it with him. In any situation, writes his grandson, "he was compulsively driven to emote, dazzle, dominate—in short, to exhibit visible personality in everything he did—generally sucking the life out of anyone venturing too near, like a black hole inhaling a star." ESB's troops were her family, friends, and fellow civic activists, and her battlefield was the city of Richmond. Even though her life played out on a much smaller stage, she, too, became a captive of her own "visible personality." One friend of hers whom I quizzed about ESB when I first started thinking about this memoir, responded, "I really didn't know her that well, I was afraid to get too close, afraid I would be sucked in."

In Mother's life, similarly, there was an abrupt and permanent dislocation—although there some of the similarity to what peacetime meant for Patton ends. The event in her case was Father's death. He died in the late summer of 1958, when she was fifty-seven years old and I was just starting my senior year in boarding school. Bessie and Bobbie had at last succeeded in having children, and Freddie was about to marry Roberta Bryan, a friend whom I had looked up to since working for her when we both were counselors at a summer day camp and I was in charge of keeping the children quiet on her bus. ESB's foot soldiers were veering off down other paths at the same time that this void in her life opened up.

Father had been ill for several years, and in and out of the hospital with what Mother referred to as a "circulatory disturbance." In fact, it was prostate cancer that had metastasized into the bone of his lower back. Mother chose to bear this burden alone, which added enormously to the pressure that built up inside her as his condition worsened. Father's friends came to Mother: couldn't he be sent to Johns Hopkins to find out what was wrong? She had looked at the X rays and knew he was dying, but she may have thought that he did not want to know; probably he made it clear to Mother that he was not interested in knowing the clinical details. Certainly her intent was to protect him. He did not go to Johns Hopkins, and how they handled it between themselves I can only guess.

Bessie remembers Mother's mysterious references to Father's illness when he was in the hospital, when she would say they had decided not to operate, but not say what they would have operated on. It was her decision not to seek any sort of emotional support even from her grown, married daughter. Bessie feels Mother may well have been carrying out Father's wishes in not talking openly about the gravity of his illness. She points out that Father would say, "If you have bad news to give me, give it to me with a cigarette"—meaning, perhaps, don't give it to me at all.

The summer that I was a rising senior at Saint Timothy's, Mother knew Father was dying, and she sent Bo and me to Europe. This was particularly cruel to Bo—she is bound to have wanted to be there to comfort her brother. Mother often victimized Bo, whose courtesy, sweetness, and schoolmistress manner seemed to conspire to annoy Mother. But Bo was no more able to say no to Mother successfully than any of the rest of us, so she and I were not part of that sad summer. We were at the Salzburg Music Festival when Father died in August.

Starting in about 1955, as Father's health was worsening, Mother had rearranged life at 909 to suit their changing circumstances. Using her own architectural instincts, she had transformed the whole back end of 909, the kitchen, servants' dining room, and upstairs bedrooms, into an elegant three-bedroom apartment separate from the rest of the house. The living room/ dining room stretched across the whole south-facing back of the house, its French doors and windows framing the beauty of the garden she worked so hard on. Father was made comfortable in a four-poster bed upstairs in these new quarters, and a television set was installed so that he could watch baseball games. Custom was reversed: she would read to him, or sit, sewing, while he dozed.

The last year of his life, much of the time Father was in Stuart Circle Hospital, five blocks up Franklin Street. Mother would make the round-trip on foot or bicycle several times a day, carrying, in one of her many baskets, the handsomest rose from the garden or some delicious soup Cora had just served her for lunch. When meetings kept her away, she would often stop en route to them, double park her car and run in when she had only a minute, just to kiss him on the forehead to give him encouragement. Before she left at night, she would write him a short love note and leave it with his nurse to hand him with his last medication, or to save for the middle of the night if it looked as if it was going to be a rugged one. She was very protective, limiting his visitors, making sure she was present for their visits, and generally watching over him like a lioness over her cub. She controlled his treatment, having many battles with his doctor, Father's cousin Wyndham Blanton, over painkillers that were not strong enough, or that had bad side effects.

In letters to me at school, she was always upbeat, recounting only the anecdotes that shed a positive light on things. I was encouraged to write frequently, which I tried to do. Once Bo and I left for Europe, I kept a diary, which I sent back as often as possible for his amusement. By the time we arrived back in Richmond, I was numb from a combination of sorrow and exhaustion. Exhaustion always has the effect of turning my emotions loose, and all I remember of Father's funeral was of crying uncontrollably while the adults around me, led by Mother, were stoic and quiet in their grief. A short time later, I was back at Saint Timothy's for my senior year.

In the aftermath of the funeral, Mother went into a period of accelerated activity that was less and less rational and more and more emotionally driven. Never hesitant about making decisions, in this period, which went on for several years, she was making them before she considered the pros and cons. It was clear that she was trying *physically* to flee her grief at Father's death, making it difficult for Bessie and Freddie to help her. She would seek their advice *after* she had made hasty decisions. These decisions involved the many businesses that her civic involvement had inspired, and relations with her sisters and brothers, particularly concerning Royal Orchard.

Despite the fact that by this time they had their hands full with their own young children, Bessie and Bobbie stepped into a larger role in raising me, making sure that I did not suffer from the fallout from Mother's irrationality. For her, 909 had become a sinkhole of memories that only heightened her realization that Father was not there to share them, so staying home made her even more unhappy. Like many people who are good at taking care of others, she squirmed at the thought of being taken care of; so she fled Richmond during the period when people would be feeling sorry for her. For weeks at a time in the summer of 1959, I lived with the Carters, and later vacationed with them on Nantucket.

After Father's death, Mother's brakes were gone. It was not only that the accustomed presence of her husband of thirty years was no longer there: with him went his steadying effect on her emotions and on the clarity of her thinking, as well as the tranquil and orderly pace of their life together. Mother without Father was like the horse who, in the middle of a steeplechase, loses its rider and careens along with the rest of the pack, stirrups and reins flapping loose, veering dangerously close to the other horses as it obeys the thoroughbred's instinct to race on. Without the need to slow down of an evening, to blend her pace with Father's, her own pace accelerated to fill the emptiness.

Recreating that period from the point of view of a fifty-seven-year-old woman whose life yawned before her as a suddenly purposeless void, her next lightning-quick move looks more predictable than it seemed at the time. Purposelessness was not a state she could abide, in others or in herself. Three weeks after Father died, she enrolled as a student in the Ambler School of Horticulture, Pennsylvania, later to become part of Temple University, which would accept her finishing-school diploma from Saint Timothy's. Leaving Cora and Garrett in charge at 909, she commuted weekly to Philadelphia, living in a dormitory along with girls who were nearly forty years younger, and beginning ten years of work toward a college degree. So in the next ten years, without charting any formal educational course, she went where it suited her to be, taking courses in what interested her. That will be the subject of the next chapter.

Her abrupt departure from Richmond in September 1958, so soon after Father's death, horrified many of her social friends and her brothers and sisters. I do not remember being much amazed, probably because I had come to expect the unexpected from her. But to her friends, who wanted her to go on meeting them at the Woman's Club or the symphony or the garden club, her action was a betrayal of sorts. As far as they were concerned, her restlessness was symbolic of a splintering of her time and focus that led to a downward spiral of overly intense interests, which left little time for them. What they held against her, right after Father's death, was her refusal to bow to convention and be pigeonholed in respectable, predictable widowhood. This tactic, of removing herself from all that was familiar, fell into her lifetime pattern of changing her plans if she ever thought anyone got the idea that they could predict what she was going to do.

Marianne Bocock, Freddie and Berta's youngest daughter, wrote a paper on her grandmother for a Dartmouth class on women's issues entitled "Leader, Conservationist, Visionary: The Power of Contradiction: Elisabeth Scott Bocock, 1901–1985." In it, she looked at two elements of her grandmother's personality—her almost obsessive sense of etiquette and her unprecedented originality—as very much part of a southern ideal of expecting females to express both their "lady" (submissive) self and their "woman" (dominant) self. Pointing out that for many women the inherent contradiction between these two selves led to confusion and frustration, Marianne goes on to argue that ESB blended these two conflicting selves by "creating a lever which she could use to create space for her ideas."

Part of this lever was what Edith Wharton referred to as the authority that beauty gives a woman; other parts of it were her position in society, her grace, and her drive. As Jack Bocock, Marianne's brother, puts it, "One of Grandmother's greatest strengths was her ability to inspire others' loyalty to herself and to her cause. She made people feel good and so she could get them on her team by her strength and force of will." But the most important part of this lever was her eccentricity, which developed in her middle age and became a striking part of her character in old age. As Marianne expressed it:

A way to envision Grandmother's eccentricity is to picture an older woman, at an Amtrak train station, wearing a suit, a green silk dress, a long raincoat, a fur coat stylishly cropped at the waist, her leather walking boots, and her green scarf. She carried her evening shoes in her hand bag. She wore all of her jewelry, some showing and some hidden amongst the under layers. It was safe from robbers there. Now, there was no need for anyone to help an old lady carry her suitcase.

The example that Marianne chose is particularly apt, because, besides showing her eccentricity, it also shows the calculatedly practical results of her behavior. When she got to Pennsylvania Station (New York often being her destination), having no suitcases to carry she could walk past the long queue for taxis and either find a cab on the street or walk the thirty blocks to her beloved Colony Club, where she was an out-of-town member. When evening came, the boots and suit came off and the evening shoes went on, to go with the green silk dress. The fancier jewelry moved up from the slip to the dress, and the daytime jewelry moved in the other direction. The strands of pearls and two or three gold necklaces stayed on, sleeping and waking, because their catches were a bother so she wore them all the time. This had been the case ever since she had asked her ten-year-old grandson Alex Bocock how old he thought she was. "You look about seventy, Grandma," he replied, "but your neck looks about ninety." After that, scarves and necklaces proliferated.

Just being in New York would transform her usually high metabolism into a pace that it was nearly impossible to keep up with. Bessie describes it wonderfully in an article that Guy Friddell wrote for the *Richmond Times-Dispatch* after Mother's death.

She was always six jumps ahead of me. On a trip to New York, I'd still be eating breakfast and she would say, "Meet me in the hat department of Lord and Taylor's." And off she'd fly. I'd go there and ask if anyone had seen a lady in a green hat and white gloves.

"Oh yes," a clerk would say, "she said she'd be in the hose department at Saks." So I'd rush there and find that she'd bought stockings for her nieces and had decided to see a foreign film. At the theater, she had left word that the film was entirely too loud, and she was returning to the hotel for lunch.

But more than shopping she enjoyed the museums, especially the Metropolitan, and she realized, after she was 75, that she enjoyed it even more sitting down, so we rented a wheelchair, which, when she got in it, immediately added thirty years [to her age] and attracted an audience, and as I was rolling the chair, she was entertaining a party of about 30 people.

We reached the bottom of a tremendous flight of stairs, and she jumped from the chair and leapt up the stairs two at a time and, reaching the top, turned and, with a grand gesture, called, "Send the chair on the elevator!" And the 30 spectators looked as if they'd seen Lazarus.

The woman that Bessie is describing, the one with such an evident "visible personality," is Mother in her old age. But the woman that went off to the Ambler School of Horticulture in 1958 was a woman running from loneliness, from a mold that she felt was fast hardening around her, and from a big empty house. To deal with the empty house she responded to the Junior League, which was casting around for an appropriate location for a senior center in the fall of 1958. The front part of 909 was the solution, and it was an immediate success, since the seniors who got together there on weekdays loved the fact that it was in a home, and a gracious, high-ceilinged home at that. It was not long before the center needed more space—the basement for a woodworking program, the breakfast room for ceramics—and instead of being freed from housewifery, ESB felt deluged by details.

The Richmond Polytechnic Institute (RPI), the precursor of Virginia Commonwealth University, already surrounded 909. RPI needed more space for offices, and before long they began to look, to ESB, like a less-invasive tenant, and one that would take care of routine matters through their Buildings and Grounds Department. ESB pointed out to the Junior League that RPI, being a public institution, could use eminent domain to take the house at any time. This was true, technically, but it was also a convenient ploy to put the Senior Center on notice that it should look for permanent quarters elsewhere. This they did, although it took until 1967 for them to find new quarters.

After they had decamped, ESB wrote the board of the Junior League:

"When . . . you opened here, this house had already become something of a grand piano into which two little mice had crept and were making unaccountable small noises. These mice were Mary Buford Bocock and your old friend ESB. . . . You made music on this symbolic piano: gave music, good to the ear of a busy old lady who came and went in the garden entrance."

* * *

ESB probably recognized that she was running from loneliness, but I think she would have found it hard to articulate exactly what she was running toward. Did she envision an eventual career in horticulture? Did she hope to teach in the field of environmental science? We have one clue that her initial goal might have been working as an environmental consultant. In January 1961, Lewis Powell, who was then chairman of the Richmond School Board and later a justice of the U.S. Supreme Court, wrote to Dr. Wilkerson, an official with the city school system, presumably at Mother's request. His letter reads:

Mrs. John H. Bocock, of this city, wishes to talk to you about the possibility of preparing herself to work with the State Department of Education as an advisor or consultant on conservation.

As I am sure you know, Mrs. Bocock has been a fine civic leader in a number of areas, and has especially interested herself in encouraging conservation of both our natural and historic resources.

Since the death of her husband, Mrs. Bocock has done a good deal of graduate study in this and related fields. She expects to attend V.P.I. during the second semester commencing in February, and is most anxious to talk to you before she leaves Richmond. She is one of our first citizens, and if there is some way that we could take advantage of her talents, I am sure the public school system would benefit.

Whether this meeting ever took place, I don't know, but whatever her motivation was, she moved, with a mind clouded by grief, in her usual lightning-quick fashion to address the one great lack she felt in her life—the lack of a formal education. Mother was not a formal planner, and would not have spent much time thinking through why she did things. This was partly a matter of operating on instinct, and partly a matter of philosophy.

Mother believed in an Old Testament God, one who could react with punishing power as well as with forgiveness, and one who was in constant battle with the devil for people's souls. I think she felt that to do too much planning was to tempt fate; that it was a sign of hubris when human beings really started to convince themselves that they were in control. As Aunt Pinkerton puts it, "She had a great sense of the tragedy of life and of evil, and kept guard against it." One of her ways of guarding against it was not to tempt it.

In my final year at Saint Timothy's, Mother, living in Ambler, Pennsylvania, was closer to my school than she had been in Richmond, and she showed up regularly for our hockey and basketball games. She bought a Japanese folding bicycle, which she rode from the college to the train station at Ambler, where she would catch a train into Philadelphia and then on to Baltimore. Going home, she would reverse the process. This routine was successful until one day the bike, with Mother aboard, folded, throwing her into a ditch alongside the Bethlehem Turnpike. She was badly shaken up, and the Japanese bicycle was permanently folded.

Meanwhile, she ran 909 by telephone during the week, and by often asking too much of Cora and Garrett when she was home on weekends. Sunday lunch was liable to be a big family gathering; and even though she was not home during the week, she continued to buy several subscription tickets to all the Richmond institutions like the symphony, opera, and ballet that she wanted to support. She kept these tickets hanging on a peg in the living room, and if she came home Friday afternoon and discovered there was an evening performance, she would pick up the phone and in the course of ten minutes Cora would have a dinner party on her hands. Tinsley was quite old by this time; he died a few years later. Cora and Garrett, instead of having fewer duties as they got older, were asked to do more and more. The ordered routine of their existence when Father was alive had been replaced by nothing to do during the week and too much to do on the weekends. There was a frenzied restlessness when ESB was around: orders given and then countermanded, guests added then subtracted then added again, unrealistic expectations on Mother's part, and confusion, sullen foot-dragging, and finally, Cora's drinking. Cora was as gregarious as Mother, and she would gladly have traded the silence around 909 in Mother's absences for a full house and the workload that entailed. The house cleaning, silver polishing, and advance cooking that she was meant to be doing during the lull in each week did not get done, and gradually the dust began to pile up on the bookshelves, and most of the silver turned a spotty gray.

Mother, when she did come home, needed people around her—replacements for her children, so to speak—to boss, spoil, instruct, put to work, involve in her projects, support, and entertain. Shortly after Father's death, Tom Clark, a young lawyer who had just moved to Richmond, heard through a colleague at work that the Bococks were looking for a reliable person to live at

909. Arrangements were made at a lunch with Freddie, and Tom moved into Bessie's old room. Tom lived at 909 for only two and a half years before he moved to Delaware, but in that short time he became a close family friend. For the rest of Mother's life, he would stop for the night en route from Delaware to his hometown in North Carolina, and he would return (not just as a guest but as a worker—a special family privilege!) for weddings, dances, and parties.

Tom was a personable, hard-working bachelor, suddenly thrown into the ingrown social scene of Richmond in the 1960s, who had the time and the inclination to take up the place offered him under Mother's wing and to submit to what he calls "the Education of Tom Clark." This homebred southern scholar came from a small town in North Carolina, brought up in an atmosphere of "no aristocrats and no peasants." Plunged headfirst into one of the best law firms in Richmond after the academic isolation of Harvard Law School, Tom encountered the polar opposite of life in Roanoke Rapids, North Carolina. Mother became his tutor in how to behave in a social world that took itself very seriously.

Mother and Cora adopted him, shooing him out of the kitchen when he was caught satisfying his addiction to ice cream, trying, against the odds, to take weight off his heavy frame with salads and fruits, and presuming on his good nature to do impossible jobs. The best example of this was Tom being asked to sleep on an uncomfortable horsehair mattress that bulked up in the middle, with the idea that if he slept on it long enough it would eventually redistribute itself into a flat surface. Despite his relatively short stay at 909, Tom left with another grandmother, and an enduring sense that his well-being mattered, permanently, to her. As important as this was to him, he adds, "However, knowing the Bococks has had a far more significant by-product: I came to see a family with substantial wealth and social position who were genuinely concerned with others, with ethical issues, and with things that really matter. Having had a strong dose of teaching at college and in graduate school about the robber barons, monster business, and the greed of the wealthy families of the late nineteenth and early twentieth century, it was enlightening and refreshing." He puts this as both a compliment to the family and as a stab at his own early social preconceptions; but Mother, who in the last one-third of her life jettisoned social rules and found her friends more and more among down-to-earth people who shared her interests, must have been equally influenced by Tom's human compass.

In the early 1970s, Freddie sent a young man who was working at Scott and

Stringfellow up to 909 to meet mother, to see if it might be "mutually agree-able" (Mother's favorite phrase) for him to live at 909. Mother was living at home, choosing college courses at Richmond institutions, and wanted to find a young person to work in the yard and relieve Garrett of some of his chores. At that point in his life, Matthew Spady was a slight, energetic young man from Chuckatuck, on the Virginia side of the Eastern Shore. Before long, he recognized that a business career was not for him, and arranged with Mother to work for her part-time while he pursued a master's degree in music, with the long-term goal of becoming an opera singer.

ESB and Matthew hit it off instantly. A gentleman to his fingertips, Matthew thought quickly and moved quickly, which endeared him to Moth-er; and his cheerful willingness to tackle nearly any job made him a hit with Cora and Garrett, too. Like Tom Clark, he was sensitive to the nuances of family life at 909, comfortably fitting in without being cloying, and absenting himself, when appropriate, without being obvious. Though there was a fifty-year gap in their ages, Matthew had respect for Mother's Victorian mores and the unique fashion in which she employed them when dealing with her every-day world.

The front of 909 was being used as a girls' dormitory by Virginia Com-monwealth University: she wanted to provide a haven for young women who did not want to be bothered by the opposite sex when they were trying to study. Every other dorm had visitation rights, but the girls at 909 did not. Mother was not trying to change what they were doing in any other dorm; that was not her business. But if the girls at 909 were going to use her house, they were going to use her rules. As Matthew says, "She lived what she be-lieved; and in that she was such an inspiration, not only to me, but to so many people who came into contact with her." Her rules, and her moral structure, reflected her unique perspective on human nature, not some manual of good behavior.

Mother had a set of rules in her mind about how a lady should and should not act, but in each different situation these rules were subject to adaptive reuse, and to the application of common sense. For example, in the early mornings, as Matthew was laying the fire in the living room, Mother would hear him at work, want to tell him something, and come halfway down the circular stairs, having progressed no further in her dressing than her slip. The first time this happened, he looked up at her, and then looked away. Catching on immediately, she said, "You don't have to be embarrassed. I have a good deal more on than most young ladies wear to the beach these days."

I asked Matthew, who is living in New York now and is openly gay, if he thought Mother had known of his sexual orientation or ever asked him about it. She had not ever mentioned it, as it turned out; and, Matthew smilingly added, "It was not something I ever felt I needed to talk to your mother about." Neither he nor I thought the issue had simply cruised right over her head; she was not naive. But it was typical that she felt no need to discuss it. What she needed to know about Matthew's character was already firmly established by the time the thought may have occurred to her.

When he had finished graduate school, Matthew had a chance to go to Europe for the summer to sing with opera companies and study voice, but the cost was $3,000. He wrote to Mother, asking if he could borrow some of the money from her, any part of it. Her return letter came immediately, and in it was a check for $3,000. Mother's letter read: "This is not a loan, it is a gift, and the only way you can repay it is by helping somebody else." Looking back on this unexpected act of generosity, Matthew said, "She always felt that the only reason that she had the wealth that she did, and recognition and social standing, was fate. She believed that she had received a lot in her life, and that she needed to give something back—which she was consciously always doing, I think."

* * *

There was a nineteenth-century context for life at 909, which was in keeping with Mother's own view that she was a Victorian at heart. Her Victorian outlook was nowhere as evident as in her approach to chaperonage for young women. Neither Bessie nor I could go anywhere where males were to be present without telling Mother well in advance not only where we would be staying and with whom, but also who our chaperone would be. I think her determination on this count had to do with remembering what a capricious, headstrong young woman she herself had been, and how, in hindsight, her parents' strict emphasis on chaperones had stood her in good stead. Early on, Bessie discovered that Mother was partial to Episcopal bishops as chaperones, and she made liberal use of any whose names she came across. When I spent a weekend away from Smith at a men's college, I would scramble ahead of time to find out the name of some unsuspecting person—a college dean, a dorm master, someone's grandmother—to give to Mother, hoping that she wouldn't call them. Uncharacteristically, she usually didn't call them, for which I was particularly thankful one weekend when I was staying at the Nathan Hale Motel in New Haven, and I, not having done my homework, told her that Mrs. Hale was my chaperone!

Despite her attention to outdated conventions, it coexisted in Mother with a willingness to ignore the conventions when they did not suit her. When she gave a party, it would be remembered for the ways in which it was unlike any other party the guests had ever been to. An example is the debutante party Mother gave, not just for me but also for my second cousin Molly Nolting (we are both named for ESB's mother's half-sister, Mary Buford Nolting, a feisty, eccentric lady who lived a block down the alley from 909, whom Mother adored).

Molly lived in Paris because her father, Frederick Nolting, later U.S. ambassador to South Vietnam, was posted there with NATO, and Mother, knowing that Molly did not know most of the people at the party, used an old technique of hers—musical chairs at the dinner table—to introduce her to as many people as possible. The technique worked—much the way it always had: Mother would reign in the dining room, wearing a decolleté, full-length, black dress, with a black-lace mantilla wrapped around her head and shoulders, which set off the high color of her animated face and her teardrop, diamond pendant earrings. Between courses, she would ring a little handbell—once, announcing that all the young men were required to move next to someone they didn't already know; twice, a short while later, to signal that this time the young women were to relocate themselves. Just as Mother planned, hilarity and chaos ensued: napkins dropped, hurrying guests bumped as they zeroed in on the same seat, and minds raced ahead of conversations as everyone planned their next move. Pretty soon, awkward nineteen-year-olds who didn't know each other very well were actually having fun.

When dancing started in the big front hall, Mother would dart in and out, finding the young men who, preferring to watch from the safety of the sidelines, held back; looping her arm through theirs, she would take them to meet girls who were sitting out the action in the living room. Or she would wade into the midst of couples looking down on the dancing while sitting on the wide staircase that overlooked the front hall, sitting down in the middle of them and challenging both a girl and a boy to go down and cut in on the dancing couples below, all the time urging them to go meet someone they did not already know.

I suspect that being a good hostess is more an instinctive talent than one that can be acquired. Wherever it came from, Mother had it, and she used it most effectively when dealing with young people. This was the age of dancing with one person all night, of dating one person exclusively, of "going steady." She didn't buy any of it, and in her put-them-in-the blender approach to parties, she defied the norms of the day. Nobody minded. Mrs. Bocock was granted a sort of cultural license to turn things topsy-turvy.

* * *

Over the course of these transition years, as Mother painfully switched gears from wife to widow, a special relationship grew between Mother and Freddie. Freddie's attitude toward Mother was touching, made up, as it was, of the chivalric ideal of the deference of a southern son. Freddie was filling in for Father, doing his best to see to her needs and to be a go-between in her business interests. After some time had passed in this role, he developed an instinctive sense of which of Mother's proposals to push onto the back burner and which to help her move on. He also became expert at interpreting for others what it was Mother was trying to do.

Garrett, interviewed in 1992, defined his own role in Mother's life at that time. "When she stepped out of her shoes," he said, "I stepped in 'em." He became the monitor of her household accounts, telling her when to close out her account at R. L. Christian, the local gourmet grocers, because Tinsley was charging his cigarettes on it, and reporting to her when Cora was not working. Occasionally, he would check on Mother herself, about things he considered extravagances. "I had to call her down, too," he said. "I took the same interest in your mother's business that I did in mine." Sometimes he found himself on the receiving end of her fury. One Sunday, she asked Garrett to drive her all the way back to Pennsylvania, following a lecture that was to be held at the Walter Robertsons' that night. In the aftermath of Father's death, her requests were often unreasonable, and Garrett said no, he would not drive her back to Ambler. "When I went to pick her up at the Robertsons'," he said, "she was so mad she couldn't speak." By the time they got to the station, she had found her tongue. "She laid me out," said Garrett.

When Father died, Garrett did just what he knew Mr. Bocock would have wanted: he began to watch over Mother. In a Richmond version of *Driving Miss Daisy,* and set in approximately the same era, he did not just follow her orders, he argued with her when he knew she was wrong, brought her tea when Cora was not there, laid the fires, swept the front of 909, fed the dogs, gave advice when it wasn't asked for, and stuck to his guns when ESB pushed him to the limit. Twenty years of service had earned him that intimacy, and in the next thirty years, as arthritis cut down on the number of trips he could make to 909 in a day, he stayed in touch with Mother by telephone, reminding her to turn on the outside lights or checking to see that she had gotten home safely. Their lives were so intertwined that Mother's death must have

Garrett Hardy, Eliza, and one of Mother's guard dogs in the garden at 909, 1979

been a great shock to Garrett, but he stayed on track by continuing to make the dish he had started making for Mother: chicken hash. To prepare it, he diced the ingredients into fine pieces, to make it easier on old teeth. I tried to get him to use a Cuisinart, but he insisted on chopping the onion, celery, and chicken himself, perched on a stool, leaning into his work, balanced with one foot on the floor and one on the rung of the stool.

After Mother died, and well into his nineties, Garrett still presided at 909, hobbling down the outdoor stairs to the basement as his arthritis got worse. When we rented out Mother's apartment in the back of the house, the chicken-hash factory moved to the old laundry room in the basement, where we added a stove and a refrigerator to the table and rocking chair that made up Garrett's headquarters. Once there, he would direct Mr. Ellis, who was only slightly younger and spryer than he, and who was paid to keep the grounds of 909 in good shape. Once Garrett was satisfied that Mr. Ellis was occupied, he would begin his morning's work—making chicken hash. Since this operation was no longer interrupted by Mother's hourly requests that he stop what he was doing and take care of the crisis of the moment, he produced gallon upon gallon of hash. When the morning's cooking was over, Garrett would drive the plastic containers of hash out to the Bococks' house on Rothesay Circle, where Berta would greet him and they would have a leisurely talk about the latest goings-on in the family. Freddie, Berta, and their four children ate chicken hash for breakfast daily, and supplied it to family and friends every chance they got.

Whenever we were in Richmond, we would seek out Garrett at his home base at 909. It was warm and cozy, with the homey smell of his hash simmering on the stove. And how welcome he made us feel!—making it inevitable that we lingered talking to him. He loved to talk about Mother and Father and the old days, and, whenever he did, I was always struck by the sense that our family formed more of his reality than that of his life away from 909; and so he came to 909 to carry on that reality by making chicken hash, until he himself died.

* * *

Carolyn Heilbruner, contributing to the Smith College quarterly magazine several years ago, wrote of a stage in a woman's life in her fifties when she goes through a period of invisibility. The more beautiful a woman has been in her youth, and the more this beauty has meant to her sense of herself, the more vulnerable she will be to this attack of invisibility. On this scale, Mother would have been very vulnerable indeed. A woman can respond one of two ways to this stage, and to its outward manifestations of facial wrinkles, graying hair, and sagging body. Either she can spend the rest of her life fighting something she can only disguise and delay but never defeat, or she can accept invisibility as a healthy transition and emerge from it, freed to move in directions that might not have been obvious to her before—directions that enlarge the scope of her interests and reenergize her. Mother chose the latter reaction with a vengeance. She did not, as she could have done, retreat at age fifty-seven, discouraged by the thought that she had raised her children, that her husband had died, and that her life was over. Instead, in these transition years, she was struggling to plan a strategy for a productive last one-third of her life.

Over the course of years, she became Mrs. Richmond, passionate in her vision of what the city could be if enough people put their shoulders to the wheel. There was noblesse oblige connected to it, in the sense of return for gifts given her, but her greatest motivation came from her drive to preserve the best of the past. In addition to leading many causes herself, she was also high on the list of people that others came to for support when they were working on a civic project. If the historic building that housed the Woman's Club needed restoration, if the symphony was going bankrupt, if there was a move afoot to start a local opera company . . . on all such projects, ESB would be approached early, and her response was usually generous. Where money was concerned, Mother cared only about what could be done with it; just accumulating money did not appeal to her. By connecting on a personal level with those who were doing the asking, ESB kept up with a new generation of leadership in the city. Many wealthy people react to requests for money as if the approach is a personal threat from which they have to protect themselves. Mother's way was just the opposite: if the undertaking was for the benefit of the city of Richmond or the state of Virginia, you were welcome and she was interested.

In addition to being philanthropically generous, she was also personally generous. Perhaps most extraordinary of all, no matter where she happened to be—at college, or learning to lay bricks, or traveling in Greece—her godchildren, grandchildren, and friends all received missives in green ink on their birthdays, usually accompanied by checks for young people and something handmade for adults, like a monogrammed dish towel, an initialed, linen pocket handkerchief, or a pincushion stuffed with her own hair, complete with every size of straight pins and safety pins already stuck in it.

The letters that arrived with these presents are jewels of originality and humor—serendipitous musings on the importance of the recipient to her, and huge pride in their potential to be valuable citizens like Robert E. Lee, Booker T. Washington, Ellen Glasgow, Thomas Jefferson, and so forth. Many people saved their letters from her because they were so unique—not just in the meandering thought processes, but in punctuation, abbreviations, and handwriting. The following letter was written, in 1979, to her grandson Jack Bocock when he was a boarding-school student at Episcopal High School in Alexandria, Virginia.

My Darling Jack Bocock of sixteen years of grandson status,

The enclosed check can be used as you see fit either on a bicycle to keep on the "Holy Hill," or food, or other "riotous living" or if you are kin to "Big Al," [his brother] maybe sent straight off to your father at Scott and Stringfellow to invest and bear interest and make you a rich man by age 95 or so.

Anyway the important thing it wants to say is that you are a "guy" I'm proud to be grandmother to—your blessings and talents are great: with your golden disposition you can wrestle almost any enemy or opponent and end up friends, like Robert E. Lee, who grew, in defeat, to world renown for his stature as a fine, strong person. You will be great too!

Mother did not limit such letter writing to birthdays or special occasions, as the following to her niece Rossie Fisher and her husband, Sandy, in February 1979, suggests. The Fishers had been helping Mother with her two very badly behaved mini-mules that were pulling a buckboard in the annual spring drive-arounds on Monument Avenue (Jane and Murray, referred to in the letter, are the Fishers' children).

Darlinks—joy-giving Rossie and Sandy,

No day in any year is wrong for a love-letter, joke, token, or wireless message, so no need to call the enclosed a Valentine (or belated Xmas).

It says clearly you must spend it on planting of whichever type you believe will make Jane's and Murray's view more beautiful: be it on your "home place" lawn or at Camp Holiday Trails or Manakin-Sabot.

Perhaps Quince, "Pyrus Japonica,"—fiery red blooms in March!—likes full sun; will survive dry, red-clay: always excites me.

Hugs, your doting ESB

drop me enc. p.c. to say what you decided!

put your effort into digging and drops of your golden cow manure, not writing— no "thank you" necessary—

A gift that generations of newborn Richmonders received from ESB was a green-leather scrapbook with hand-bound linen pages, made up especially for her by Mr. Atkinson, whose shop was at the lowest point of the U that Broad Street makes going east from downtown before it climbs to Church Hill. The covers of these volumes were engraved in gold lettering, stating the child's name, date and place of birth, height, and weight. The first page generally was inscribed to the child, in Mother's outsized, bold handwriting. The following is an example of what she might write.

1971
WELL COME! Welcome! darling Jane Thornton Fisher
to this wicked wonderful world, with
the hope that this book will hold a
fine record of your sayings and doings
and bring you pride to read when you
grow up.
From your great-aunt and fan
Elisabeth Scott Bocock
your ready-to-wear friend.

As with everything else, her generosity was susceptible to swings of erratic and wonderfully illogical thinking. Mother gave Freddie and Berta their first house on Rothesay Circle soon after they were married. Several years later, she bought it again—buying it back from them—so that they could buy a larger house, around the corner on Rothesay Circle. Her theory was that she could live in their old house in her old age. But it is a low-slung, one-story bungalow, as different from the high-ceilinged spaciousness of 909 as it is possible to be, and she knew in her heart that she never wanted to live there. So—Fred and I having a daughter, Eliza—she gave it to Eliza, who was then aged ten or so, as if to say, "Your Mother and Father were foolish enough not to live in Richmond, but now you needn't make that same mistake."

On Jack Bocock's twenty-first birthday, ESB offered to join his mother and father in giving him part of a car to take to college. When he asked if he could get a Ford Bronco, she said yes, indeed. He went to pick it up at the Ford dealership and drove it to 909 for her to admire. Everything was fine until she discovered that it had only two doors, and that in the case of fire or a crash, the people riding in the back seat would be imprisoned there. The Bronco was to go out the driveway and not come back, as she had no idea of helping to pay for such an unsafe car. The Bococks, who had already agreed to buy the car, ended up paying for all of it since it was the ideal vehicle for Jack in the far-north woods at Dartmouth.

There was literally nothing that Mother would not have done for her own children and grandchildren. Had she needed to give her own life to save one of ours, she would have, willingly. When it came to bravery, she had enormous follow-through. But the one thing that we often would have traded for cars or for houses or for opals and pearls was a peaceful, relaxed visit, and most of the time this was just not possible for her. I referred above to Carolyn Heilbruner's stage of invisibility: one important aspect of that transition is that a mature woman emerges from it more able to blend with those around her, to listen to others, and to hear new voices; she no longer needs to dominate a conversation or a social scene, to dazzle a crowd or to be in control. In this, Mother failed, and it was the only tragic aspect of a life that both gave and received an extraordinary amount of happiness. Blending was something she just could not do. There had been too many years of the cultivation of "visible personality" for it to be possible. When she arrived at the Bococks' or the Carters' for a family dinner, the whole atmosphere would change, and the focus—wherever it had been before—would shift to her.

Particularly in regard to her relations with her grandchildren, I remember often wanting to shout, "STOP! Stop issuing dictums about bad posture and good manners, stop hijacking conversations that have barely gotten started, stop manipulating the very air waves in the room. Listen, just listen!" When I asked her grandson Bobbie Carter about his reaction to these visits, he said, "I do remember a sense of conflict. I don't really remember if that was just teenage rebelliousness, or rebelliousness against the command performance expectations that she had."

* * *

Many of the command performances took place at the Homestead, the hotel in Hot Springs, Virginia, where, for years after Father died, Mother took all of us for the New Year's holiday. One of the great hotels of the world, the Homestead turns the holiday season into a child's paradise. The Great Hall is decorated with poinsettias and running cedar, and the focal point at the end, where the corridors meet, is a two-stories-high Christmas tree. For several years, Mother would extend her visit until January 3, when the hotel took down the tree by stripping the trunk of its branches. She took the denuded trunk to Goose Chase, her property near Royal Orchard, and "planted" it as a keepsake of another happy New Year's vacation, having Bill White, the director of the carriage museum, carve the year into its wood.

At the Homestead, blazing fires are kept going all day in the two huge fireplaces of the Great Hall, where benevolent grandparents sit reading newspapers, saving seats on the sofa beside them for their grandchildren, who burst in at teatime with cheeks aflame and tales of the fun they have had that day on the funny little Homestead ski slopes, or riding horseback, swimming, or bowling. Teatime, with the sound of the piano playing, the fires crackling, and the voices of excited children coming into that warmth and cheer from the cold of early winter darkness, is my standout memory of the Homestead. Once while we were there, a notice came around announcing that tea would be served not in the Great Hall but in the dreary Homestead Bar. The decision caused a revolt. Few of the old regulars went to tea in the new location, and Mother circulated a petition to protest the move. Bob Schieffer of CBS News signed it first, which was effective, and in the following months enough people badgered management that, the next year, tea was again served in the Great Hall.

The Homestead is a secure and pampered world. A stay there is akin to an ocean voyage. Five-year-olds roam the halls in packs, room keys tied around their necks with ribbon. When a child forgets the family's room number or gets lost in the vast reaches of this marvelous Victorian resort, a maid, a waiter, or another guest will reconnect the child to its family. The headwaiters know many visitors by name, and with high Virginia decorum assign tables near the dance floor not simply on the basis of tips, but taking into account the number of years the family has been coming and "has always been in Captain Mack's section."

This visit was surely the highlight of Mother's year. It was a matriarch's delight: for a few days, she had her family all under one roof. Aware of how thoroughly we were all being spoiled during our five-day stay, she took it upon herself to add a little discipline to our daily routines and to set up ground rules for grandchildren. Since what she was paying for included three superb meals a day, high tea, and hot chocolate after the movies at night, grandchildren were not allowed to charge soft drinks. The same rules applied to activities: anything that was "free," like swimming or ice skating, we were encouraged to do; bowling was frowned upon, and skiing was an extra that parents were expected to pay for.

Usually, Mother arrived driving several grandchildren, because after a few years of overregimentation, Freddie and Berta and Bessie and Bobbie dropped out. Fred and I, not living near Mother all year long in Richmond, could deal with the short but intense burst of Mother's regime that our annual foray to the Homestead involved. In the early years, she would be driving her green Mercedes; later, when the car's antiquity confined it to short-range use on days when it did not rain, she would be in her miniature yellow pickup truck, named Daffodil. The children would be dressed in heavy parkas, with ear-muffs, scarves, and gloves, because their grandmommy never turned her heater on so as not to be asphyxiated by carbon monoxide that might slip in with the heat, and always rode with the windows open, even if it was below freezing. What should have been a three-hour trip from Richmond took twice that. Mother usually stopped to eat hard-boiled eggs and drink tea, sometimes took a nap, always took them on an architectural and historic tour of the town of Staunton, and often checked out the junkyard opposite the cemetery to see whether it might just have an interesting mantel or some homeless shutters. Once past Buffalo Gap and into the mountain highlands, she would insist that they pull over, turn off the engine, and listen to the sound of cascading water where the road parallels a mountain stream in the George Washington National Forest. Finally, winding slowly up the sides of Warm Springs Mountain, she would reminisce about a terrifying moment in her childhood, when her Uncle Cole Scott's horses had not been able to hold the carriage back on that same mountain one icy winter night.

She always took with her several books—histories and biographies—from which her grandchildren could choose when out-loud reading time came, which was every morning at 10 A.M. in a secluded hallway outside her room. Mac McElroy, who came with Andrew Carter one year, remembers being fas-cinated, as a teenager, by a biography of Golda Meir. And when our daugh-ter, Eliza, who was by four years the youngest grandchild, took her turn in the reading circle, the older children were hard-pressed to keep from laughing: she read with the exaggerated verve and animation that she knew pleased her grandmother.

Children were expected to be at the table for all meals (no hamburgers to be charged at the ski chalet!), but the afternoon was theirs to fill as they wished. They were on duty again at six o'clock, when the eldest grandchild would go to the dining room and take the menu to Grandmother's room so that we could all order ahead of time. Although Mother often kept people waiting, she could not stand being kept waiting herself, so when she arrived in the dining room at seven o'clock, ahead of the wave of cocktail-bound guests who streamed in half an hour later, she wanted to see the first course already on the table. This was the responsibility of the eldest grandchild, who was to see that the menu, with its check marks beside the ordered items, got into the hands of our waiter in time to have this happen.

The uncomfortable command performances that Mother's grandson Bob-bie Carter remembers usually had to do with meals. As he puts it, "It was not something that in itself was particularly important; she would want something and would ask me to go up to the waiter and get it, and it was usually not worth creating a scene over. I remember thinking that no one has the right to make the type of scene that she was making." Quiet, thoughtful Bobbie then summed up in one sentence the root not just of her commanding presence at the Homestead, but of the way she approached life. "I guess," he said slowly, "I don't see myself as someone special because of the way I was born . . . as how I present myself to the world. Her situation was quite different." Mother's parents clearly thought she was special; her husband did, too, and countless people when I interviewed them said, "Your Mother was special." Expecting her not to think so herself may have been unrealistic.

Bobbie, talking about her need to be in charge, went on, "I remember later in her life, when she began having heart fibrillations, sometimes she would get so excited from talking that you would notice she was short of breath. I would want to say to her, 'It's the time in your life now to find a little peace and grace.'" When I asked him if he had ever experienced any peaceful moments with her, he remembered being at Goose Chase, the mountain home she built in the 1960s: "There were times when she would slow down and become reflective. I remember her sitting inside in the evening, reading quietly. It was a powerful sort of feeling that for once she was quiet—we were listening to each other, maybe because no one else was around."

Mother's eldest Bocock grandchild, Natalie, at least in her school and college years, found that Mother was almost always supportive of her on her own terms. When she begged Natalie to give up hockey and lacrosse because she had broken her nose so many times, and the advice fell on deaf ears, she still showed up for many of Natalie's Princeton games. And at that time she was over eighty. At one particular game, against Temple University, in the worst weather November can produce, Mother, wrapped in scarves, stood on the frozen, windswept field. She eventually had to retreat to sit and watch from her taxi.

My own frustration with Mother's lack of peacefulness usually had to do with juggling her needs with those of Fred and 'Liza. One Thanksgiving weekend we were at our house at Royal Orchard and Fred was trying to administer a practice SSAT test for 'Liza. His mother was visiting us, and Fred had already had some difficulty convincing Liz Hitz that he needed absolute quiet in the house for the next couple of hours. In burst Mother through the back door, carrying a sidesaddle that she wanted to give 'Liza. I remember thinking, "*Help!* I want out of here." I knew it was hopeless to ask Mother to come back later, and equally hopeless to expect Fred to be anything but impatient. The tension that had built in the house had nowhere to go, and Mother's arrival was more than that house, at that moment, could hold. Fred exploded; Mother retreated, hurt. The sidesaddle, however, now sits in its place of honor on a saddle rack in the living room, and the young girl who took the SSAT test is herself a teacher.

ESB and Fred Hitz pulling vines out of trees at our house site

7. A Flash of Green

MOTHER WAS a woman of many talents, but in one area her touch approached that of genius: she had a very special way with *flowers*. When it came to flower arranging, Mother could do more with less in less time than anyone else I know, except possibly Bessie. Her membership in the James River Garden Club came about because of her interest in conservation, not because she wanted or needed to study decorating with flowers. Most likely she felt in her bones that either the Lord had made you so that you could arrange flowers or he hadn't, and if his attention to this talent had been lacking, there was nothing anyone here below could do to remedy the situation.

Her materials for flower arrangements started with the garden forsythia of early spring, stark and graceful when it was brought into the house in late February, and put in warm water to force its buds. Her favorite month was April, before the first wave of summer heat that always came in May, wilting the blooms on the azaleas and making the late tulips droop. Her garden blazed in April, a repayment for all the planting that had gone on from November well into January. ESB believed that mass was the most important principle in creating beauty, and so bulbs were planted in groups of fifty, not five. Color flooded the backyard: tulips by the dog yard, a painter's palate of primrose and grape hyacinth in the triangle off the path to the garage, daffodils around the water fountain, and hyacinths marching all the way down the driveway to Franklin Street.

But no matter what combination of hyacinths, tulips, and daffodils she carried in her left hand, she knew instinctively which vase to reach for with her right hand. Not just color, but shape and size were always right for what had been picked, and all kinds of odd objects that could never be defined as vases served to hold flowers. One of these was a big, warped wooden salad bowl that she and Bessie had cut off of a diseased hickory tree on a riding trail at Royal Orchard. For years afterwards, whenever we passed the tree on horseback, Mother would remind us about what a hard job it had been to saw off the bowl; and how embarrassed Bessie had been the day they were working on the tree, when an impossibly handsome suitor named Tyler Kohler, following directions given him by Cora, came around the bend of the Erskine Trail in his clean white suit and white bucks, catching Bessie sweaty and dirty in her overalls at the work site.

When Mother arranged flowers, she often worked with a large plate and several small containers of different sizes so that she could combine nuts and berries, small eggplants, persimmons, or grapes with the flowers. Cuttings of poets' laurel or nandina would peek out between the fruits, vegetables, and flowers, hiding the containers and making the whole look organically grown. If the arrangement had nuts in it, a nutcracker would be invitingly visible between the greenery; a knife would be stuck in between the navel oranges and the handles of scissors barely showing amid the grapes. Her eye for beauty was visceral, unerring, and immediate. She gave no thought to what flowers she was going to put where; as with so many other things, she acted instinctively in response to the beauty that she saw, and her instincts, in being so unpremeditated, shared the graceful spontaneity of nature.

ESB's favorite flower and favorite scent was lily of the valley. It reminded her of her own mother, and, unlike all the other flowers that brought spring inside the house, it was seldom mixed with anything else. Lily of the valley went in two small, antique glass jars with sailing ships etched in them, the flower's white bells begging a passerby to lean down, inhale, and lock in that intense fragrance. Mother did so, frequently; and when I saw her bent over those white blossoms, I knew she was conjuring up her mother.

Mother and Father both hated heat and tried to escape Richmond as much as possible in summertime, so spring was the garden's finest season. But no matter what the time of year, flowers were as ever present as food. Roses cascaded from the trellis that went from the second-floor balcony at the back of the house down to the garden. With their southern exposure, they bloomed well into December. When they gave out, poinsettias took over, and between the reds of Christmas and the whites of stately Easter lilies came weekly boxes of fresh-cut flowers from Ratcliffe Florists. Flowers, and Mother's way with them, did a great deal to make the formality of 909 more livable.

* * *

Father loved Church Point Farm for its duck hunting, but for Mother it offered the chance to experiment without having to answer to her brothers and sisters, as she did at Royal Orchard. Raising pigs was a project of the war years. In order to begin the breeding program, Mother and Freddie drove a gargantuan sow down to the farm in the back of the old, wood-sided station wagon. Every time the sow shifted its weight, the station wagon would lurch to one side.

Many years after the event, Mother wrote a college English paper about what it was like slaughtering pigs at Church Point during the Christmas holidays in 1943. Manpower was scarce, so Freddie and Bessie were enlisted to help. Instructing them was the manager, a man Mother suspected of being a draft dodger. In her paper, an extract from which appears below, she referred to him as Mr. Laylow.

Mr. Laylow's plan was to get all the mature pigs into one large, fenced in area, take a BB gun and shoot one between the eyes so as to hit the brain and paralyze him. Then he, Mr. Laylow, would move in with his huge sharp knife, cut the pig's throat, and, assisted by the two big children and me quickly dunk the pig into the already boiling hot cauldron. This sounded hard enough because the pigs had been so well-fed and were so huge; but the sound of it was simple in comparison to the execution. To remove the nearly dead porker from the corral, or to lure him to die close to the improvised wire gate, so that we could drag him out, was equally difficult. Even after we had him dragged, pushed, shoved out of the corral, near the cauldron by super human efforts, it looked and felt (in our back muscles) that we would *never* get him lifted into the cauldron.

But Mr. Laylow had a lot of ingenuity, and he improvised a sort of five-level platform so that we could roll our over-fed friend onto the bottom level, then lift one end of those three boards (three of us lifting altogether) and hold it up long enough for a couple of bricks to be shoved in underneath.

But we succeeded finally! As soon as the whole huge creature hit the boiling water it ceased to boil, of course, so we had to hurry and build up the fire, so long neglected, or the skin would not be quite hot enough to make the bristles easily removable. Right away the hideous question arose: how to get him out? Our hog, now waterlogged, looked more like a young hippopotamus. The very thought of lifting him now with the added risk of near-boiling water spilling all over my innocent children (not to mention me) made me blanch.

Just as I opened my mouth to say "this is impossible, we will have to give up," Mr. Laylow said in his quiet, lazy way, "We'll all get over on that side and shove, when it's time, and turn the cauldron over away from the fire, that way, and let the hog roll out by his ownself." "Oh, how clever!" I said, but my heart sank in spite of instructions to the contrary. This was surely a lazy man's way, and while it saved us all from the boiling water, it exposed us to the very flames themselves, if we should fall forward with the cauldron as it went over, face down in the fire. Mr. Laylow said we were not to do this by hand, but by *poles*, which to my surprise, were nearby.

Obviously, the four of us could manage only two of these green heart-cedar posts. So we divided up according to size, Mr. Laylow with twelve-year-old Freddie manning one, and Bessie supporting me. So we huffed, and we puffed, and we nearly blew the kettle down, but it didn't turn over, because Bessie made me laugh so hard by saying, "Mother's not trying," when any idiot could see that I was shoving with all weight, and every muscle in me. Our "men" got the giggles too, because Bess and I kept falling down whenever our post would slip off the kettle.

But you will be relieved to hear we did finally succeed. So there lay the hot inflated hog, on the frozen earth with a biting cold ready to freeze him solid if we left him long, which seemed "a mighty good idea" to the young ones, not to Mr. Laylow though. How we got him hung up is too much like our agony getting him into the boiling cauldron to repeat. Only it was quicker because we could use ropes—that is Mr. Laylow could, and did, very cleverly—first sending Freddie up a tree to put the center of the rope around the strong crotch where a large limb branched off. By this leverage, Mr. Laylow, with us three tugging on the rope behind him, *hauled* the carcass to the proper height to cool, but not to freeze, and set out to repeat all that we had done only with a *new*, and this time slightly smaller, poor pig. After the second slaughter we returned to our first victim.

In a jiffy he had his powerful butcher knife out, and was down on his knees cutting vigorously—zestfully. It seemed to be the high moment of his career; he had such ability, skill, aptitude and ease. The children stood back appalled (So was I). To set an example, I had to pick up another knife and ask with all the force I could muster in my voice, "Where shall I cut?" Freddie came forward and said, "Can I do it, Ma?" Proud of his manliness, but also full of relief, selfishly, I said, "Fine!"

Mr. Laylow wanted help from Bess and me to move the now two-piece carcass from the ground to the farm wagon which he had wisely left waiting for just this moment. Loading the farm wagon was a comparatively easy operation after we understood that a dead pig is not carried in the arms as one would carry a beloved pet dog (if one's dog had been murdered) but by the feet, one person at each end of the split carcass. Because he was still so heavy, even half of him, Mr. Laylow humored us by taking hold of one foot himself, so Bess and I together had only one quarter of the whole hog's weight to lift into the wagon.

By now, Freddie, with harness over his slight shoulders had brought our horse, Twinkletoes, and put her between the shafts of the wagon. Mr. Laylow helped him make the harness right, buckled down the traces, the crupper under her tail; and with the reins in one hand gave Freddie a hand up and off they rattled the half-mile over the frozen ruts to our house. Bess and I running behind, still hypnotized and anxious to help and to see what was coming next.

Much encouraged that Lucy James, our cook, and Cora Gardner, Mary Buford's nurse, could now help, Mr. Laylow set about cutting up the sides with knife and saw. Lucy and Cora had been getting lonely in the farmhouse with no telephone, no electricity, no neighbors and only a baby to talk to, so now they were in a sort of heaven-sent return to childhood. They knew as much about butchering as Mr. Laylow, and they enjoyed it every bit as much, or more, because they had each other and worked as partners now, as always.

After removing my butchering clothes it was bliss to take my two-year-old, Mary Buford, in my arms, and do the nursing job, while brewing and serving tea with lots of brown sugar and warm milk in it (the Irish way) while still watching the butchering. By the end of the day the six of us had all the tenderloin, sausage scraps and fats for lard separated, as well as cut up and weighed and all the large pieces trimmed and salted down, packed in the coffin-shaped pine boxes Mr. Laylow produced before we went to bed that night. When my husband arrived for a quiet weekend in the country, he, loving ham, bacon, sausage, chitlins and scrapple, was very pleased with us and proud of our achievement. *So were we.*

Her interest in husbandry and horticulture made her question, year after year and decade after decade, the common wisdom about the connection between nutrition, health, and the environment. Dating back to her efforts at organic gardening at Royal Orchard, she became convinced that poisoned soils, water, and air were unconvicted criminals in the increased incidence of cancer and modern diseases. Way ahead of the granola children of the 1960s and the Green Movement of the last thirty years, for half a century ESB fought a stubborn battle to raise public consciousness on environmental issues. In the years of prosperity and consumption that followed World War II, even as she knew that few were listening, she insisted on whole-grain breads and unprocessed foods in our diet, worried about the carbon monoxide that was polluting the air from new, gas-guzzling cars, and urged the garden club to put conservation on its front burner. ESB became fascinated by her own and others' experiments linking nutrition to the value of the soil that produce is grown in.

Mother was a recycler before there was any public consciousness about that topic, and she was especially interested in the reuse of biodegradables by turning them into fertilizer. Our compost pile was a source of fascination to her; and although meats were not meant to go on it because of rats, Mother was always experimenting with what would degrade. As Freddie puts it, "Mother's recycling instincts were stronger than her fear of rats."

Mary Tyler Cheek McClenahan wrote a series of vignettes about Richmond characters, one of which, reproduced here, is about Mother (although she changed the name to Penelope).

Penelope Gray Newbold is the most beautiful woman in Richmond. Tall, accurately described as willowy, with enormous dark eyes set very deep in a face of classic outline, she has never passed unnoticed anywhere except among the blind. . . . Penelope lives in an atmosphere of her own creation composed of relentless moral purpose, a compulsive sense of civic responsibility, and an intense curiosity about almost everything. She is pure without being innocent, wide-eyed but not naive. . . . She is given to unpredictable fads. One of these is compost.

Her experimental station was in her garden. Circles of wire fencing six feet high were set up in an irregular row. Each cylinder contained compost of a different type; some received only kitchen waste, some only garden rubbish, to one was added boron, to another cobalt, etc., etc. ad infinitum. As the various elements were put in, yellow tags identifying them were tied to the wire, and the effect was of an unearthly assemblage of weird sculpture always in motion as tags fluttered in the breeze.

As the levels of compost mounted, Penelope did not hesitate to avail herself of the services of the state chemist, who in Virginia is at the mercy of the public for soil testing. Sometimes she sent him several samples a week, and waited with eager impatience for the mail to bring the long printed forms filled in with the percentages of precious minerals. Since she never saw the chemist who did the testing, he had no way of knowing how rare a creature was keeping him so occupied. Had he ever seen her, of course, he would never have indulged himself in the small expression of exasperation that so wounded Penelope. There is no counting the number of samples, perhaps it was the hundredth, but the form came back, typed in neatly under the heading Type of Sample: "Pain in the neck garden soil." Penelope's hurt was matched only by her incredulity that anyone could ever weary of exploring the enthralling possibilities of compost.

On a very hot morning in July Penelope read a small notice in the newspaper that the Bureau of Fisheries would deliver free of charge truck loads of spoiled fish eggs of which it wished to rid itself. She picked up the telephone and ordered three carloads, which were delivered late that afternoon, a Friday.

The large houses of the residential neighborhood in which her own house stood had gradually been absorbed by the branch college of a state university, and a record enrollment of summer students was inhabiting every dormitory. Penelope's telephone rang at six o'clock in the morning, and the chief of the City Health Department made only a transparent gesture of apology for waking her. He had had no sleep at all, he informed her, because his telephone had rung all night complaining of an unbearable odor in her backyard. One girl student had sobbed that she was suffocating. . . . The chief's patience was threadbare and he ordered her to remove the nuisance or expect a summons.

Only Penelope could have persuaded the head of the street cleaning department before breakfast to send the men and trucks assigned to clean the ball park to clear her garden, but she did. Four men and two vehicles arrived at seven, and at seven-thirty they rang the back doorbell. Penelope was shocked and offended by the language that one of the men used in telling her that they couldn't clean up the —— fish eggs,

that the —— stuff was so —— slippery that it slid off their shovels and they could-
n't even get the —— mess into the trucks. Penelope lifted her head, thanked them
briefly and formally and asked them to depart. She would dispose of the eggs herself,
she told them. When they left she turned on the hose, and with the assistance of a
large bottle of Clorox, restored the summer sweetness to the air.

ESB could not resist trying to persuade others that frozen foods were
poor, not just from the point of view of nutrition, but also because they were
possibly linked to cancer-causing agents. Her musings on the subject tend to
leap way ahead of what scientists had to say—although ESB would herself
quote scientists—which often made her thinking suspect to businessmen like
Uncle Edward Anderson, who raised turkeys when he was not engaged in investment banking. In a letter to him dated May 29, 1950, ESB wrote:

In December at a party you asked why I objected to frozen turkeys. My answer is
built on reading, as well as observation and respect for students of nutrition, some of
whom I will quote.

Fairfield Osborn's book "Our Plundered Planet," cautions against processed
foods. Faulkner in his book "A Second Look," speaks of the under value of over-
processed foods. In the April Garden Club of America Bulletin, page 48, "Research
in Compost," by Mrs. James Inglis, you will find the best of all condensations of this
enormously intriguing subject. . . .

In Bromfield's "Out of the Earth" much of it can be boiled down into a great
faith, that primitive peoples and old fashioned intelligent farmers, often through ignorance have allowed to live, the secret and often unknown processes of nature,
which give to animals and humans, if left to their own instincts, self-protection from
degenerative diseases of which scientists are every day becoming more aware. . . .

As you know, Dr. Asa Shield has written very interestingly on the subject of food
values in connection with nervous and mental illnesses. (His children take whole
wheat sandwiches to school, which the humorous tell me they sell at some profit to
their friends for white bread! Even so, they are educating or nourishing their friends
if not themselves. . . .

This is not to say that you or anyone else interested in farming can by himself do
a great deal, but by the study of these subjects, all so closely related to prevention of
disease in the soil, like Bangs, disease in cattle, fowl and humans, (much of it due to a
lack of manure from the animals that used to take the place of our modern automobile and tractors)—but we can follow "a word to the wise" and spread some good
will, health and profit to the world by using the concrete some of us carry on our
shoulders called brains!

Hugs and kisses, ESB

I took particular interest in the bit about Dr. Shield's children selling their whole wheat sandwiches to their fellow students: I never had any luck pawning off mine, probably because of what was in them—lots of lettuce and smelly cheeses like Leiderkrantz and Limburger.

Even in her formal invitations, she used a conservation theme. The following one was to a birthday party for herself, Zach Toms, and Virginius Dabney, all of them turning fifty on February 8, 1951:

> To speak of your age is considered bad taste
> If you're feminine, fifty, with lines in your face
> So we'll slur over that in ladylike haste
> And beg you to come to us, bringing your waste
> Paper and cans old rags and dead cats
> To add to our compost, (we're really quite "bats")
> But fifty we'll be on February eight
> So come to our party come early or late
> And celebrate with us, the wise and the sage
> Not the old age of youth, but the youth of old age.
>   Elisabeth Barrett Browning Bocock

Father was heard to say that he figured he'd better not die before Elisabeth, because the temptation to put him on the compost pile would be too great.

* * *

Organizationally, much of her interest in conservation was carried out through the Associated Clubs of Virginia for Roadside Development. The Associated Clubs were organized in March 1937 with the purpose of beautifying state roads by restricting the growth of outdoor advertising. The intent was to survey the billboards on highways, to ask advertisers to restrict their ads to within city limits, and to help to create and lobby for the Outdoor Advertising Act of 1938.

The Associated Clubs, with ESB pushing the organization in a direction she wanted it to go, also focused on beautification of highways through plantings, working with the state's landscape engineer, a Mr. Neale. One such project, close to ESB's heart, was to sponsor Neale's plans to beautify Route 60—a road that carried a lot of tourist traffic, from the "new" capital, Richmond, to the old capital, Williamsburg. With this project, as with many others she would later be involved in, ESB took the bit into her teeth, confusing and sometimes alienating those she hoped would be interested in helping. Usually this was because she tended to overlook the committee process.

ESB wanted to approach the Rockefellers, to ask them to participate in the Route 60 project, as they had been so generous to the Colonial Williamsburg Foundation. She wrote Susa Snider, the president of the Associated Clubs in 1955, about this idea. Snider's return letter reflects her fear that ESB had jumped the gun.

Dear Elisabeth, When I returned last evening . . . your letter was awaiting me. Because I found it a bit bewildering, and because so little of it answered what I had written you about two weeks ago, I am going to take it up paragraph by paragraph. . . .

As for writing to Mr. Rockefeller with regard to *your* project to beautify Route 60 from Richmond to Williamsburg, *don't think of writing to him.* Perhaps you have forgotten that you sent me the letter from the Garden Club of Virginia in which Mrs. Thorne told you that her Board of Directors could not undertake the project you proposed.

ESB had not "forgotten" Mrs. Thorne's letter. More likely, she had pressed on despite it, scornful of its lack of imagination.

Characteristically, being told no did not stop her efforts to bring things about. Her handwritten note on the bottom of Mrs. Thorne's letter read, "This is sad, but no reason to give up." Hence, she continued to lobby Susa Snider. Her maneuverings in this instance give a clue as to why she was never elected president of the many organizations she was associated with over a lifetime of civic activism. She became chairman of the conservation committee, and of committees for finance, nominating, development, and grounds, and in the early 1950s associate director of the William Byrd Branch; but she never became chairman of the board.

On the one hand, her guerrilla tactics made her process-oriented co-workers nervous; and on the other hand, she, by the 1950s, had figured out that she operated best on her own—often in concert with others as far as ends were concerned, but seldom in concert as to the means of achieving those ends. Add to this that she was always in a dreadful hurry, and it becomes obvious why she began to operate more and more as an individual, and less and less as an organizational loyalist. It was not that she was afraid of the work involved: she was the most indefatigable worker I ever knew. It was because she saw where she could make her greatest contribution.

In the 1950s, it seemed to those who were interested in conservation that President Eisenhower and a cooperative Congress were about to pave over large portions of the United States. The Interstate Highway System had just been conceived of, and ESB was in almost monthly touch with Virginia Senator Harry Byrd and Representative A. Willis Robertson, lobbying, with other members of the Associated Clubs, to see that the system would have legislation banning billboards. ESB lobbied with poetry.

> Let no one say
> And say it to your shame
> That all was beauty here
> Until you came.

In the same period, she put enormous effort, under the auspices of the Associated Clubs, into seeing that the new Richmond–Petersburg Turnpike be made as attractive as a toll road could be by tree plantings on its banks and multiflora roses in its median strip to cushion vehicles in crashes. As we drive interstate highways today, our eyes are accustomed to the many plantings and wildflower patches that Lady Bird Johnson initiated, but in the 1950s the road builders were mainly concerned with infrastructure, not aesthetics.

ESB took on the job of raising the money for the plantings from the James River Garden Club and Associated Clubs members, personally writing hundreds of letters. When much of the first round of plantings, which the toll-road authority had cooperated in, died for lack of watering, ESB began organizing bucket brigades to keep what was left alive. I remember a period, which lasted for months, when no matter what direction we were headed in Richmond, our first stop was the toll road, with me holding buckets in the back seat of the little green Mercedes to keep them from sloshing, as we veered up banks and over median strips to treat the worst cases of the drought.

* * *

ESB was particularly concerned about odorless pollutants, and the health hazard of poisoning by carbon monoxide from car exhausts. If a friend drove into the 909 driveway and stopped to talk, ESB would reach across the driver and turn the motor off, and then continue talking. She also lectured her friends about turning off their engine in a traffic jam, turning off unused electric lights, using public conveyances, a bicycle, or their feet instead of their car, and never walking behind the back of a car when the engine is running.

One day, Freddie was driving ESB and Jim Whiting on a tour of Church Hill in Daffodil, ESB's pickup truck. She was sitting in the middle, and every time they had to stop at an intersection, the diesel motor rattled so much that she would reach over and turn the motor off. "Mother, don't do that," said Freddie. She responded quickly, "but I can't hear." Freddie turned the motor back on, they proceeded another block, and she turned it off again. On. Off. On. Off. It was a slow journey across Church Hill. When ESB was herself driving, anybody riding with her would pray she would not park on a hill, because she would jump-start her old Mercedes by pointing it down a steep street, letting up the clutch into second gear to spark the motor to life. She seldom bothered with first gear.

City employees were frequently her unwitting adversaries on conservation issues. Jesse Reynolds was head of City Parks and Trees in the late 1960s and early 1970s. ESB had a polite but running battle with him, just as she had had with the turnpike authorities, about doing extensive planting and then letting it die for lack of water, compost, and mulch. In the fall of 1969, when she was chairman of the James River Garden Club Committee on Air Pollutants as Affecting Horticulture, she was increasingly interested in the need for city planners to be horticulturally informed. She had an ally in Mrs. Pendleton Miller, from Seattle, Washington, who was chairman of the Committee for Urban Planning of the American Horticultural Society, of which ESB was a member. They devised a questionnaire to be sent to urban planners and horticulturists in major cities across the United States, gathering information on what types of trees and plants had proved to be hardiest in their particular climate and urban setting. Writing to Jesse Reynolds about this questionnaire on December 13, 1970, she says:

Thank you so much, Mr. Reynolds, for your clear answer to my questionnaire, by which I am trying to learn so that I may pass on this valuable information to organizations which cover much larger territory and are endeavoring to help in the horticultural education of all city planners throughout the United States. Each of us—you in your job, and I, in mine, are all city planners to some degree; you, because of your professional standing; I, because of my financial investment in real estate, both where I live and on Fifth Street and, more extensively, on Church Hill.

Her sentence, with its eight commas and two semicolons, may set some kind of record.

The tone in her letter to Mrs. Pendleton Miller is strikingly different—a blunt assessment of Reynolds's lack of training for his job: "Since Mr. Jesse Reynolds is the overall head of parks and trees in our city and is seven or eight years too young for retirement and since some of us who have tried to get him 'promoted' to teach English in the public school system have failed, we are locked into this uncongenial marriage. Mr. Reynolds has no education in horticulture, botany, or city planning and seems to have learned nearly nothing from observation of his own department's failures. Nothing is gained by irritating him." I hope she felt guilty about trying to pawn him off on the public school system.

* * *

With the postwar population explosion, unrestricted suburban development began to eat up the countryside. There was a dawning awareness that we were losing the natural habitats that plants, animals, and birds depend on; and that we needed to act to preserve those habitats while it was still possible. In 1951, the Nature Conservancy, a national nonprofit organization, was founded with the goal of creating land preserves that would protect the habitats that plants, animals, and birds need to survive. It set about raising funds for the purchase of land and persuading landowners to place farms and ranches under open-space easements.

The impetus spread and state chapters, chartered by the national organization, started forming. In 1960, the former director of the national board, Donald Stough, wrote his friend Gerry Bemiss, then a Virginia state senator, about the possibility of starting a chapter in Virginia. Gerry wrote back on September 19, 1960: "To my mind, Mrs. Bocock is the very best person to actually get this program started." ESB often called herself a bulldozer, and in this case she was glad to start the engine. She held an organizational dinner meeting at 909 on October 12, 1960, inviting friends she knew were interested in conservation from all over the state. The Virginia chapter had its first meeting in February 1961. ESB was one of eleven original directors.

George Freeman, another director trying to schedule the next meeting, wrote: "I would strongly recommend, however, that the meeting be held on the day most convenient to Mrs. Bocock. She is certainly the driving force in Richmond for the Nature Conservancy and I believe that her complete cooperation and assistance are necessary if the organization is to succeed in this part of the state." Succeed it did, and in 1999 had 27,500 members. Approximately 250,000 acres across the state are now protected by the Nature Conservancy.

* * *

ESB's biggest battle on the environmental front was fought against the Richmond Metropolitan Authority (RMA), which was determined to build a downtown leg of the Interstate Highway System. It was to be a toll road, separating downtown from the James River as it whisked affluent commuters from the western suburbs downtown to their offices, drastically shortening their commute. City planners had studied the area from Main to the James and recommended a surface-level boulevard, a recommendation ignored by both the RMA and the city council. A group put together to protect the James River and the Kanawha Canal that runs alongside it protested the toll road vehemently. The group's president, Eugene B. Sydnor Jr., said in an advertisement: "It's not too late to stop the expressway. It is too late to build it. Our society is changing. The expressway is obsolete. Help stop the expressway before it destroys Richmond's secret treasure. Then help us build a better Richmond."

ESB, horrified at the plan, founded the Committee for the Alternative (that is to say, an alternative to the expressway). Fred and I were just back from West Africa and Fred was between jobs, so ESB hired him as legal counsel, bought time on local television and radio, and sent him out to raise the profile of the issue so all Richmonders would be aware of it. The symbol of the Committee for the Alternative was the picture of an enormous python wrapped around the expressway, ready to destroy downtown Richmond. It was accompanied by ESB's marvelous purple prose: "City Council plans to go forward with the RMA's python. Must we be buried under concrete and debt?"

More studies, including one paid for by the city and the Main to the James Committee, reinforced the recommendation of a surface-level boulevard. They pointed out that ramps for the expressway would pave over the historic canal, and emphasized that the expressway had been conceived and planned in the 1950s and 1960s, and represented thinking that the gas crisis had rendered out of date. The more ESB sensed that they were losing the battle, the more purple her prose became, and the more she began to emphasize that here was an issue of fairness to the politically powerless, as well as one of urban planning and preservation. "For nearly nine years," she wrote, following the start of construction on the first leg of the expressway, "nine men of RMA, all of them white, given power of life and death over private property and public parks, have prevailed over the little people. The fires of anger are lit. Who will defend these nine men? The barbaric destruction of Byrd Park has infuriated a peace-loving populace."

ESB was a great believer in neighborhoods, and one of the things that bothered her most about the expressway was that it was splitting Oregon Hill, a blue-collar neighborhood, into two pieces in order to get wealthier Richmonders to their offices faster. She was also concerned about the fate of the Pulliam House, which had been built in 1858 by the manager of the Tredegar Iron Works, which, a few years later, produced many of the munitions manufactured in the South during the Civil War. The Pulliam House had particularly handsome ironwork on its porch and fence, and lay directly in the path of the expressway. ESB was one of several preservationists who saw to it that the house was dismantled and moved to Church Hill. Sadly, despite the best efforts of the preservationists in trying to stop the expressway, the RMA had a stranglehold on the city council, and triumphed.

Several years later, as a freelance writer, I did an article for the *Richmond Times-Dispatch* about the ingenious ways that Portland (Oregon), Seattle, and Vancouver had found to celebrate their waterfronts, including, in Portland, tearing down an old expressway to reopen the city's access to the water. By this time, Richmond's Downtown Expressway had already sealed off much of the city's access to the James River. At the millennium, the downtown that I knew as a child is ghostlike, its two big department stores boarded up, its vitality sucked away to the suburbs. But another downtown center is taking shape, in an area as near as the expressway allows it to get to the river. Old warehouses are being renovated into restaurants, chic stores, and offices. Under the looming shadow of the expressway interchange, a pedestrian walkway is being built along the old canal lock.

Once the expressway was built, ESB tried to get Virginia Commonwealth University, which needed to expand its campus, to put a deck over the expressway, as had been done in Seattle, and use it for open space. This, if it had been part of the planning process for the expressway, would have been an imaginative way to make green space in the inner city. ESB also felt strongly that VCU should expand to the north and east, aiming eventually to hook up its undergraduate school in midtown with its medical college downtown. Thirty years later, that is exactly what is happening, as construction to the tune of $100 million (including a biotechnology park) is being planned along that same corridor.

Even ESB's "failures" produced small successes. She did not stop the library from expanding, but she did move houses from its path; the Expressway got built, but not without the whole city focusing on its distinctive qualities and how to preserve them; years after her effort, VCU is fulfilling her idea of the institution's manifest destiny; and trolleys may yet be resurrected in Richmond. If she had been alive these last ten years, ESB would be so cheered by municipal recycling, by Bessie's hard work on conservation and her presidency of the Garden Club of Virginia, and, most of all, by the movement of environmental issues into mainstream consideration.

It is fitting that this chapter end with a recognition of her efforts, even when she lost. Just inside the entrance door to her apartment in the back of 909 sat a heavy granite rock with a gold plaque, inscribed

Solid as a Rock
Presented to Elisabeth Scott Bocock
On October 3, 1974
By Fellow Citizens of Richmond
In Appreciation of her Untiring Efforts
Towards the Preservation of
The James River and Kanawha Canal

ESB driving her basket phaeton at Goose Chase in July, 1969

8. (Wild) Goose Chase

ATHER'S DEATH took the referee out of ESB's relationship with her brothers and sisters. As with any game lacking a referee, the play soon turned rough. The irrationality of her behavior increasingly irked the other "little Scotts," and when they tried to impose their will in matters having to do with Royal Orchard she reacted defensively, feeling, in the isolation of her widowhood, that the other four were ganging up on her.

At the heart of this conflict was ESB's relationship with her brother Buford. Bobbie Carter may have thought that he was the first person in ESB's life since her parents' death to say no to her, but, in truth, Uncle Buford had a jump on him. ESB and Buford were the most willful of five siblings, and as young people they egged each other on and shared an approach to life that milked every day of its last bit of gaiety and humor. Trying to reconstruct the parting of their ways, I would guess that the beginning of it was Grandfather's death, and Uncle Buford's comfortable assumption of the mantle of family patriarch. ESB, as an adult, was willing to take orders from her father, but not from her brother.

Uncle Buford married Mary Nixon, a Philadelphia beauty, brought her to Richmond to live, and expected her to graft herself into a very strong family and an ingrown society, mostly on her own. The graft did not take. Aunt Mary had a fragility and sweetness that gave her no natural protection against Uncle Buford's teasing. She scandalized the ladies of Richmond and her mother-in-law by insisting on smoking in public; later in her life, she told her daughter Leezee that she had not been coached by her in-laws in the Richmond dos and don'ts, and never developed close friends in her adopted city. She and Uncle Buford produced five children, but not an equivalent amount of marital happiness.

By the late 1950s, Uncle Buford had developed serious medical problems, which led to his having a substantial length of his aorta and renal arteries replaced in an operation that lasted fourteen hours. With poor health, his temper shortened, and he had less and less patience with ESB's high-handedness. For a time, the five siblings took turns running Royal Orchard, and when it was ESB's turn she made changes that often got changed back again when the next sibling in line took over. After Father died, the Royal Orchard meetings turned into pitched battles, with Aunt Isabel trying, unsuccessfully, to keep the peace, and Uncle Freddie and Aunt Rossie trying, equally unsuccessfully, to talk some sense into ESB and Uncle Buford. At some point, ESB suggested that they divide Royal Orchard up among the five families, but her brothers and sisters argued that that had not been the intent of their parents in building a family gathering place, and that if she would only agree to operate by consensus it would be possible to share it harmoniously.

By the early 1960s, relations had grown so strained that they agreed to hold a silent auction among themselves, and to sell Royal Orchard to the highest bidder. Characteristically, ESB made the highest bid, and her intent was to go ahead and do what her sisters and brothers did not want done—to divide the place among the five families. In the course of the meeting, tempers were so frayed that Uncle Buford, to his credit, disbanded the meeting, insisting that they all go home. With time to reflect, ESB must have realized how thoroughly she was the odd person out, and that she was the one who needed to pack up and move elsewhere.

For many years, the Scotts had had an uneasy truce with Sam Goodloe, who lived at the foot of Afton Mountain. He also owned a beautiful pasturage just to the southwest of the Royal Orchard line, distinguished by its springs, which never went dry, and the kopje, or little hill, that jutted up treeless on the crest of the mountain. Uncle Buford had tried time and again to get Goodloe to sell his property to Royal Orchard, since a tiny wedge of it impinged on our entrance road, providing him with the right to come through Royal Orchard herding his cows to their summer pasturage. Goodloe had had a grudge against the Scott men ever since Grandfather Scott had made him angry by searching in the Goodloe pasture for moss-covered stones to use in the construction of the Big House. He sent Grandfather a bill for $500 for "Construction Materials," which Grandfather countered by sending him a bill for $500 for "Pasture Clearing." Neither bill was paid.

Goodloe continued the feud after Grandfather's death with Uncle Buford. It is easy to imagine Uncle Buford's reaction when he learned that Goodloe had sold ESB his lovely mountaintop land—350 acres—at $19 an acre. According to Freddie Bocock, Mr. Goodloe had a particular affection for ESB, who had foxhunted periodically with the Goodloe Hounds, and so approached ESB when he was ready to sell his mountaintop property. According to Buford Scott's son Buford, the five Scott siblings learned that Goodloe was offering his land for sale, met to discuss it, and delegated Edward Anderson to negotiate the sale. When he began the process, he learned that it had already been sold to his sister-in-law, Elisabeth.

Despite their chagrin at not adding the land to Royal Orchard, Mother's brothers and sisters must have been relieved to realize that her attentions would now be focused on what she herself named Goose Chase, knowing that the prefix wild would inevitably be added to it. At about the same time, the management of Royal Orchard shifted down a generation: it was made into a family land corporation and run on a much more businesslike basis.

In creating Goose Chase, Mother was, in a literal as well as a figurative sense, contradicting Royal Orchard. Goose Chase was as haphazard, rustic, and informal as Royal Orchard was planned, domesticated, and formal. She wanted to create a place where her grandchildren could learn firsthand how to milk a cow, make butter, or gather eggs. As each summer's projects were added to those of the summers before, Goose Chase became an expression of Mother's increasingly antimaterialistic philosophy. If it had had a motto, it would have been "Recycle, Reuse, and Restoration," and these three Rs would be applied not just to what went into the building of Goose Chase, but also into the use of nineteenth-century techniques in the operation of a farm. The woman who, in her fifties, had been known for the high style in which she lived and dressed, in her seventies was likely to be found in her overalls, with wisps of gray hair escaping her sunbonnet and dirt under her fingernails, weeding her vegetable garden. The sunbonnet even went to church, although a clean cotton dress replaced the overalls.

The first project that Mother undertook on her new property was a 100,000-gallon water reservoir, sited up on the crest of the mountain so that water could be supplied by gravity feed to the three houses she was eventually going to build. The storage capacity of the reservoir was intentionally large: Mother felt sure that Royal Orchard, with greater and greater usage by a larger and larger family, would some day need to augment its own supply. Mr. Brockenborough (called Mr. Brock because his construction firm was Brock and Davis) was her contractor for the several years that Goose Chase was being built. He remembers that no sooner was the reservoir built than she wanted to put sheds around it for her carriages. When the sheds were in place around the huge, poured-concrete structure, it looked like a wide-brimmed lady's hat set into the base of the kopje. The view into the Rockfish Valley from the top of the water tower is magnificent, and Mr. Brock still has in his mind's eye an image of ESB "sitting up there one day, eating her lunch, when a bear came up and was eating strawberries in the field."

The construction traffic went through Royal Orchard, so ESB decided that the next thing she needed was a road. Initially she had a surveyor lay out a bicycle path to Goose Chase, and when this needed to be upgraded to a road fit for heavier traffic, she asked Freddie to build one. He took a week off from Scott and Stringfellow and, by Wednesday of that week, when ESB paid a surprise visit, he was making good progress. As he explains it:

When Mother came up and said she wanted to see the road, I told her it wasn't a good idea, that it wasn't completed. But she wanted to see what was happening. She looked, and said, "This is a nice job," but then she heard the noise up in the woods. I had a man there with a bulldozer who was used to working on logging roads in the mountains. She said, "What's that noise?" and I answered, "That's the machine helping us build the road." "Get rid of it," she replied, "I thought you said you'd build the road." I said "I did, Mother, but I didn't say I'd build it with my bare hands."

What she objected to was that the machine was going to wreck the environment so the road would eventually erode. I had to tell the bulldozer operator to stop. So the first part of the Goose Chase road took three days, and the second part took seven years, and untold amounts of money with all the handwork involved in building a rock retaining wall for over a mile, and filling in above it.

Mother wanted grass in the middle of the road, so blacktop was to go only on either side of the grass median strip, which meant that a machine could not do it. "That's probably the only blacktop done by hand in the state of Virginia in the last fifty years," says Freddie.

Although he was excused from road-building duty, Freddie was part of another remarkable operation when Mother wanted to build a dam to make a goose pond, having decided to raise geese for eventual sale to the Commonwealth Club kitchen. Mother had hired lots of men, because she wanted it done in one day, so there would be no seam in the hand-mixed concrete. When the men got low on gravel, she would take the pickup truck down to the gravel pit at Waynesboro, waiting in line for supplies. But the man in charge kept letting big dump trucks go in front of her. Eventually, she got out of her truck, went up to him, and said, "What have you got against grandmothers?" Then she asked: "If your grandmother had a truck and she needed gravel, would you treat her the same way you're treating me?" "No ma'am," he said, and every time she returned after that, he waved her to the front of the line.

"It was a huge job with a lot of men, everybody pouring gravel into the wood frame," says Freddie.

Every hour, Mother would come along with a choice of water or her favorite drink, Russian tea, which was iced tea spiced with orange rinds and cloves. Starting about 9:30 A.M., she'd pull one or two men out and say "You've got to take a nap now." They'd usually say "I don't take naps," to which she'd reply "You have to have a nap or you don't get paid." She had a pad and checked them off, and everyone had at least two naps in the course of the day. As a result, all these people worked from 5 A.M. until 10 P.M., and got the job done.

Mr. Brock did the hiring, but Mother, often, did the firing. Anybody caught smoking on the job was a goner, ditto for working shirtless, killing a snake, using crude language, or being a shirker. Bill remembers one of the boys getting into trouble when the road was being built. "He was trying to pretend he was doing something," says Bill, "so when she came up he cut down a dogwood tree—he was history after that."

Things had to be done by hand. That was only one of her requirements for how Goose Chase was to be built. As Mr. Brock puts it, "She wanted everything done the old-fashioned way." What this meant for her, in many instances, was the way her Father had chosen to do it. When it came time to build a septic field, she wanted it to be made of loose rock, like the septic field for the Big House. Mr. Brock tried to explain to her that that method would not pass code, but this was immaterial to ESB. "So when the inspector came up to look at it," says Mr. Brock, who later became an inspector himself, "we had quite a discussion. Finally I said, 'Forget about your regulation, Inspector Casey. Will this or will this not serve the purpose?' He said, 'Well, yes.' And I got by with it."

But if Mr. Brock thought he had seen it all in the early summers at Goose Chase, he would admit later that it was not until the summer of 1967, when they started building the houses, that he realized what he was in for. Looking back on it, he says, "We could have built a place as nice as the Big House at Royal Orchard if we could have used machines and modern methods and had something to go by. But that wasn't her way of doing it." Her way of doing it was to describe to Mr. Brock what it was she wanted, as with the 100,000-gallon reservoir. When it came time to build the houses, he protested: "Mrs. Bocock, I have got to have some kind of a plan, some kind of drawing, give me something to go by."

Her eldest Bocock grandchild, Natalie, happened to be reading Hansel and Gretel at the time; after she had showed Mother pictures of the steep A-frame cottages in the book, those pictures became ESB's mental blueprint of structures that, in size, simplicity of design, and materials used, fit most gracefully and harmoniously into the natural setting. The setting she had in mind was a hickory grove on a knoll that was on the same parallel as the knoll that the Big House sits on, a mile and a half to the east. She wanted to be able to see her parents' bedroom from her own new bedroom, to keep Royal Orchard in her sights, fondly, but at a distance. So Mother would describe to Jacquelin Robertson, son of her Richmond friends and at that time an architect serving in Mayor Lindsay's administration in New York City, what she had in mind. Jacquelin would make vague sketches, which Mother would turn over to Mr. Brock, who was supposed to do all the measurements and the drafting. As he puts it, "I might as well have been the architect of it since I had to do all the work on it."

Goose House was the first to be built, and because it housed Cora's kitchen below and her bedroom and bath above, it was the heart of Goose Chase. It was later connected by a curving, wooden walkway to Mother Goose House, where ESB lived, which had a living room with an elegant fireplace below, and above just enough room under the steep eaves for her bed, a daybed for a grandchild or two, and a bath. Often, ESB would spend the morning raiding junkyards in her pickup truck and come bumping back up the Risky Road to Goose Chase with swamp cypress boards, shutters, paneling, doors, windows, or mirrors to go in a section of one of the houses that the workmen had thought was complete. Before Goose House was stained a uniform brown, it looked like the winner of a competition to see who could use the greatest amount of recycled material in a new structure. Mary Tyler Cheek McClenahan, who points out that a sense of economy was very much a part of Mother's upbringing, says that "in her houses at Goose Chase she just loved seeing what she could make out of scraps."

Mother, I am sure, tried to justify her expenditures in her own mind, to not be overly extravagant or wasteful of the fortunate position she found herself in and the resources that were available to her. Had she been asked, directly, about the stewardship of her own resources, I think she would have been quick to say that she wanted to make positive use of them and not waste them so that her descendants would be equally able to help out in their lifetime in projects that were of civic merit. Nevertheless, her build-first-and-change-later philosophy was costly. In the words of Fred Hitz:

By approaching projects like Goose Chase, the Hand Work Shop, or the Early Virginia Vehicular Museum impulsively, she spent far more money than she probably had to, or wanted to, to get done what she was trying to achieve. And again, that goes back to the whole issue of training.

What I'm talking about is discipline—discipline of mind, discipline of habit in terms of analyses of these things, and a willingness to rein oneself in when instinct and impulse were overpowering. That, unfortunately, was not part of her training or upbringing, and she probably spun her wheels and spent her resources more lavishly than she had to, to achieve her goals.

Everything about the architecture of Goose Chase was distinctive, original, and in many cases, impractical. This was truest of the bathrooms. In both houses, not enough space had been allotted for them—and that was true even before Mother returned from England with the soaking tubs, six feet in length, she was so proud of. Even though these fittings were odd sizes, Mr. Brock managed to hook them up. Workmen had the devil of a time getting the tubs up to the second floors of both houses, and once they were in place there was not enough room for the toilets. In Cora's bathroom, this meant that the toilet had to be placed on an elevated pedestal. I found it was necessary to walk up two narrow steps, turn around, and then perch precariously on the "throne." It was wisest to hold onto one of the towel racks to keep from falling off, because your feet were suspended in air. In ESB's bathroom in Mother Goose House, the tub was jammed up under the steep eaves, so that getting in and out of it required the moves of a contortionist. Reaching for the soap meant banging one's head, and on stepping out there was barely room to fit the towel around oneself. The old-fashioned, wide-rimmed porcelain sink always had a bar of Pear's soap on it, a bottle of bay rum that Mother used on her hair (she did not approve of washing out the natural oils; after all, Cleopatra hadn't washed her hair), and an eggcup filled with salt and soda for brushing her teeth.

Whenever I went to spend the night with her, I would marvel that ordinary, daily routines could be made to be so taxing, and would wonder to myself who, besides Mother, could possibly ever make those houses their home. At the same time, when there, I was very aware of the distinctiveness of everything—that it was Her Place, and that she and it were encouraging me, willingly, usually, to drop back to an earlier age and a simpler time, when nature played a greater part in human lives. Eliza, our daughter, who was eleven when Mother died, saw Goose Chase with the eyes of a young child; she says, "Everything is so easy now in our culture, you push buttons and an instant image pops up; it's easy access. I think it's to be respected when somebody still thinks the hard way is the way things should be done. There was something honorable in having guidelines like that."

Lying in bed at night, upstairs in Goose House, I loved the combination of sounds that reached my ears as I sank into sleep: somewhere fairly close to the house, a whippoorwill; the occasional heavy-footed squirrel racing across above my head; the branches of the hickory trees brushing the tall roof as the evening breeze overcame the heat that had built up in the rafters during the day. Around me in the walls, mice, and coming up the curving stairwell, the

ESB entertaining on the walkway between houses at Goose Chase

drone of Mother's books-on-tape, or the eleven o'clock news. Mother and I were just two of the many creatures occupying that house, and if nature seemed too intrusive, that was the way Mother wanted it. It was her way of doing battle with a world that had become overly comfortable, antiseptic, and mechanized.

Both houses were small, in terms of square footage, and nearly every inch of wall and ceiling was taken up. In the one-room space on the first floor of Goose House there was a central chimney that served, on the living room side, a fireplace with a cast-iron mantelpiece, and, on the kitchen side, a cook stove. Baskets of all sizes and gardening tools hung from the living-room ceiling, and along the walls, bookshelves competed for space with saddle racks, walking sticks, coats, dog leashes, hats, and farming implements. On the kitchen side of the chimney, pots, pans, colanders, and kettles hung within arm's reach, and the herbs and spices that Cora knew how to use so well were on shelves over the stove. There were no cabinets; the refrigerator was small and hard to get to; and the only real storage space was in an oubliette—a hole in the floor that was reached by pulling up on a brass ring. There was barely room to turn around in between the stove and the sink, which was under the window facing up the mountain. It was a kitchen that had been designed by someone who did no cooking.

There was clutter, too, in Mother Goose House, but it had a rustic elegance about it. The fireplace was on the wall opposite the entrance, so the space did not have to accommodate a central chimney and, although small, was unbroken. The ceiling was high, and the windows gave onto the staircase, which was open to the room below as it curved around to the second floor. There was a fluid grace to the room that spoke to me of Mother's potential as an architect, had her instincts for beauty been disciplined by the formal training required in that field.

In the early years of Goose Chase, Cora moved up with Mother for most of the summer, just as she had been used to doing at Royal Orchard. But unlike Royal Orchard, conditions were primitive; she and Mother shared cramped quarters, and since Cora did not drive, she was stuck there. Cora had grown up on a farm, and the back-to-nature approach that Goose Chase represented held little romance for her. Going over to Royal Orchard to swim was part of Mother's daily routine, and whomever she encountered at the pool she was likely to invite over to Goose Chase for tea, or cocktails, or a meal. The numbers would be relayed to Cora at lunchtime, then Mother would go cheerfully across to Mother Goose House for a nap, leaving Cora complaining to Bill about how she was supposed to produce dinner for twelve when nobody had been to Waynesboro, shopping, in a week.

Many people would have said, "Now Cora, you can stay home and I will send you a check once a month, I think you should retire." But Mother knew that it was not in Cora's makeup to retire. No matter how much she complained, she wanted to be there. Eventually, Cora's health meant that she went to Goose Chase less and less, and long before she died, in 1982, Mother began advertising in the Virginia Commonwealth University campus newspaper each spring, looking for young women willing to work for the summer. The ads ran along the following lines: "Help wanted cooking and cleaning for the summer at a rustic place in the mountains. Do not bother to apply if you're afraid of rattlesnakes, bears, spiders, or manure." The students at VCU knew the woman next door by reputation, and only the hardy applied.

One of these summer helpers, Melissa Whey, got a rude introduction to life at Goose Chase. At lunchtime on her first day, when she was getting hungry, she said to Mother, "What shall we have for lunch?" Mother said, "Chicken would be nice." So she looked in the fridge, and all she could find were smelly cheeses and leftover salads. Melissa asked where the chicken was, to which Mother answered that the chicken was outside, running around. "But I don't know how to kill or pluck a chicken," said Melissa. "That's all right," answered Mother, "Bill White will show you how." So Bill showed her how, and at about 4:30 in the afternoon they had chicken for lunch. Melissa lasted the whole summer. Bill White recollects that the most successful summers were when Mother had hired two young women. "A lot of times, it took a couple of them to handle Mrs. Bocock," he says, "because one could be doing something while the other had time off, and they would kind of take turns. She had a way of making people want to please her."

Our daughter, Eliza, agrees. Whenever her grandmother made demands, "it never seemed silly or stupid or without reason," 'Liza told me. "For instance, memorizing Robert Frost" (which was Mother's standard form of punishment for 'Liza and her friend Rosi Kerr, my college roommate's daughter who spent part of her summers with us). "As much as we grumbled and didn't want to do it and swore that we would burn Robert Frost when we got older, eventually I enjoyed it, and it was a real addition when I studied Frost in college."

'Liza remembers: "We had to memorize 'The Runaway' and 'The Road Not Taken' and 'Stopping by Woods on a Snowy Evening'—'The Runaway' because it was about horses—she always picked wonderful ones. And we didn't just have to memorize them, we had to be able to give her a recital that was not rushed, and that was well articulated and done with emphasis. She had such a sense of purpose. Even when you didn't understand you knew there was a reason for it . . . it wasn't as if she went around making things difficult without a purpose."

Some of the young women who worked for Mother at Goose Chase could feel the sense of purpose that 'Liza refers to, and would stay the course for the whole summer. Others would stay only long enough to glimpse an eccentric older lady whose demands seemed incomprehensible, and left, usually within a few days. Most of the girls who stayed had as little cooking experi-

ence as Mother herself had, so eating at Goose Chase was always an adventure. Bill kept chickens, planted a small vegetable garden, and bought a cow—
named Bossy, of course. In Mother's effort to live off the land, these were the
sources of much of what got to the dining table. Bossy's production was
made into butter, buttermilk (one of Mother's favorite drinks), and something that Mother euphemistically referred to as cottage cheese. It was white
and lumpy, but otherwise bore little relation to its namesake.

Guests would arrive hot and thirsty from the walk over from Royal Orchard, since for many years the road was in too primitive a state for anything
but four-wheel drive trucks. Mother would come out to welcome the guests
in one of the sunbonnets she lived in in the summertime, and take them by
the hand to show off her varieties of lilies growing along the rock wall up the
hillside. Bossy would lumber past, looking for grass to graze on; and the two
mountain goats, Bonnie and Clyde, would swish their stubby tails to keep the
flies away as they surveyed the scene from their favorite perch on top of the
picnic table. Lilies admired, Mother would sit the guests down on a bench in
the shade of the hickory trees that overhung the wooden walkway between
the two houses. In one hand a guest would be given a glass of Russian iced
tea, and in the other a colander filled with peas to shell—or it might be a cutting board, with green onions to chop, or a bowl with strawberries to hull. It
would gradually dawn on the visitor that lunch, or dinner if it was evening,
was a long way off. Time seemed to slip at Goose Chase, and houseguests
coming over from the more conventional daily rhythms of Royal Orchard had
to make allowance for it.

Goose Chase became famous for Mother's "grass soup." Made up of
whatever was growing in the garden at the time, she would throw into the pot
wild onions she had pulled from the grass around Goose House, and various
roots and herbs she had gathered in her pockets while directing workmen that
morning. Whatever seemed suspect for having languished too long in the refrigerator also got tossed in, often without positive identification. The first
few things to go into the pot would be nicely diced, but as time and conversation slipped by, the last ingredients would go into the pot whole. And the
whole would bubble away at full boil on the back burner of the little electric
stove. A great believer in bouillon cubes, Mother would toss in four or five,
hard as rocks from wintering over at Goose Chase, before she took her guests
on a tour of the two-story harness house that Bill was building, up the hillside from the houses. She was proud that the construction materials were
cobblestones salvaged from when Richmond pulled up its old trolley tracks,

Royal Orchard contradicted—goats on the picnic table

and prouder still of Bill's skill in expertly rounding the corners of the distinctive little building up the hillside from the house.

Once back at the house—with whoever was helping Mother that summer perhaps still struggling to locate the big pewter soup spoons and set the table (which listed because its legs were made of apple-tree limbs of uneven length)—Mother would taste the soup and declare that it was coming along nicely. A child would be sent to look in the back of her truck for the suitcase that carried laundry back and forth from Richmond, and get out of it neatly ironed napkins (the use of paper products was frowned on). The laundry often was in Richmond when the need was at Goose Chase. Eda Williams remembers, one visit, finding a beautiful lace tablecloth substituting for a top sheet on her bed. Then, to take the edge off of everyone's hunger, she would offer sherry and some Stilton cheese that looked as if its transatlantic passage had been by sailing vessel. One explanation for Mother's extraordinarily good health was that she ate so much natural mold as a regular part of her diet of overripe cheese that she was permanently on a low dosage of penicillin. Finally, the grass soup would be served, along with some of Cora's stale Sally Lunn that Mother had brought up from Richmond, now sprinkled with water and rejuvenated in the oven.

Despite the food, a trip to Goose Chase to pay a call on Aunt Elisabeth, also often called Aunt Flighty, was an important part of a Royal Orchard stay for most of her huge extended family. Her great-niece Margie Springer told me:

She would always invite us over and we loved it. She would have some good goat cheese for us, and grapes in bunches. Once I was plucking the grapes from all over the bunch, and she said, "You should never eat grapes like that. Peel off one stem and eat the grapes off that first, and if you want more peel off another stem," which I always do now because of her.

She showed us how to milk her cow. I'll never forget the time we were going to have chicken for dinner, and we saw Bill White wring its neck.

All my friends remember your Mother; they thought she was the finest example of an older woman.

Another great-niece, Alice Massie, remembers being out jogging with three of her female cousins when they came across ESB "in her buggy with her sunbonnet on and her gloves. She waved us down and said, 'Stop! Please—you're jiggling your female parts.'"

Alice's aunt, Rossie Fisher, recollects: "Anytime you came to Royal Orchard, no matter which house you were in, there would come Aunt Bocock, with a green wine bottle full of magnificent lilies that she'd raised at Goose Chase. My friends would ooh and aah, and I'd say 'Oh that's just my aunt, she always does that.' Then after you've grown older and tried to raise lilies yourself, you realize what that meant." I can remember having an even more negative reaction than Rossie's, because Mother would give lilies to me at Goose Chase to take back to Royal Orchard, and by the time I had bumped back over the Goose Chase road, the pollen from the center of the blooms would have made yellow smudges all over me. But for Mother, the joy of the lilies came from sharing them, and the further she was able to spread their beauty the more pleasure she got out of growing them.

Mother's generosity with her work, whether it was from her gardening or her handwork, was as legendary as her generosity with her financial wealth—wealth she knew she had inherited, not made, and in relation to which she felt herself to be somewhat of a conduit. But beyond these two obvious forms of giving, she also had a generosity of spirit, which showed up as acceptance when things she had been counting on did not turn out the way she had hoped. Fred and I had wanted to build a house in the mountains from the time we were married. Mother knew this, and encouraged the project by offering to help us build a stone tower on a rock outcropping at the edge of the Goose Chase meadow, one-third of a mile up the mountain from her houses. After going back and forth on it for several years, we finally decided, with permission from the board that ran Royal Orchard, to build a house in the Royal Orchard apple orchard. Instead of trying to talk us out of it, or complaining about being deserted once the decision was made, Mother accepted our reasons for it, realizing that she herself was responsible for my attachment to the piece of land we had chosen. Whether or not she thought it was wise, she knew that it was a decision of the heart, and she respected that. Genuinely delighted in our delight, she took pleasure in coming to watch the construction of Rockfish House, and gave us a house-warming party when the frame was up.

Meanwhile, the building projects at Goose Chase continued. It was part of the terms of Bill White's employment that he live at Goose Chase during the summer months, so the construction of a larger house for Bill and Betty and their four children was the next priority. Humpback House seemed to grow organically, sprouting a wing here, a porch or balcony there, according to what supplies Mother came home with that week. Like the other houses, its architecture was long on originality and short on practicality, but because it was larger, it seemed even more eccentric. When ESB and the Whites were not at Goose Chase they left the houses unlocked, on Mother's theory that vandals, if they wanted to get in, would break in despite locks. One day in June 1971, the following note was found on the table in Humpback House, the house that Mother had built for the White family.

TO WHOM IT MAY CONCERN—

We weary wanders of the wild, warm and wonderful wilderness ventured into Humpback House thinking it to be a plush shelter. (Gimme shelter) We thought that private homes could not be built on Federal land and all the doors were open. So . . .

After careful consideration we came to the cataclysmic conclusion that we must have crossed a border, and that this was (is) in actuality, a country retreat for some moderately to aristocratically wealthy people.

We stayed two nights. We used and cleaned some of your cooking utensils. We lounged in the greatest of country comfort in your living room. We took nothing and cleaned up slightly. Your taste in architecture (sic) furnishings, and literature is excellent.

Thank you very much for your courtesy, cordiality, and hospitality. Very trusting people. A rarity these days. If we pass this way again we will try to bring something of use to you.

> Taz Delaney
> Geoff Ryan

In case you're interested we are adolescently attempting to become artists and writers.

Knowing that it was hard on the White children living at Goose Chase when their friends and baseball teams were all in Waynesboro, Mother had Mr. Brock build a swimming pool. But instead of building one that was rectangular, square, or even circular, the pool was in the form of a very thin sliver, the shape of a new moon, and looked like a slice of honeydew melon clinging to the hillside. The White children could not possibly have all swum in it at the same time; in fact, there was no way for two people to pass each other in the water. Mother called it the Cool Pool, and thought of it as a place to get cool, rather than a place to swim.

When 'Liza and Rosi went with Mother to Waynesboro on an errand, she would let them sit on the tailgate of her truck on the way back up the mountain, once they were off the highway. 'Liza reminded me, "You wouldn't let us do that going uphill because you thought there was more of a chance of being run over." But her grandmother would:

Starting at the bottom of the mountain . . . five minutes later she would completely forget that we were back there at all.

She would turn onto the Goose Chase road, and go up that last hill over those rain drains that were built in. They were built in diagonally for runoff, which meant they were extra bumpy. She kept the truck in second, going about twenty miles an hour, and we were bumping up and down and laughing so hard that I fell off. We were both screaming, but Bumma didn't hear us, and she didn't stop 'til she got to Goose Chase.

Bumma was the name Eliza called Mother by. Mother gave herself the nickname when 'Liza was only a few weeks old and staying at Mother's in Richmond. A marvelous baby-nurse known as Cookie was working for Mother, staying in Eliza's room to give her a feeding in the middle of the night; but 'Liza, according to Mother, had taken one look at her and screamed with fright at Cookie's flowing white hair and angular features. Mother blamed herself for not getting up to feed her grandchild, and nicknamed herself Bumma, as in "a bum substitute for Mother."

At Goose Chase, a hay and tool shed was built where the road turns back on itself for the last long pull to the top of the mountain, and down near the Goose Pond where the livestock lived, an open barn and a greenhouse. From her father, Mother had acquired the habit of naming and dating every structure, so one summer when a bobcat kept stealing chickens, Bill built a hen house onto the side of the barn, displaying a large sign announcing "The Bobcat Incubator."

By the end of the 1960s, the major construction at Goose Chase was finished, and Mr. Brock and his large crews had been replaced by Bill White supervising two or three boys that he had hired for the summer. Every summer there were different projects, building carriage trails, clearing pastures, putting up fences and putting in gardens. Mother, in Daffodil, came and went, often making the trip to Waynesboro to the hardware store or the Augusta County Cooperative to pick up supplies that the crew needed. Bill recalled a particular day:

We were working up on the mountain and she drove up. She left the truck on just a little slope. It was an automatic, but it was loaded down with posts and cobblestones and a lot of heavy things. It started off rolling right toward a wall. She thought she could catch it, and she did. She got part of the way in, but then the truck dragged her and it ended up hanging over the wall. Her leg was up under the truck. We had to dig her out, when she was out she just wanted to lay there on the ground.

She wouldn't let me take her to the doctor, but she wanted to know if we had any beer down in the cottages—this was at nine o'clock in the morning. I said, "I believe there is some down there," and she sent me to get one. I went down to the house and got one and took it back up there. As I opened it and handed it to her she said, "Where's the glass?" I'll never forget it. So I had to go back and get the glass.

Mother would not go to the doctor for several days, although her foot had stiffened up badly. She kept telling Bill that, as with a boxer's jaw, the swelling would go down in a week. Her foot was broken in three places, and the doctor had to threaten amputation to get her to take it seriously. Mother was not a Christian Scientist, but she often acted like one where her own health, and sometimes others', were concerned. As a young girl, Bessie one day was thrown from a horse that, according to her, "ran away with me every time I got on him." Although she had taken a particularly nasty fall, onto a rock, she was required to get back on Rockaway, Shamrock's colt, for the ride home. Only when they reached Royal Orchard and Bessie's jodhpurs had to be cut off of her was she treated as hurt and taken to the doctor, where her severely broken leg was treated. Mother's ideas about bravery and killing fear at its source sometimes got the better of her common sense. Not surprisingly, the closest Bessie gets to horses today is the road side of a pasture fence.

On the subject of what would happen to Goose Chase after her death, Mother talked in as matter-of-fact a fashion as she did about who might work for her the following summer. She had a gardener's philosophy about "dust thou art, to dust returnest," and a faith premised on the belief that, for humans, to have faith is not to understand but to be steadfast in hope. Stuck in the mirror of her dresser, in her own handwriting, was a quotation from the book of Hebrews: "Faith is the substance of things hoped for, the evidence of things unseen." Later, the words were carved on her tombstone. She never said it in so many words, but I think she herself had made a leap of faith, believing that her death would reunite her with those she loved who had "gone before."

This faith led her to do the things others put off, like making sure that her will was up-to-date, and that her children understood the reasons behind what her will made explicit. Mother stayed in regular touch with her lawyer, Tom Word, on the subject of her will. Like the buildings she built, it was continually subject to change; but Tom made sure that, whatever the cause of the moment, it was represented in ways that took advantage of the tax code. Bessie and Freddie and I were in agreement that Freddie would inherit most of Goose Chase, but while we did not say so in front of Mother, none of us could imagine anyone but her actually living in those houses. Every detail in them was so modeled on her eccentricities that it was impossible not to wonder what would happen after her death. We need not have wasted time wondering. The two connected houses, Goose House and Mother Goose House, burned to the ground in September 1984, fifteen months before Mother died, in what was believed to have been an electrical fire. Mother absorbed the shock with her usual resiliency. That chapter had ended, and if someone else wanted to continue the book they would have to write the next chapter. At eighty-four, she was not going to begin again. In some ways it may even have been a relief.

She had grown increasingly frail as calcium disappeared from her bones. She had shrunk several inches in height, and her arm, when one held it in a handshake, felt almost weightless. Pulling up hills made her out of breath, and living at Goose Chase was probably becoming a chore that she was almost—but not quite—not up to. The fire took it out of her hands.

Again, her acceptance had to do with faith—faith that, though we do not know why things happen, there is a cosmic purpose, and things will turn out for the best. The last summer of her life she rented California Cottage at Royal Orchard, living happily in it each day, doing a lot of reading and sewing, and making gallons of applesauce from the apples that rolled from the foot of the June apple trees down to her back door. The applesauce was chunky, and potent with fresh ginger, cinnamon sticks, and whole cloves. Mason jars full of it were in every refrigerator on the mountain.

'Liza was ten that summer, and we were often able to coax Mother up to meals at Rockfish House. Bumma knew 'Liza well from taking care of her as a baby, but after that summer 'Liza, likewise, knew her grandmother well. 'Liza said to me: "I think to a certain extent she had missed being a part of the scene at Royal Orchard. My fondest memories of Bumma are of that summer. Sometimes we would go down to have dinner with her, you would bring your guitar, and Rosi and I would sing with you. We would sing 'Matthew' and 'California Cotton Fields,' Rosi and I jockeying to see who could sing lowest and softest, and Bumma always enjoyed that."

When Freddie tried to give her an electric golf cart, she protested that she did not want one and would not use it even if he got one. But when Freddie did get one for her, after a few days of spurning it she became a convert. She discovered that she could sneak up on people without them hearing her, and she loved the fact that there was room for two and it had a roof, so she could sit and watch the tennis players while she and her partner in conversation were in the shade. The golf cart was nicknamed Bumma's Buggy.

Rosi was as horse crazy as 'Liza, so when the three of us rumbled back up the mountain from one of the little local horse shows, Bumma would hear us and appear in her buggy to find out how we had done. That summer she was as peaceful as I ever remember her. In the fall of the following year, like the period being placed at the foot of an exclamation point, Humpback House burned to the ground. The cause was never pinpointed. Friends had spent the weekend there, and Sunday evening after they left, Bill White, who was living in Waynesboro, had gone up to walk through and make sure the fire was out in the fireplace and that all was well. In the first light of morning, Wilson Bryant, the father of the current manager at Royal Orchard, looked up from his house in the Rockfish Valley and saw the flames, stark against the dark hulk of the mountain. I doubt that Mother let the possibility that Goose Chase could have been destroyed by arson seriously disturb her. She recognized that nature had just finished reclaiming Goose Chase. She took comfort, I'm sure, in Longfellow's completion of the line about dust, which reads: "Dust thou art, to dust returnest was not spoken of the soul."

Cora, Andrew, Natalie, and Jack at play

9. Grandmother the Undergraduate

OTHER SCRAMBLED so fast, in the month after Father died, to arrange her transition to college life that a month later she was a live-in student at Ambler Junior College of Horticulture. That first year, she kept an on-again, off-again diary, whose short entries give a peek into her new life.

Sept. 19th: Ambler has just become a section of Temple University, and will expand, offering liberal arts education. Ambler has cut out agriculture—cows, chickens etc. this year in order to do this—but still teaches all phases of horticulture and horse husbandry—it offers no athletics except riding and bicycling!!! It seems the angels made it for me!

There is an immense difference in the mental maturity and native ability of these students. . . . This cloistered life would be ideal if so many of us "novices" were wise enough to choose the subjects we need in order to develop our minds rather than those offered for credits. So many of these students need stimulus rather than requirements.

But soon the difficulties of being a student when she could not shed her former roles of mother, housekeeper, and civic activist began to weigh on her, and to show up in her grades. One entry in the winter of 1959 tells of her being "off to Baltimore" (she was en route to Richmond) to see her "coltie" (that is, me) play on the unbeaten Saint Timothy's Varsity team,

only six on a team, indoor basketball. . . . Monday they will play Oldfields, but I cannot possibly go—have mechanical drawing, my most difficult subject—so am especially glad to be allowed to go today—Miss Anders was awfully nice and understanding—Dean Fisher was too, as always—being a widow who had to create a new life for herself she never fails to see my problems—i.e. how torn I feel between family and old jobs at home, and college.

Oct. 21: Bad news in Botany class—test papers returned with bad, worse, worst marks! Especially after the hideous family perplexities of Oct. 6th weekend. It would have been better just to have been away—at least my body would not have led other people to believe my mind was here—it stayed at Royal Orchard in emotional "condition."

(The weekend she refers to was probably spent in meetings with her brothers and sisters about the future of Royal Orchard.)

The English Department turned out to be the most comfortable milieu for her college career. Because she was so intuitive, it was easy for her to leap into the mind of an eighteenth-century poet or novelist. She was already acquainted with the works of Shakespeare and a good deal of nineteenth-century literature. She was also used to putting her thoughts on paper; she wrote with grace and ease, although she was frequently called down for jumping from subject to subject. A friend once described hers as a "frolicking intellect"; it had its advantages in conversation, but was less adaptable to academic pursuits.

Freedom to interpret the work of others fired her always-lively imagination: "Oct. 3rd: soon I'll be thinking 'pride goeth before a fall,' (Mr. M gave me an A on English). One A does not mean all A's, as one sparrow doesn't necessarily mean Spring." The mechanics of the English language were not as fascinating to her, however; and the sciences were difficult because of her lack of background. With her usual optimism, she took on both botany and chemistry her first semester at Ambler. But the biggest handicap she was fighting was that she had not given herself any time to absorb Father's death.

Oct 8th: Today I did abominably on two tests: on English—parts of speech, very simple test for which I was unprepared—I got a 72 out of a possible 100! And this afternoon in Botany I did worse (I suspect) but these two black moments may be good, in the end, if they awaken me to the knowledge that I am suffering from fatigue and brain fog that is part of the shock and sorrow of the past year's tragedy, and trying to stand on my wobbly-without-Jack decisions. So I've written a note tonight to Mrs. Fisher, Dean, saying I am not "quitting," only "postponing" the study of Chemistry until such time as my brain has been brought into some discipline and order. The meeting of the student body this evening broke my heart—our freshman class needs leadership—is this my job at fifty-seven years old? God forbid.

She managed to sidestep the leadership void and, by the end of the academic year realized that the only way she was going to pull off her dual careers was to move herself closer to home base. She chose Mary Baldwin, an all-female college in Staunton, Virginia, which was a two-hour, rather than a five-hour, trip from Richmond. I was now at college in New England, and, although we were in constant touch by telephone, because I was far away I took up less of her time. She stopped keeping a diary, but when I visited her at her college in Staunton, I could see that she had made a real place for herself there. Mother lived in the Stonewall Jackson Hotel, down the hill from the campus, and drove herself home to Richmond on the weekends. She became a familiar figure on campus and walking up the steep streets to the houses of her various tutors; she made some close friends in her two years there. When she left, her classmates, supposing that she was too poor to buy new clothes because she was forever wearing her wrap-around, green corduroy skirt and a well-mended sweater, took up a collection to buy her a new sweater. Mother's main reason for caring about how she looked was gone; and more and more her clothes reflected her determination to reuse and recycle. Practicality took over, and she dressed to suit what she was going to do that day—root around in her favorite junkyard in Staunton, walk into Goose Chase, or go on a geology field trip.

At Mary Baldwin, Mother came to depend on the advice of Dean Martha Grafton, who encouraged her to focus on what it was she wanted to do with what she was learning. As Dean Grafton put it in a letter to Mother, "I'm amazed at your tenacity about getting a college degree. Naturally, I admire you for wanting to complete the work, but I think you should always ask yourself, 'for what end?' Sincerely and with love, Martha Grafton." This letter, I think, was aimed at drawing to her attention the fact that, given her difficulties in science courses and her strengths in the humanities, she might want to reexamine her desire to be a school-system consultant on conservation issues. She had tackled chemistry her second year at Mary Baldwin, earning an E grade the first quarter, but, with countless hours of tutoring, bringing it up to a C—pretty good for someone who had not taken any chemistry in high school forty years earlier. In a letter to Dean Grafton, Mother, on vacation in Richmond, describes the suspense of waiting to hear if she had passed a chemistry exam. "Dr. McAllister was kind enough to call here at my request the day that the girls got back from their vacation," she wrote, "and he reported to my severest critic, twenty-six year old Mary Buford Hitz, that I had just squeaked through with a 'D' for 'Done It.'"

Shortly after that, she began to take more English courses, accompanied by forays into courses on urban problems, pollution, and natural-resource conservation. She had to meet course-distribution requirements, but after satisfying them I think she abandoned the idea of emerging with teaching credentials in the field of conservation. She was beginning to sense that her vocational interests were secondary to her desire to be better informed in her twin avocations of conservation and historic preservation. Also I think a strong underlying motivation was her wish not to be the only member of her family without a college degree. After two years at Mary Baldwin, she must have considered that, having been away from Richmond for three years, she could move back confident that she would be thought of as a student. I think she also realized that there were not enough hours in the day for her to be a full-time student and still keep a hand in her many civic interests. She now found that taking two or three courses a semester while living at home had real appeal.

From 1958 to 1969, Mother took courses at six colleges, and her grades ran the gamut from A to D, with a preponderance of Bs. Neither Ambler nor Mary Baldwin seem to have worried much about Mother's degree from Saint Timothy's being a finishing-school degree; but when she wanted to take courses at Westhampton College, at that time the women's college of the University of Richmond, they were insistent that any entering student must have a high-school diploma. Saint Timothy's perjured itself with the statement that "the individual student records for those years are too sketchy to evaluate credits precisely, but a diploma for the college preparatory course was given to Mrs. Bocock." This was a convenient fiction: Grandfather Scott did not allow his daughters any consideration of college, much less preparation for it. I find it amusing that two of her lowest grades were in courses on the Bible—a C and a D, from Westhampton College and from Mary Baldwin, respectively. She also got a C and a D in an American history course at the University of Virginia. Both these subjects, Bible and history, require analytical skill and the ability to absorb quantities of factual material. Neither was her strong point; they had never had to be, as Father had always been there to supply them.

One summer, when Fred was in a months-long training course and I was working toward a master's degree, Mother and I lived together at Royal Orchard, both of us taking courses at the University of Virginia, and one semester, Mother commuted to Mary Washington College in Fredericksburg, Virginia. But by the mid 1960s, most of her course work was being done at either Westhampton College or at what was to become Virginia Commonwealth University.

By 1969, Mother had been taking a circuitous but personally satisfying tour of the garden of learning and had accumulated enough credits to graduate. Her degree was in English; but I think she looked at her higher education from the perspective of the Alexander Pope quotation that she loved: "The proper study of mankind is man." She took whatever improved her understanding of humankind—plumbing relationships in literature, absorbing a sense of human perspective from history, and exploring man's partnership with the earth in the sciences. In whatever she took, she looked for beauty, for that is what replenished and refreshed her. She did not feel obligated to learn about what she considered ugly, which included all versions of the Bible other than the King James, much of twentieth-century music, and explicitly sexual literature.

As it happened, 1969 was Virginia Commonwealth University's first degree-granting year, and graduation was held in the Mosque, around the corner from 909. The degree-granting ceremony was preceded by making the usual request that applause be withheld until the last degree had been granted. The first person whose name was called, a Mr. Abrams, was not present. The second name was Elisabeth Scott Bocock. Before her last name was out of his mouth, the shouts and applause erupted, and ESB headed across the stage to collect her diploma. It was not those of us in her graduation party that were clapping, but her fellow students, who knew her as the older lady whose hats and sunbonnets made her easy to pick out around campus and whose eccentric behavior included climbing in the window when she was late for class (she said to keep from attracting attention). It was fitting that she should receive the first degree to be handed out by VCU, her next-door neighbor, and it was a while before the dean was able to get the audience back under control.

Mother's college career, in the decade of the 1960s, when she, too, was in her sixties, introduced her to the racial diversity that was finally penetrating segregation's barriers, particularly at the college level. She had a huge jump to make, since the only African Americans she had known had been servants. The best way to get across her childhood experience is for me to reproduce her own description of her family's relationship with John Fauntleroy, the family's butler and, for the children, banker and confidante. It was published in *The Richmond Quarterly* as part of a series of vignettes about her childhood.

OUR BANKER (1912–1919)

Most banks require deposits before their customers can draw on them. Not ours. Not John Fauntleroy. He kept his money hidden in his own bedroom at 909 West Franklin.

It was easy to borrow from John on a weekend, and cheap. He charged no interest. If a sudden need arose, we never went to either parent because they felt our allowances were generous and should suffice for all our luxuries and whims. Instead, we went quietly to John after any meal while he was washing and drying dishes with the help of his second-in-command, Arthur Wood, and asked, "Can you lend me . . . , John?"

"Sure I can; de question is, when you gonna give it back?"

This simple request and his never-failing reply, affirmatively, gave us all great freedom of action when we had overspent our allowances; but far more important was the prestige he maintained by his importance in the household.

In another vignette, she again touches on how close she and her brothers and sisters were to John, and yet how isolated he was from them in his life outside of 909.

JOHN FAUNTLEROY'S SNOBBERY (1901–1921)

Isabel had been consistently courted by a young man of known ability and wealth. His father had died long ago and he, an only child, had already inherited a fortune with no one dependent on him. John smiled on him and often gave Isabel strong hints.

When she instead announced her engagement to handsome Edward Anderson with those "big brown eyes" which poignantly reminded Mother of her adored mother, John's disapproval was clearly shown.

I asked him in the pantry "Why?" He said she should have chosen the young suitor of known wealth. I said, "But she's in love with Mr. Anderson." To which John replied, "Marry for money and de love will come. . . . Marry for love and de money fly out de window."

He had a firm attitude toward women. His day off he went to his own apartment a few blocks away, but he never told us about anything he did for fun. He never married.

As our intimate friends grew up and married, he invariably sent each a handsome, silver-plated six-sided serving tray. Each bride was immensely gratified and surprised by John's generosity and that made him happy. After our parents died and Brother Freddie and his lovely wife Elizabeth Pinkerton Scott bought 909 West Franklin, John was retired on account of his age; but he responded to any call to help at 909 until his knees began to give way under him. When he died in the hospital in 1945, still without complaint, none of us knew his age. He left a small fortune but no family of his own. One wishes there had been more compliments given him for his sweetness and unselfish service, and for his friendship.

ESB's childhood memories, plus Cora's and Garrett's being back at 909, working for her in ways far beyond a servant's role, supporting her even while she was going to college, made race relations much more than an academic question. Ambivalence was there, I am sure, but Mother made a genuine effort to take individuals as they were, in any given moment—without context or assumptions, in the same way that she hoped to be taken as a fellow student, not as a woman too old to be in college.

As the civil rights movement raised consciousness and brought slow change, Mother's usual attitude applied: that change should be approached positively. Sometimes, however good her intentions, old habits reasserted themselves. Lee Switz, a close friend from college who moved to Richmond, tells a story that illustrates this. She and her husband gave a dinner party for the first black Episcopal bishop in the United States—he was visiting Richmond to give a series of sermons during Lent. As Lee recounted it to me:

Your Mother had come to dinner several times, and she was always perfectly nicely dressed. But this evening she was dressed in a lacy cocktail dress with lots of jewelry on and with her mink tippet over it all. She was at her social best, and it was fascinating to see her honor the bishop that way. She was there with bells on, so to speak. What she was doing, at age seventy-odd, was to give him the greatest respect she could muster.

Meanwhile, at the table, she'd talk about her "chocolate friends." Fortunately, he was of a generation and a gracefulness that it was all right. I cringed but he didn't . . . but she was certainly of her generation.

Mother's relationship to Cora Jones was always that of employer to employee, albeit a valued and beloved one. However, as I reached adulthood I yearned to leap over the forms that governed my relationship with the one black person I knew intimately, Cora. We were very close, and I knew she loved me as much as I loved her, but we were happiest working together in the kitchen, and she would not have felt comfortable being a guest at our table. I dreamed of it, however, and finally it fell into place one summer when she came to visit us vacationing on Deer Isle, an island in Maine's Penobscot Bay. Finally, she was able to see that I needed her as a friend, not just as all the things she had been for me in the past—cook, mentor, servant, mother, teacher. In that week, we bridged much more than the forty years between us, sitting down together to devour the seafood feasts that she and I had cooked up in the large, square, sun-filled kitchen, rocking in the armchairs on the porch overlooking the water, talking about nothing and everything, keeping an eye on Eliza as her plump toddler's legs propelled her around the porch, and just enjoying each other's company. We had crossed an abyss. The importance of it in my life was only heightened by her death the following winter.

Among the family photographs in our bathroom, I have the most wonderful picture of Cora on the wall by the sink, so I see it daily. She is sitting in Fred's little sailboat, off with us on a picnic sail to a nearby island, untroubled by the fact that she does not know how to swim. She has on a hat to shade herself from the sun, pearl earrings, and an old, blue sweater to cut the wind's chill. Her expression is serene, trusting, happy. Six inches away from the picture is a two-sided magnifying mirror, on a trestle so it can be extended, that

Cora sailing with Fred and me on the Penobscot Bay

Fred uses for shaving. When he has finished with it, he pushes it back against the wall in such a way that when I come in to brush my teeth or wash my hands, Cora is smiling at me from the magnifying glass, larger than life, and the memory of her warmth comes flooding back at me. I get the comfortably eerie feeling that she is, literally, watching over me.

* * *

Following the advent of feminism, when I looked, as an adult, at Mother's operating principles and philosophy of life, I saw a strong feminist, but one who came at it, if not backwards, at least in ways that rejected the operating principles of the feminism of the latter half of the twentieth century. Men were not to be put down, they were to be exalted, using all the powers of charm, guile, and intelligence at a female's command. But at the core of this seemingly sweet, old-fashioned view of how to deal with the other half of the human race was a raging, deep-seated chauvinism.

Lee Switz first encountered this when she was one of the first women to run for the vestry of Saint Paul's Church, in the 1970s. Mother and her sister Aunt Isabel both told Lee that although they had voted for her they did not approve of women being on vestries. When she asked why, Aunt Isabel's reaction was that we ought to leave that to the men, poor dears, because they need to sit there talking about pigeons roosting in the columns, getting high visibility and prestige—all that stuff—otherwise how would we ever get them to church? The underlying rationale for this kind of thinking has been at the heart of strong female leadership, particularly in the South, for centuries; in essence, it is an attitude that regards men with a good-humored near-contempt similar to that applied to children. Women, being naturally strong, so the rationale goes, do not need to take these ego trips. Men need to be sent downtown every day so they can read the *Wall Street Journal,* have lunch, make a few trades, and come home feeling important. If a woman is smart, she runs the man and does not need to run the organization.

In an unguarded moment, Mother once expressed this approach when she said to a group of Historic Richmond Foundation preservationists looking for ways to raise money, "Men are like wheelbarrows. They are only useful if there is a woman to pick them up and push them where they need to go. On their own they're not going anywhere." Mother's wheelbarrow had room in it for her grown children, as well. Despite the fact that I no longer lived in Richmond, Mother made me a life member of the Richmond organizations she cared most about, like Historic Richmond, the Virginia Museum, the 2300 Club, and the Woman's Club. Sometimes I reacted by not paying my dues, sometimes by resigning—part of the adult process of distinguishing my own interests from Mother's. Perversity was my strongest weapon against the force of her personality, as an adult just as when I was a child.

Lee, on the other hand, was in Richmond, and was happy to absorb all the nurturing, nudging, and grandmothering that Mother loved to provide. Lee had lost her mother at age fourteen in an automobile accident, an event so cataclysmic in her life that its worst toll was delayed until she herself had children. Mother systematically introduced her to everything in Richmond that she might possibly want to be a part of. Lee's telephone would ring, and the bell-like urgency of Mother's voice would be on the other end of the line. "Lee," she would say, "the annual meeting of the garden club is six months from now. I want you to have it on your calendar, and I'm going to pick you up and take you and introduce you to people." Lee did not know a dandelion from a tulip, and, in her naïveté, thought garden clubs were about gardens. At that point in her life, she had come straight out of the civil-rights movement at college into a very different world.

For Lee, being adopted by Mother meant much more than simply the opening of doors. As she puts it: "She was part of my education. She took me under her wing and said, 'Hey, this is what you do here, and here, and here.' I was looking for friendship, for roots, for involvement, for the love and attention of an older woman who would teach me the things that I had missed. I was hungry for what your Mother was offering and she offered it with such abundance." The Switzes were immediately part of our family parties, and, when Mother sensed Lee was overwhelmed by three young children and the fact that her doctor-husband was always at the hospital, she would send Garrett out to Lee's house to deliver a delicacy, like fresh peaches cut up in brown sugar.

Mother was constantly urging Lee to relax about how she was raising her children. The Switzes' eldest son was a bright, rebellious iconoclast who did not see why either his thinking or his behavior should conform to what he saw around him. When Lee was concerned about Neil's table manners, or sitting still in church, or shaking hands, Mother would say, "Lee, don't worry about it. He's ten years old, it will come." This was fascinating to me because, although Mother could bend the rules for Neil, she was rigorously demanding of her own grandchildren. With her own flesh and blood she was unable to take the long view, and to look for manners to develop naturally.

By the time she had grandchildren, her own eccentricities had become pronounced, and because she worked hard at staying in close touch, each of them has stories about how acutely embarrassed they were when she was interacting with their friends. When Alex Bocock was in the fifth grade, Mother one day made a date to take him and a friend to dinner at McDonald's, a trip that was a first for her. When they arrived, Mother strode up to the counter and ordered a gin and tonic, inquiring at the same time about what kinds of fish they served. When presented with a McFish sandwich, she opened the styrofoam container, removed the bread, scraped off the tartar sauce, and cut up her fish with a fork and a knife.

ESB valued her exposure to adolescents and enjoyed playing the devil's advocate with them, knowing that it would get their dander up and make them struggle to explain their point of view, whether it was on abortion or the Vietnam War. Luckily for her, she died before the linguistic virus of peppering sentences with *like* struck; but the closely related phenomenon of following every statement with *y'know?* drove her crazy. When she heard it, she would pounce, grasp the arm of the disconcerted young person, lean forward, and, looking them straight in the eye, say sharply, "No! I *don't* know—that's why we're having this conversation." Looking back, Alex says: "I think the older you got, the more able you were to feel comfortable with her eccentricities. As young people, we were self-conscious about how everything appeared to everybody else. It always seemed like she was making waves needlessly, but the older people, who appreciated what she was more than we were able to, just took it in stride. She died right as I was emerging from my self-conscious period."

Andrew Carter played drums in a rock band following college. Mother, learning that he would be playing late one night nearby, decided she wanted to go hear him play. She hired a VCU security guard to go with her and, he in uniform and she in high heels, fur tippet, and white gloves, they walked around the corner and appeared in the back of a smoke-filled Broad Street dive. Andrew saw them out of the corner of his eye, but before he could worry that Mother was going to try to make her way up to him, they left: the noise hurt Mother's ears.

Andrew's brother, Jack, recalls an overwhelming sense of frustration when ESB would take a seemingly small issue and blow it out of all proportion in order to make her point. Mother felt strongly that, to know her grandchildren, she needed to do things with them without their parents being part of the outing, so Mother and Jack, when he was thirteen or thereabouts, were going to a movie at the Bryd Theater. They parked on the street, about a block away. As they made their way toward the theater, she turned and walked up to a window display. Jack, not being interested in that window, kept going then stopped at another window, figuring she would catch up with him. That was a bad mistake. In a minute, Mother was walking up the sidewalk toward him with her head tilted forward, arms swinging at her sides, her legs stretching out in long paces while her boot heels sounded a staccato thrum. "My dear Jack," she began, wiping her nose with a handkerchief, "do you have any idea what could have happened to me back there? I could have been kidnapped by hoodlums. I could have been robbed and beaten, and you wouldn't have any idea about what happened. You treat your old grandmother like a piece of furniture. We are not going to the Byrd Theater, we are going straight home to your house and you are going to explain to your mother and father why you deserted your grandmother." He didn't put up any argument; nor did he fare any better at home.

Mother lived long enough to know Natalie, the eldest Bocock grandchild, not only as a child but as an adult, too. Mother was in her eighties when she went to visit Natalie at Oxford University in England. She treated herself to a trip on the Concorde, to see what everyone was talking about (she also treated me to the trip, but I was in Oxford only briefly, traveling on to France to meet Fred). Mother wanted Natalie to hire her a tutor for the time she was there, so she would not be in her niece's hair during the day—a tutor knowledgeable in architecture, art, and the history of England, and available for a week. So Natalie went to the dons of her college and eventually was put on to someone at the Oxford Union. The arrangements were made and Mother approved them, including the fee the tutor was to be paid. Mother wanted to ride double-decker buses and have the tutor lecture to her on the bus, so they did this for several days. Natalie managed to meet up with her grandmother in between examination sessions. One day Natalie showed up to be told by Mother that she had had to fire her tutor because he had gotten too expensive. This seemed odd, because the price had been agreed upon. After a little sleuthing, Natalie figured out what had happened: the tutor had fallen in love with his pupil and started fawning over her. He wrote her an epic poem on two huge legal sheets of paper—verses about her and about their tour—and she just got bored with him.

Natalie feels strongly about the importance of her grandmother as a role model.

Repeatedly, in different environments I've been in, whether it was Princeton or Oxford or different places outside of the South, people have said, "You don't strike me as a being a southern woman. How did you grow up in that environment and not be like that?"

And it always seems such a surprising question to me, because the southern women that I knew intimately were these incredibly strong, eccentric people. They didn't fit into any mold. When I look around at my friends from Saint Catherine's School who are still in Richmond, most really didn't have that kind of woman in their life. They lead such different lives from me. I think grandmother is a big part of that, and I think my mother [Berta Bocock] is a big part of it, too.

There definitely is a link between Natalie's grandmother and her mother, despite their not being related by blood. Both of them held loyalty highest among human virtues, practicing it down to the minutiae of daily life, and in Berta's case this extends to the animal kingdom as well. For both of them, decisions were matters of the heart, instantly arrived at through a highly personal, visceral instinct for telling right from wrong. Most importantly, for both of them compromise was out of the question.

It is proof of how tough Mother was that she did not concern herself with whether or not she sometimes made other people—even her closest kin—feel that they were swimming upstream in her company. If she had a point to prove, or saw manners that needed correcting, or had a job to do, she was not to be deterred. Like her father, she was as interested in being feared and respected as in being loved. She could look at her grandchildren's world and see that, in this new world, anything goes—a fact that only heightened her determination to impress on them that good manners are immutable.

Most of the grandchildren's friends were fond of Mother, even when they were embarrassed by her, because she took such a sincere interest in them, wanted to know all about what they were doing, and made them feel as if they were a part of her life. Much of her beauty was in the part of her character that made you feel that she was very interested in you. This was a message that came through her eyes. She never gave the feeling that she was talking to you while looking elsewhere to see who else was in the room. People from all different walks of life sensed this interest. Alex, in Richmond on his way back to Episcopal High School after Mother's funeral, was signing his name to the credit-card slip for his Amtrack ticket back to Alexandria. The ticket agent saw that his name was Bocock and asked if he was related to Mrs. John H. Bocock. Alex replied, "Yes, she was my grandmother." The ticket agent, who knew ESB as a regular train rider, said, "I want you to know how sorry I am. She was a great lady." Alex was touched to hear a man that he had never seen before express his sense of loss.

Mother, Eliza, and me with our dog, Gusti, in the garden at 909

10. Mother and I

*I*T WOULD HAVE BEEN easier for both Mother and me if I, at least as a child, had not looked so much like her. Coming out of church on Sundays on the steps of Saint Paul's, the ladies would peer down at me as I fidgeted at her side and remark, "My dear you *do* look so like your mother." This seemed to require some response from me, and when I asked Mother what I should say, she replied, "Say politely, what can't be cured must be endured." So, having no idea what it meant, I would look up brightly and chirrup my retort, scandalizing the ladies, to Mother's great amusement.

As an adult, I have neither Mother's chiseled bone structure nor her deeply set brown eyes, which, along with her grace of movement, were the seat of her beauty. But because the resemblance was clearer when I was a child, she and I both expected more similarities between us than actually existed. I was her "coltie," and she looked on my tomboy antics with amusement; but she was extravagant in buying sophisticated dresses for me right out of the display windows of New York stores, and gave both Bessie and me her most beautiful jewelry, recreating, perhaps unconsciously, the encouragement her parents had given her to step from being a schoolgirl into the role of belle of the ball.

She took me for the extrovert that she was, which, to complicate matters, I could make a fair pretense of being, mimicking my funny Aunt Rossie or cutting up with my cousins. I was amazed to read recently in the Saint Timothy's yearbook for 1959 that I was our class clown. I can recognize it now as an easy route to popularity, but the frame of extrovert was not a good fit. Mother was a ladylike coquette; I got so little of this gene that even in Italy I never got pinched. She was happiest as hostess of a large party, I at a party of eight— or better yet, six, and not as hostess either. Her talents lay as a visionary and a catalyst, mine as a realist and a chronicler. She thrived on turbulence and unpredictability; it seemed to me that life itself offered quite enough of both without having to stir the pot further.

I was, however, a very active child, and she dealt with my energy with common sense, using her operating principle of keeping those around her busy. She was realistic about how fidgety children got in formal settings: so if we were traveling and dinner had been ordered but was taking a long time to appear, she would send me off on imaginative missions—to the front desk to find out what time the museums opened the next morning, or out into the street to take a poll of how many ladies wearing hats came by the hotel entrance in a five-minute period. When I returned to the table, I would be expected to make a report that was accurate and articulate; the museums paired with their hours of opening or the hats described. To bob up and down on such errands as these was acceptable; to ask to be excused to go to the ladies' room during a meal was not.

Bessie remembers the dizzyingly rapid way she, as a child, went from being an angel to a moron in Mother's eyes. By the time I came along, Mother had had more experience as a mother, and most of the time I was her sugarplum; at least, I do not remember being called a moron. Mother had the ability to change a child's approach to ordinary things—to look at a patch of ground and find seeds to plant in it; to make a trip to the bookstore into an exploration of the bookseller's restored apartment above the shop; to go, in a day, from reading about General Lee's childhood home, Stratford Hall, to visiting it. Setting off with her, you never knew where you might end up.

As I write this, I am in a rear corner of the porch on our cottage in Maine that looks out over a back cove called the Mill Pond, a circular body of water formed by islands connected to the mainland of Deer Isle by sandbars. At high tide, it is a beautiful saltwater pond, where we swim and kayak. At low tide, it empties out completely and becomes a mudflat. For an hour or so, either side of the tidal change, there is a gurgling noise as the outgoing or incoming tide in the narrow passageway called the millrace becomes a stream over rocks, a perfect place to wade in and collect mussels—mussels that are cleaner than most because they are scrubbed four times a day by wave action. For each tide there is a moment that is often missed because it arrives with an absence of sound, when the gurgling is overwhelmed by the tide moving in the other direction, reversing the flow of water with the quiet, unquestionable authority of the Moon. Mother's authority was like that of the Moon, unquestionable in its forcefulness, and quiet in the sense that, although she often gave orders to her children, she gave them in a clear manner in her lilting voice. She did not yell. She did not have to, anymore than the Moon needs to announce each tidal change with a thunderclap. We went where Mother's tides took us, and we went places many children do not have the privilege of going, not for lack of means but for lack of imagination and time.

Mother spent a great deal of time encouraging me my freshman year at Saint Timothy's, when I found that I was almost a year behind my northern counterparts in academic preparation. When I entered the door of Carter House at lunch time, there was a green-ink letter in my mailbox nearly every day to boost my morale. Letters would often contain second- and even third-hand scraps of correspondence, or newspaper clippings that she thought would interest me. For her, the real objective in a day's work was to light brushfires of interest in other peoples' lives. Often a stamped, addressed envelope would be included so that the news chain to assorted godchildren and nieces and nephews did not get broken. Although I had been sent off to be educated, the apron strings were gently tested every so often to make sure that I was still attached to Richmond.

Fred and I married shortly after I graduated from Smith College, and as a young, married woman in my twenties and early thirties I often seesawed between loyalty and independence, seeking the golden mean but settling, mostly, for awkward lurching between the two. My twenties and thirties corresponded to the 1960s and 1970s, when the expectations of females caused friction in what had been previously unquestioned relationships. As it evolved, the language of liberation sounded sweet, but to those of us who graduated from college in 1963, it had the exotic appeal of a foreign language that we could understand better than we could speak.

The tenth reunion of my class at Smith I remember for all the vivid stories of broken marriages, bitter custody battles, and struggles to pursue careers. It seemed that an enormous amount of flotsam and jetsam had washed up on the beach. The class had married under one set of expectations, most of us within six months of graduating from college. Within five years the world was laughing at those expectations, and most of us were trying, some in small ways and some in large, to renegotiate them. The ways I did this were small. Loyalty came before self-fulfillment; I had things that were embarrassingly rare in that era: a happy marriage, no need for money, and, as far as I could see, no burning talent that needed to be pursued. What I did not realize was that, aside from a few geniuses, most of us have to construct talent through constant use of the abilities we have been given. If I could go back to college now, I would major in English, and pursue the writing of creative nonfiction. At the time, I chose history as a major because I got better grades in it. For many in my Smith class, renegotiation failed and divorce resulted. I look at the Smith *Alumnae Quarterly* today and know that the judges, symphony conductors, and corporate executives got where they are at great personal sacrifice. What strikes me, when reading their biographies, is that one of their greatest interests is in mentoring younger women.

Fred and I spent part of this period teaching in Nigeria, in the tumultuous 1964–65 year that led up to the Biafran civil war. Fred was teaching law at the University of Ife, then in Ibadan in the Western Region, and I was teaching history and English at Yedije Girls' Grammar School. Not speaking Yoruba, we missed the hints of the storm that was coming, until faculty meetings in my school broke out in fistfights and Biafran teachers began fleeing the Western Region. I arrived at school one Monday to find that French and library science had been added to my class load, because Biafran teachers of those subjects had left over the weekend. This was an important year for Fred and me, as we depended on each other to help make sense of the craziness going on around us and we settled into married life far from the influences of home and family. I learned to cope with daily tensions, such as driving to work across a city of a million people. Had I hit someone, I was instructed to keep going, as justice often did not wait for the courts. While we were in Ibadan, a young man in the Peace Corps had to be sent home, having become unhinged after witnessing a thief have his hand cut off with a machete for stealing food in an open-air market.

When we returned home, I got a master's degree from George Washington University. Thinking I wanted to teach in public school, my degree was in the art of teaching English. By 1969, we were again living in West Africa, this time in Abidjan, the capital of the Ivory Coast. I was teaching English in a civil-service college and working with a friend organizing tours of the Ivory Coast for American teachers of French. Toward the end of the second year, I became sick. I went home on medical leave to find out why I felt so rotten and had lost ten pounds. Tropical diseases were the natural suspects, and I spent the fall and winter being tested for one after another. Mother, believing that worry is the most corrosive illness of all, fastened on the need for a diagnosis. When the doctors did not come up with one, she dispatched one of her young tenants to the library of the National Institutes of Health. He returned with the theory that I had tropical sprue—a disease of unknown cause.

I lived at home for those six months, and during that period came to know Mother adult to adult, and to benefit from both her constant attentions and her relentlessly positive attitude in the face of an illness that we could not explain. Mother loved the theoretical diagnosis because the cure for tropical sprue is folic acid, found in strawberries, and it was springtime and strawberries were in season. So she and I had strawberries on our oatmeal for breakfast, strawberries and cream for lunch, and strawberries mixed into rhubarb for dinner. The actual culprit, it turned out, was more mundane—a bacterial imbalance from an overdose of antibiotics. But while this health mystery was being cleared up, another, bigger one, was making itself felt. After Fred had come home and gone back into law practice (we had decided we did not want to spend most of our lives living abroad), I began having recurrences of a painful shuddering sensation that would roll in waves from my shoulder down my right arm. I had first felt this as a freshman at Smith College, but in the late summer of 1974, when I was six months pregnant, the occasional shuddering became a constant, searing pain. Being pregnant, I could take little in the way of medicine, although for the last month I was allowed pure codeine. The doctors thought the pregnancy was causing a nerve to be compressed, but things did not improve after the birth of Eliza.

Mother was so worried that for the last month of my pregnancy she sublet an apartment in Washington, D.C., driving out to our home in McLean to be with me during the day or ferry me to the doctors, disappearing as soon as Fred got home from work. Her joy over Eliza's birth was huge. She loved the old-fashioned name and the fact that it was chosen as a compromise: one of Eliza's grandmothers was named Elisabeth, the other Elizabeth; Mother spelled hers with an *s*, Liz Hitz spelled hers with a *z*.

Once Eliza was born, I was given a myelogram, a radiograph that charts the progress of purple dye inserted in the spinal column. It revealed a large, benign spinal tumor, which was removed a few days later. From the age of eighteen to thirty-four, when pregnancy finally forced the tumor out of its hiding, I had subconsciously thought of myself as the weak link in a strong family chain. I did not share in the enormous physical stamina I saw around me in my family. This had a subtle but powerful effect on my thinking about what I wanted to do with my life because I never knew when the pain would reappear. I was in awe of friends who made intricate plans and then were able to carry them out—like getting pregnant in December, finishing a graduate degree in June, moving in July, and having a baby in September. My life did not seem to proceed on such an orderly track. The end of this seventeen-year mystery, which had colored my view of myself for all of my adult life, fundamentally altered both how I saw myself and my relationship to Mother. The shackle of the weak-link theory fell away. Up until then, I had been the cared for and she was the caregiver, and no one could possibly have been more generous with their care. When I was thirty-four, Mother was seventy-four—an appropriate time, in terms of who was caring for whom, for the tables to be turned. She lived another ten years, and our pleasure in each other deepened enormously over that period. I was as liable to telephone her as she was to call me, and to try to show up in Richmond for the many events she put on.

In 1975 we moved from McLean to Old Town, Alexandria, the part of the city that had been a thriving port on the Potomac River long before Washington, D.C., existed. When Mother came to visit—usually for not more than a night—she would stay in the back bedroom that she called "the grandmothers' room" (it was also used by Fred's mother). In her eighties by this time, she tackled the challenges of old age with a bemused amazement that she should have lived long enough for them to happen to her. Sitting on the backstairs to catch her breath on the way up to her room, she would comment that she had lived longer than her father and her mother and say she hoped to be "promoted" before another decade went by.

On one visit, she reached up above our sink to get a pot down from where it hung, to cook her oatmeal. Having shrunk slightly as her spine compacted in old age, she was not quite tall enough. She reached for it anyway, and managed to slip the pot off the iron hook that held it, but in bringing it down, her fingers slipped and the pot hit her on the mouth. It hurt, a lot. Mother—usually impervious to pain—kept referring to what happened—what a dangerous place it was to keep heavy Le Creuset pots, and how we should take them down and store them under the sink. I could not understand why she kept on about it, and had no intention of changing the arrangement, for it suited us, both aesthetically and practically. It was not until I myself first experienced a diminution of physical strength due to aging that I understood why that incident bothered her so. But that did not come in time to tell her. Although she was ready to be "promoted," she was not ready to be perceived as weak or frail. In retrospect, my insensitivity to that amazes me.

* * *

Having a child causes a fundamental change in one's relationship to a parent. Feeling the new weight of another human being's dependence brings a fresh appreciation of the weight that one's own parents carried. In my case, I saw Mother in a new light. I was now the middle rung in this female ladder, loving both upwards and downwards, and feeling, in this cozy positioning, that the love I gave Eliza came bolstered with double reinforcement from the rung above. Eliza was Mother's youngest grandchild by several years, and since she had been eleven years in the coming, she was truly the apple of Mother's eye.

As Codi Noline, the main character in Barbara Kingsolver's novel *Animal Dreams,* says in describing her pregnancy, "You find you're not the center of the universe, suddenly it's all flipped over, you have it in you to be a parent. You're not all that concerned anymore with being someone's child." For me, Eliza's birth was the beginning of the loosening of the stranglehold of self-consciousness. We were living in northern Virginia in the mid-1970s, and Mother was one hundred miles away in Richmond, but her sphere of influence extended north. To me, it felt like her world was a huge switchboard,

Mother, Eliza, and me at Eliza's christening, Royal Orchard, June 1975

with every single wire plugged in and with many of the wires so tangled and intertwined with my own and those of other people that I found it difficult to trace either the original connection or those that had blossomed out from it. Methodically, I set about unplugging connections—resigning from organizations of which Mother had made me a member, refusing to join garden clubs and the Junior League. But I was not yet able to see where, on my own switchboard, I wanted to plug in all the loose wires.

At the same time that I was busy unplugging connections, I was still looking at myself through the example of Mother's life, as a civic activist in a specific social setting. I had not, however, inherited the peculiar blend of character traits that fired her activism. I tried teaching in public school in Fairfax County, but washed out of the system as a hopeless disciplinarian, unable to keep order in a classroom of thirty-six junior-high students. In West Africa, classes had been as large, or larger, but the British and French systems were so strict that discipline was not a problem. If I had been smart, I would have

Fred, Eliza, and me riding up on horseback to visit Mother at Goose Chase, 1977

looked for a job a few yards up the road from where we lived, at Madeira, an independent girls' school, where smaller class sizes and more mentoring might have made the difference.

I was still trying to get life back to normal (I was not able to pick up Eliza for a year) and to figure out something I could do reasonably well on a part-time basis while raising a child. I had been active in a civic battle in Alexandria to establish tenants' rights during the condominium craze in the 1970s. Former renters were being treated shabbily in a local instance of condominium conversion, and I went to a good friend who wrote for the *Washington Post*, Alice Digilio, to alert her to what I thought was an interesting story that might help embarrass the city into regulating the process.

It was a fairly complicated story, and halfway through the details that were spilling out, she stopped me and said, "You know so much about it, why don't you write it. I'll help you if you get stuck, and I'll edit it for you. This is something you care about, and you'll write a more interesting story." So I did, and she did, and fair treatment to tenants in condominium conversions became an issue in the "Virginia Weekly" section of the *Post*. It was the first instance of shifting from the role of civic activist—one I had moved into almost automatically—into that of freelance writer. From the start, the transformation felt right; it is one that is still going on.

Since then, I have worked as a freelance writer for magazines and newspapers, writing anything I could sell—profiles, feature articles, inn and restaurant reviews, pieces on cooking, and travel articles. At one point, I wrote a series for the *Richmond Times-Dispatch* on weekend trips a family could do on a limited budget within a day's travel of Richmond. These I based on expeditions that I had made with campers during the two summers I ran a camp for family children and their friends at Royal Orchard. The downside of freelance writing is the poor pay; the best aspect of it is being able to follow one's interests and, usually, one's own timetable.

I inherited some of Father's ability to create consensus, and used it during the years that I was president of the board of Saint Timothy's School, the vestry of Saint Paul's Church in Alexandria, a social service agency made up of forty churches and synagogues in the city, and the family land corporation that runs Royal Orchard. Whereas Mother operated on the periphery of organizations, acting as a visionary, a fairy godmother, and a goad, I am happiest in the center of the things that I'm involved in, trying to establish common ground.

* * *

Looking back, I can see that I was slow to mature, which is something of an extended family trait. I married straight out of college, which on the one hand allowed me my own identity separate from Mother's, and on the other was an "out of the frying pan into the fire" event, for Fred Hitz is also passionate and of strong opinions. Luckily for me, Fred and Mother got along well, with disagreements erupting from time to time, but not disturbing the basic respect each had for the other.

Sometimes Mother and Fred tried to keep their arguments from me, as when, shortly after my spinal-tumor operation, Mother came to stay with us over Christmas. We were living at the time in an eighteenth-century sheep drovers' inn—a log cabin called "Drover's Rest." I was on the sofa in the living room and they were in the tiny kitchen. Fred and Mother—neither one a cook and neither one a nurse—were in charge of me, a recuperating patient, of Eliza, age seven weeks, and of cooking Christmas dinner. Through the wall between the two rooms, amid the clattering of pans, I could hear whispered consultations about what to do with the goose that Mother had brought, and what to do about the baby, who was crying. The fat from the goose was threatening to burn down the house, smoke was billowing everywhere, and the temperature had suddenly dropped twenty degrees as Mother had thrown open doors and windows to get rid of the smoke. The consultations went from a whisper to the din of a full-fledged argument, toning down again as they reminded each other that I was not to be disturbed. It was one time that I was glad that I was not able to take care of the baby, the mother, or the husband.

In terms of my own personal growth, it is hard to overestimate the importance of three events: the discovery and removal of my spinal tumor, Eliza's birth, and, eleven years later, Mother's death. The first two occurrences removed a lingering sense of inadequacy; and the third challenged me to make something of my life, of my own invention. As Eliza grew to womanhood, it became clear that in her six-foot frame and strength of will she inherited much from her father and grandmother; I was still sandwiched between two people, but one of the pieces of bread had changed. While Eliza was young, I clung to the role of peacemaker; but at some unidentifiable point I got angry at my assigned role and could not, would not, play it any longer. I can, when required, throw a respectable temper tantrum, but most of the adjustment I made was learning to remove myself from the sandwich. I was no longer a compliant ingredient.

Rosalie Kerr, my college roommate, comments: "It would have been awful for you if your mother and Fred hadn't gotten along. The thing that has always interested me is how you managed to chart a course of your own, and not seem to rebel from, or especially be like, or react to your mother. You look a lot like her, but I can't think of the two of you in the same way. You make life work, and are easy to live with. Your mother would have been extremely hard to live with, she was so much the center—everything radiated out from her."

It took years for me to discern the lessons that I needed to unlearn, and then years more to unlearn and replace them. The superficial ones, like being late, and entering a room with a panache that automatically made one the focus of everyone in it, were not hard to slough off, since they were not part of my personal makeup. Harder to live without was the prearranged peace of the 909 household, where arguments were cut off before they happened. Life at 909 was so dignified, so deeply civil, as servants, three children, and Father moved in an unspoken conspiracy to preserve the peace around Mother. It was a long time before I recognized that disagreement did not equal disaster, and that if you strongly disagree with someone you love, you owe it to yourself to put it into words.

Verbal sparring as an intellectual exercise was foreign to the family I grew up in, but integral to the family I married into. It took years to turn myself from a silent adjudicator into a participant. To be fair to Mother, I should point out that becoming a participant was not just a matter of learning not to avoid controversy; it was also one of overcoming a kind of conversational laziness. I suspect that Father, like me after him, fell into this habit, and that we both did so for many of the same reasons. Mother often did the heavy lifting, conversationally speaking, for us.

Some lessons needed to be unlearned, and others—equally fundamental—were finally absorbed. All through my early adulthood, I prized anonymity above all else, deliberately moving away from a context for my life that Mother had been at pains to establish, and being most at ease in situations in which I knew I was without context and could presume that people would have no set of expectations about me. I think I was trying to create a clean slate, partly in a perverse overreaction to the density of Mother's connections, partly as a necessary precondition to figuring out who I was. I was into my thirties before I began to plug in the wires on my own switchboard, and into my forties before I could see the value of living in a situation rife with connections. Part of the freedom to make such an adjustment came from having a child, and realizing the importance of family in the context that I wanted to create for her. And realizing also that she, in turn, would inevitably slough off the parts of it that did not fit her.

One of the ironies of human relationships, particularly intergenerational ones, is how resistant we can be—in the name of independence—to a philosophy of life that we subscribe to when we are older and when the person who has influenced us is gone from our lives. It is as if their going is the entering wedge through which their ideas penetrate, for good, the minds of those they love. It was not until after Mother died—when the telephone no longer rang in the late afternoon, and I was no longer on the receiving end of a five-minute synopsis of family affairs—that I recognized to what extent she had been the yeast in my life, and in our family's life. It was not until then that I actually had to call my sister to know what was going on in her life; that I traveled to another city, or country, without a list of Mother's friends to look up; and that I realized, by trying myself to keep some of the connections going, how much psychic energy she had put into her role as Command Central. I had been a taker, all those years when Mother was in my life, sometimes a complaining taker. And suddenly it was my turn to try my hand at the switchboard.

The Bococks, Carters, and Hitzes in the garden at 909 the day of Mother's funeral. Left to right: Andrew Carter, Fred Hitz, Bobbie Carter, Jack Bocock, Jack Carter, Fred Bocock, Bobbie Carter, Alex Bocock, me, Bessie Carter, Berta Bocock, Natalie and Marianne Bocock, and Eliza Hitz

11. One of This World's Originals

OTHER'S MOST STRIKING characteristics were self-confidence and energy. What was her confidence built on? I find it is a question with many different answers. In Langhorne Gibson's biography of Fred and Elise Scott, Mother's parents, he describes the effect on the family of Mother's early bout with tuberculosis. In the era before antibiotics, TB was truly a life-threatening disease. Gibson writes: "Elisabeth's sickness was the first family crisis they had faced together. Their near loss of her, plus her beauty and wit, made Elisabeth always special to her parents." Elsewhere in the book, commenting on family dynamics, Gibson points out that her father nicknamed her Beautiful. "Like her mother," he writes, "Elisabeth knew how to handle her father. She was quick-witted and full of sparkle. She was her father's favorite daughter." Mother's version, also in Gibson's book: "One of the reasons that I am so used to getting my way is because I always did. When I was young, I was very sick with tuberculosis, and when children have T.B. they have a high fever that makes their eyes and their cheeks very bright, so they're very pretty."

Mother's self-confidence was often relied upon by her parents to counteract her sister Isabel's timidity. Basing his description on family letters, Gibson describes their childhood relationship. "Isabel and Elisabeth, so different in temperament, were very close. Though younger, Elisabeth was the dominant of the two. Isabel was reserved, sensitive, shy and vulnerable, whereas Elisabeth was boisterous, self-assured and strong-minded." Once, when they were in their teens, Mother and Aunt Isabel were waiting at Afton to catch the train that would take them two hours west to the debutante dances at Hot Springs. Mother was too young to participate: her role was to get Aunt Isabel there and persuade her to enjoy herself. While they waited on the station platform, Aunt Isabel started studying her feet. Soon she was gripped with panic over how big her feet were. "Elisabeth," she said, gripping her sister's arm, "I can't go, I just can't." Mother, thinking Aunt Isabel was sick, said, "What is the matter?" "My feet are so big, they'll stick out beyond my dress," said Aunt Isabel. "I can't possibly make an appearance in public." "Nonsense," responded the younger sister, "my feet are every bit as big as yours, and nobody notices feet, anyway." With difficulty, when the train arrived the younger girl got Isabel aboard and spent the entire trip talking up the advantages of big feet.

This sense that she was being relied on to give others confidence served only to magnify other character traits that probably came straight from her father: the tendency to be action-oriented and to think positively, an unwillingness to compromise, and the almost complete absence of doubt from her range of moods. Whereas Father, with his built-in skepticism and legal training, saw the world in subtly shaded hues of gray, Mother's world was black and white, whether the issue of the moment was discipline for a child, a civic crisis, or help for someone in need. Taking action was, for her, a metabolically determined response. There is a currently popular bumper sticker that reads, "Practice Random Acts of Kindness"; every time I see it, I think of how many such random acts Mother's action-oriented generosity initiated. She had a keen eye for detecting things that she could do for other people, of the type that Hill Brown, the rector of Grace and Holy Trinity Episcopal Church, describes.

One blustery, cold, winter's day, he was conducting a burial service at Richmond's Hollywood Cemetery. Mother, once she got out of her car on the windswept hillside, could see that Hill was shivering in his clerical robes. She reached into her jacket, pulled out her green wool scarf, and, going up close to him, whispered, "Hill, put this around your neck so you won't get pneumonia." Regretfully, he whispered back, "Thank you, Elisabeth! I'd love to use it, but I can't do the service in kelly green." By that time, Mother had given away most of Father's clothes—he had been dead for several years—but she had kept a few pieces of clothing that were precious to her. Later in the day, she dropped off a box at the rector's church office, with a note that read: "I hope my husband Jack's dressy white wool evening scarf will make both appropriate and warm funeral garb. Stay warm! Affectionately, Elisabeth S. Bocock."

Mother's confidence gave her a knack for encouraging the same trait in others. In letters to her children and grandchildren, she always accentuated the positive, making an effort to isolate the characteristics that made each of us unique, and liberally sprinkling in praise and encouragement. This might have gone to our heads had the outside world not corroborated our own perception that our talents were in fact pretty average. Mother sent the following note—typical in its spontaneity and in the way the recipient is made to feel special—to 'Liza when she was eleven years old (the note was presumably accompanied by a silver dollar):

The enclosed was printed by the United States Mint especially as a prize for the first
person to write an essay in beautiful, simple sentences about American Crow Tribe
Indians. You have won it. Congratulations!

Bumma.

That there were not many fortunes of the magnitude of her father's in
Richmond when she was growing up contributed to Mother's self-confidence.
The Scotts' willingness to throw a little seed money to support this or that
had enormous impact because there were not that many private alternative
sources of getting things done. When it was her turn, she knew how to use
her position and her eccentricity to great advantage, and she was very cagey
about it. She was way ahead of her time in knowing the impact of hard-nosed
opposition coming from somebody that was as stunningly beautiful and
striking as she was.

Confidence gave her the willingness to tackle the seemingly impossible, to
insist when told no, and to bring anyone she met into her caring and critical
focus. The closer her ties to a person, the less lenient she was in what she
would put up with—one form of her expression of love. Her love was
adamantine, weighty, inexhaustible, and involving; and, once bestowed, it was
for life.

* * *

Mother's phenomenal energy level was a combination of her metabolism
and, as detailed in an earlier chapter, her ability to ward off exhaustion by taking frequent short naps. Although she used her energy productively, it was
also a curse of sorts. Jack Bocock, when asked what he thought his grandmother's greatest weakness was, responded, "I think she had a lot of energy,
and she had a hard time controlling it sometimes." Pascal said that "all human evil comes from . . . man's being unable to sit still in a room." Mother
might have gone so far as to say that sitting still in a room was a lot easier for
her when Father was reading aloud to her. Had Father not died early, I think
it is safe to say, the second half of Mother's life would have been very different, and I would probably not be writing this memoir. But he *did* die early, and
Mother entered a period where her remarkable energy became the propelling
force in her life. It drove her late-in-life college career, her civic influence, her
building projects, and, most importantly, her blossoming eccentricity. In
searching for the sources of this energy, a look at family history is helpful.

There is evidence that both Grandmother and Grandfather Scott suffered
intermittently from nervous depression, the cure for which existed for each of
them in the other. Of their five children, three suffered from depression, Aunt

Rossie at the end of her life, Uncle Freddie similarly, and Aunt Isabel in the middle of her life. Aunt Isabel, always the sweet, vulnerable one, suffered from acute, long-lasting postpartum depression after the births of her children. With the best medical care and long periods of hospitalization, she recovered. Aunt Rossie, the fun-loving, high-spirited baby of the family, changed character so completely in the last five years of her life that at first the doctors thought she had Alzheimer's disease. This was ruled out because her memory was fine. Her behavior became manic, making manic-depression the only possible diagnosis. She spent her last years protected from her own erratic behavior by a team of around-the-clock nurses.

Uncle Freddie was the most sensitive of all the Scott children. When I knew him, as a grown man, he was a perfectionist, hard on himself, and often seemed moved to pain by other peoples' problems and hurts. He and Aunt Pinkerton would often rent Clover Cottage at Royal Orchard in the summertime, and when I would stop by the porch to say hello, his interest in my well-being always seemed keener than anyone else's—as if his very existence depended on it. He was happily married and had three sons, whom he loved and was proud of, but in his seventies he could see the sad progression of old age in people around him and in himself, and he became obsessed with not becoming a burden to his family. Perhaps, also, the woes of the world became too much for him to bear. In an act of chillingly calculated bravery, he took his own life, putting a bag over his head, and, for scientific interest, marking an envelope with a pencil for each breath he took before he asphyxiated himself.

Uncle Buford and Mother inherited their father's competitive streak, which, coupled with an Irish toughness and stamina, gave them immunity to their brother's and sisters' vulnerabilities. When Mother was in her eighties and visiting Natalie in England, an Englishman asked her how she was; smiling, she replied: "Tough." In all the time I spent with her, I do not remember Mother ever being depressed. Discouraged, maybe, when someone she was trying to persuade did not see the light, or when tragedies happened to other people, but never depressed. Her philosophy of life was incredibly positive.

On the other hand, I do think that Mother, after Father died, came perilously close to being manic in the frenetic pace she kept, and in the need she had for a multitude of overlapping projects. It is interesting that the person who had the most influence over her at this stage of her life was Emily Cheston, a horticulturist who was a few years older than Mother. They met while she was studying at Ambler Junior College, the year after Father died. Mrs.

Cheston, whom Mother called Mrs. Wisdom, had a Quaker calmness about her, and long after Mother left Ambler and the haven of the rocking chairs on her friend's porch, she depended on Mrs. Cheston for advice. Rosalie, who knew Mother only after Father had died, says emphatically, "Oh yes! She was manic. The depression side, I never saw that, but she was certainly manic. When I was with her, what I saw were her sense of fun, her gregariousness, and her energy, strength, and vitality. The force of her energy, a life force, was exemplified by the brightness of that green dress. She would be running, putting up her beautiful hair, buttoning her dress, putting on a broach—running to something, full of fun and of incredible energy."

Rosalie sees a big difference between Mother and her three children—Freddie, Bessie, and me. "All of you," she says, "exhibit a public reserve that is almost the opposite of your mother." We may not be manic, but neither are we patient: we lived too long under Mother's influence to respond stoically to everyday inconveniences. Freddie will drive over front lawns to get around a traffic jam; Bessie will drive from Richmond to Charlottesville twice in one day rather than miss an interesting lecture or an important meeting; and I would much rather go pick up tickets ahead of time than stand in line. We shy away from such great American monuments to mass culture as Disney World, not because we would not have as much fun as the next person, but because we have been conditioned to have trouble moving at the same speed as the crowd around us. We direct taxi drivers, order ahead, and cut corners with the best of them. We were taught by a master.

All of Mother's grandchildren are adults now, and their appreciation of her, while loving, is more dispassionate than her children's. They agree that, to them, she was egocentric, but when this characteristic was mixed with her equally strong sense of the common good, a very odd mixture was created. Perhaps *charisma* is a better description than *egocentricity*, since the ego side was often neutralized by—by being mixed with—her concern for others, which made it both palatable and attractive. She had to have a stage, always, but she made great use of whatever platform she had; she was not cut out to be a selfless, behind-the-scenes person.

When she was over eighty, Mother created stages and scenes to play on those stages whenever the fancy struck her. Some of these performances are remembered to this day. One of them took place in the dining room at the Commonwealth Club, which had recently been renovated. Mother was disapproving of the renovation in general: she thought they had spent a great deal of money to replace dowdy gentility with pompous formality. In particular, she was disapproving of the huge, we-are-all-tycoons armchairs, whose over-sized arms kept the sitter from being able to pull in close enough to the table. She also hated the window coverings—tightly gathered curtains that were at-tached at the top and bottom of the big windows, blocking the diners' view of Franklin Street, down which General Lee, numerous U.S. presidents, and Winston Churchill had approached Capitol Square.

At this point in her life, Mother was an almost daily user of the Common-wealth Club. Althea McKnight, who is now manager of the Engineers' Club in Richmond and who remembers being a waitress at the Commonwealth Club in that period, was one of those who recalls the "scene" involving these curtains. "I loved her," says Althea, who was usually the one to wait on Moth-er. "She was different from anyone else. The first time I met her I said, 'Hi, I'm Althea.' And she said, 'What is your last name?' I answered that she could call me by my first name. She wanted me to use my whole name and to be proud of it. She herself was a proud and striking woman."

Here the story is picked up by Mary Anne Harrison Lindsay, wife of the mayor of New York City, who was one of Mother's guests one daylight evening in early summer. Mary Anne, who had been raised in Richmond and known Mother since childhood, told me:

I can see her now—in her blue suit with a jaunty little blue beret on her head. I just adored her, she was one of the most delightful woman I ever knew. I was in Rich-mond because my Dad had died and was going to be buried there, and she invited me and my younger brother to dinner at the Commonwealth Club. She thought our Richmond background had been sadly neglected, living in the North, and she was irate that she couldn't show us Franklin Street, where so much Virginia history had taken place, because the tight, sheer curtains blocked the view. She had a valid point—you couldn't see a bloody thing out of the window.

Your Mother went to the waitresses and borrowed a sharp knife. They were so in-timidated that they didn't dare stop her. I was laughing so hard—I couldn't believe her. She slit the seam of the drapery so that you could see Franklin Street. It was wonderful, just wonderful.

Mary Anne may have thought the waitresses were intimidated, but Althea knew better. "I was watching out for her while she did it," she remembers, "looking to see if anybody was coming. I knew nothing was going to stop her. I didn't even try. She didn't cut the material, just the seams." Berta, Moth-er's daughter-in-law, recollects that Mother felt penitent enough, the next day, to go down to the club and sew up the seams. Franz Mayr, the diplomatic, Swiss-born manager of the club, had by this time known Mother so long that nothing she did could surprise him. Mother had, after all, after introducing the Commonwealth Club to outside catering, been the one who had sent his waitresses into shock when a rat scampered across her carriage-house floor as they were serving a party; it was she that he had found, the morning after the party, rebagging the ice his bartenders had thrown out, and who proceeded to lecture him on wastefulness. Why did Mayr put up with all this, much less with an old lady cutting holes in his curtains? The reason is one that he expresses best himself: "Everybody who worked with her or for her she would never treat as a servant, always as a friend."

After Mother's death, Althea had a white-flowering Althea bush, also known as rose of Sharon, planted at ESB's graveside in Hollywood Cemetery, in tribute to a woman who had made a deep impression on her.

* * *

Mother came across to others as exceptionally strong and independent. I think that the complexity in her personality, and the source of the contradictions that often surfaced in her behavior, arose from her ambivalence about the most fundamental issue in a woman's life—the sharing of power. At an unconscious level, this issue was, I think, behind her marrying so late, and in her choosing a husband who had no problem with her being, from an onlooker's point of view, in charge. To what extent the onlooker had it right is a secret that died with Father, but Freddie, who knew Father ten years longer than I did, told me: "I think you were marching to Father's music more than you were aware of. When there was something important that he didn't agree with her on, he influenced Mother behind the scenes. You never realized the power of that influence, because it was Mother giving the orders."

From my perspective as a child, their relationship seemed very natural, because each of them was comfortable with the way the other operated. From the perspective of the 1950s, whether their friends regarded them as suspect or as a model couple probably depended on an observer's own level of comfort with the idea of role reversal. For my part, I can say that their marriage certainly created a felicitous home life. I remember no battles and precious few arguments. Mother knew how fortunate she was to be married to someone of Father's temperament. Hindsight can add how fortunate she was that her children are more Bocock than Scott. Though we are possessed of varying degrees of sociability, all three of us are what the late Edwin Friedman, a Washington rabbi turned therapist, called *peacemongers*. Had any one of us been cloned from Mother, our household might not have been such a happy place.

Her ambivalence arose, I think, because both instinct and experience told her that nothing is as important as the creation of a strong family—not education, not travel, not work, not even power sharing; and that those who do not succeed at it cannot hope to make up for it in any other way. Mixed messages were often detectable in Mother's approach: expose yourself as widely as possible to other cultures, but always come home to Richmond; get the best education available, but apply it at home; go out with as many people as you can, but remember to marry a Virginian. Although the messages were mixed, the bottom line was not. It read: *Family comes first*. She and Father lived this belief and passed it on to their children, so that we were on the lookout for partners who felt as strongly about family as we did. Luck played a part: I have to give some of the credit to luck, because I now realize how immature we were when we fell in love. But we did wind up with spouses who felt as deeply about family as we did, and for that it is hard to overestimate the influence of Mother and Father. They created the impression that building a family is life's most rewarding goal.

Natalie (now Natalie Bocock Turnage) felt the mixed messages; and because she felt the strength of her grandmother's attachment to her, she tried to decipher them. In her words:

I think she was really proud of my wanting to achieve things and working hard, and I know she was proud of my success at Princeton. But there was always this part of it that maybe I wasn't going to be devoted enough to have a family, and why was I interested in working for the government, and why was I buying a house in Alexandria when I wasn't married?

A lot of the things that I kind of wrestled through with her, I still wrestle with now . . . wanting to have a career and to be just like my male counterparts, but then dropping out of the workforce in order to have a family. Even though she was really supportive of me all of the time, it was difficult for me because I saw her as a mold-breaker, and I wanted to be a mold-breaker, but sometimes it didn't seem like I was breaking the mold in the right way.

When Natalie was working for the U.S. Senate Intelligence Committee, Mother was worried about the secretive nature of the work, the amount of travel, and the possible danger involved. At one point, she asked Natalie how much she would have to pay her to quit her job. "I was at a loss," Natalie told me. "I never really resolved any of that with her. The last time I saw her we were at Saint Paul's Church. She was circumspect and quiet . . . when we got up to leave I remember her just looking at me." The next week, Natalie was on a trip to Brazil with the Intelligence Committee. Her father called her at eleven o'clock at night, and before he could properly tell her, she knew her grandmother had died. As she puts it, "It was one of those things that probably would have stayed unresolved, because I think she was a really complicated person, but I always wished that I could go back to that Sunday, and just sit in church with her."

* * *

So we have, by the time Mother was in her eighties, a genuine character. But on top of that, from childhood onward, her beauty and confidence in herself meant that she developed into a woman of authority. It was not just a matter of having watched her father and of having absorbed the lessons well, it was a matter of genes. Berta, whose reference points are often animals, pays Mother the highest compliment in her lexicon by comparing her to Secretariat, America's greatest thoroughbred racehorse, whose heart, stamina, and stride have not been equaled since he won the Triple Crown in 1973. "It's rare that genes come together the way they did in those two," she says, "and it happened in our lifetime."

Hearing Mother referred to in such outsized terms makes me wish that, when I was in the most self-conscious period of my childhood, someone had taken me by the scruff of the neck, shaken me hard, and gotten across to me that I, by happenstance, was living with one of this world's originals, and that I should relax and enjoy the roller-coaster ride instead of wondering why I got overlooked when they were handing out conventional mothers. As an adult, I came to prize Mother's originality, even as I knew how to escape its frequent demands. It was not until after she died, and the world was a grayer place, that I knew how much I had loved it.

Mother was a flamboyant fish swimming in a small pond, in that all her efforts went into her city. To invoke that image is not to minimize her work; in fact, the limited locale had an intensifying effect on her impact. Ten years after her death, in a single day I heard two pieces broadcast on National Public Radio that were directly related to her efforts. One was a piece on Richmond's Hand Workshop, and the way that its broad reach into the community through the teaching of handwork was being copied nationally; the other had to do with the Valentine Riverside Project, an expansive, multimuseum tour of nineteenth-century Virginia history along the James River. Although the Riverside Project ran out of money, during her lifetime Mother's was one of the most persistent voices warning Richmond against cutting itself off from a physical connection with the James River and the rich industrial history of the warehouses and factories along its banks. A newly opened Canal Walk in Shockoe Bottom is proof that, in the new millennium, Richmond is rediscovering the James.

Cities, like people, need guardians, and at some point in her middle age,

Mother moved into that self-appointed role. She raised issues no one wanted to consider, lost as many battles as she won, and was a thorn in the side to generations of city bureaucrats, council members, and sometimes those on her own team. But by the time she reached old age, Richmond recognized that it was the beneficiary of Mother's energies, and was generous in its appreciation of her accomplishments and tolerant of her excesses. She had made a place for herself, and in eighty-four years of living had succeeded in her goal of escaping predictability. Miss Néné, whose search for stimulation was right up there with her lifelong friend's, once hissed at Mother in a fit of loving exasperation: "Oh, Elisabeth! Why can't you just be bored, like the rest of us?"

* * *

Essie Simms worked as Mother's secretary on evenings and weekends when she was not at her regular job at an oven-controls company. She was middle-aged and unmarried when she came to work for ESB, and for many years she devoted her workaholic energies and meticulous conscientiousness to keeping Mother straight. As with anyone who worked for ESB, Essie would often find herself pulled away from her typing or bookkeeping to meet a guest at the airport, deliver Christmas presents, or lay a fire; and even as she was taking dictation ESB would be pressing a glass of sherry on her, and interrupting the dictation to lecture her on working too hard.

Halfway up the circular stairs that connect the first and second floors of ESB's apartment at 909, there was a dimly lit, stuffy, five-foot-high crawl space with built-in cabinets that overlooked the living room. It was full of boxes filled with store catalogs filed alphabetically and stacks of old *New Yorker* and *National Geographic* magazines tied up in twine, waiting to be donated to the public library. Out of this claustrophobic space called the mezzanine, ESB made an office for Essie, outfitting it with a typewriter, a desk, and a rolling stool that Essie had to ride in order to approach the desk. When I was home, I could hear the sound of Essie's stool as she rolled toward the stairs to run up them to make late-afternoon tea for ESB, or down them with something for her to sign. Mother relied on Essie, whom she insisted on calling Miss Essie, and treated her sometimes as a daughter, sometimes as an indentured servant. For many years, Essie spent more time with Mother than Mother's own children did.

It fell to Essie to find Mother, dead on the sofa, when she came to work on the evening of Monday, December 10, 1985.

Mother died of a heart attack, probably in the late evening hours Sunday.

She had spent the day doing things that she particularly enjoyed: going to church, taking her grandson Alex and his friends out for brunch, going straight from there to an event at the White House of the Confederacy, and then straight on to an evening concert. Freddie is convinced that she died because she had no nap that day.

Mother left life just as she had lived it—in a terrible hurry. When she took Alex and his friends out earlier that day, they had happened to have a discussion about her death. Alex told me: "Grandmom didn't have any qualms about talking about death. I remember her having said [when he had visited her in the summer of 1985] that she hoped she died on a schoolday so that I could get out of school to come to her funeral. During brunch with my friends, Grandmom was talking to us about when she was going to die, and then she died that night. It seemed that she seized death just the way she seized life; it was just part of the continuum."

After spending what was left of the afternoon at the White House of the Confederacy, she showed up at the Saint Christopher's School Glee Club Christmas concert, held as a fund-raiser for Monumental Church (a downtown landmark that had been built in memory of those who had died in a disastrous theater fire on the same site). Monumental Church and its neglected upkeep had been a nagging worry to Mother most of her life; she was probably particularly glad to rally around it that night. Jack Zehmer, then director of Historic Richmond Foundation, remembers: "It was a big concert and the whole church was decorated. Mrs. Bocock arrived—not late—and I can see her now, walking down Broad Street, in that green satin blouse with the ruffles, and her furs. She came in and [afterwards] told me how much she had enjoyed it." Not a bad way to make an exit.

Index

Note: Streets, addresses, and buildings are in Richmond unless otherwise indicated. Kinship in parentheses is relative to ESB. Page references to photographs are printed in italic type.